HOW FIRM A FOUNDATION

How Firm a Foundation

A Gift of Jewish Wisdom for Christians and Jews

Rabbi Yechiel Eckstein

FOREWORD BY
Dr. Lloyd Ogilvie, Chaplain, U.S. Senate

PARACLETE PRESS
Brewster, Massachusetts

Unless otherwise designated, Scripture quotations are based on the Revised Standard Version of the Bible, copyright 1946, 1952, 1971 by the Division of Christian Education of the National Council of Churches of Christ in the USA. Used by permission.

Scripture quotations designated KJV are taken from the King James Version of the Bible.

Library of Congress Cataloging-in-Publication Data

Eckstein, Yechiel, 1951—
    [What Christians should know about Jews and Judaism]
    How firm a foundation : a gift of Jewish wisdom for Christians and Jews / Yechiel Eckstein ; foreword by Lloyd Ogilvie.
        p. cm.
    Previously published under title: What Christians should know about Jews and Judaism. Waco, Tex. : Word Books, 1984.
    Includes bibliographical references and index.
    ISBN 1-55725-189-4 (pbk.)
    1. Judaism. 2. Judaism—Relations—Christianity. 3. Christianity and other religions—Judaism.   I. Title.
    BM580.E34   1997
    296.3'96—dc21

                            97-23688
                                CIP

About the Cover:
The image on the cover of this book is an example of early Castilian illuminated manuscripts taken from the Cervera Bible. The image depicts the vision of the prophet Zachariah. The restored Jewish state, symbolized by the menorah, receives oil from two olive trees representing the renewed lineage of King David and of the High Priest.

10 9 8 7 6 5 4 3 2 1

Published by Paraclete Press
Brewster, Massachusetts
Printed in the United States of America

To my Christian friends who
inspired me with their faith
strengthened me with their support
and enriched my life with their friendship.

><+•>—O—<•+-<

How good and how pleasant it is for
brethren to dwell together in unity.

PSALM 133:1

Give thanks to the Lord for He is good,
His steadfast love endures forever.

PSALM 136:1

CONTENTS

A GIFT OF JEWISH
WISDOM FOR CHRISTIANS
AND JEWS

Recently, Jewish and Christian Senators of the United States gathered in the Capitol for a Seder dinner. The Rabbi invited to lead the Seder was the distinguished author of this book. Rabbi Yechiel Eckstein led us through a delightful, inspiring, informative evening. We experienced profound shalom as Yechiel led us in singing and an in-depth explanation of the Seder. We relived the Exodus, the first Passover, and the traditions passed down through the generations. He forged a bond between us all and helped us in grateful praise to the God of liberation and hope in whom we all believe.

This is what Rabbi Eckstein does throughout this book. I have found it one of the most helpful tools in my ministry to both Jews and Christians in the Senate. It has helped me compose my prayers for Jewish holy days and holidays to be prayed for the Senate. This book is rich in information Christians need to know to be responsible and affirming friends, neighbors, and fellow citizens to Jewish people.

Most important of all, this book is brimming with Jewish wisdom that will enrich and strengthen your faith. Your knowledge of God will be deepened and your appreciation of Judaism will be heightened.

Yechiel Eckstein has become a close and trusted friend. It is a privilege to work together on Christian and Jewish relations and the soul-sized issues that confront our American society and the world scene. He is my brother, friend, and fellow adventurer in the exciting pilgrimage of spiritual growth we share.

I commend this book to you. It will become one of the most valued and used books in your library.

Lloyd John Ogilvie
Chaplain, United States Senate
Washington, DC
June 1997

Kol hatchalot kashot, all beginnings are difficult, claim the rabbis, and fostering more favorable relations and better understanding between two peoples who have been estranged from each other for almost two millennia is no exception. Just as physical birth and spiritual growth involve pain, effort, and a profound dimension of mystery, so too is the creation of a relationship between Christians and Jews, whose historical interaction has, more often than not, been fraught with polemic, misunderstanding, intolerance, and even bloodshed.

We should be pleased with the advances that have taken place, awed and humbled by the mystery of this continuously evolving relationship, and increasingly encouraged to pursue it further. Admittedly, there is much yet to be done. But while the rabbis of Jewish tradition maintained that all beginnings involve difficulty, they also insisted that the greater the degree of hardship, the greater the reward—in this case, the deeper and more fruitful the relationship. It is important to remember that Christian-Jewish dialogue is still in its infancy stages. When seen in that light, the achievements that have already been made in bringing about a genuine reconciliation between the two groups can only be described as truly remarkable.

There is a Jewish story told of a young man who visited his rabbi and became so overwhelmed by the emotional experience that he cried out, "Rabbi, I love you dearly." The rabbi, who was both touched and amused by his student's sincerity, asked him, "Tell me, my son, you say that you love me, but where do I hurt? What ails me?" To this the perplexed young man responded, "I do not know where you hurt, Rabbi, but, nevertheless, I love you dearly!" The rabbi then replied, "But how can you say you love me when you do not even know where I hurt and what brings me pain?" This touching story illustrates well the truth that our first obligation in dialogue is to explain to one another the nature of our faith communities—who we are and what we believe—and to tell of that which brings us joy and of that which brings us pain.

Errors will undoubtedly be made and sensitivities unwittingly trampled upon as Christians and Jews pursue dialogue and rapprochement in what is still essentially uncharted terrain. Language can become a source of either comfort or grief, pride or embarrassment. Words invoked in the context of one group can, in the context of another, have nuances that are bitingly inappropriate and even offensive. A pastor at whose church I had just spoken and where I was greeted with an enthusiastic response followed my remarks by saying, no doubt with tongue in cheek, that he would bring me back to speak at one of their crusades. He was totally unaware of the image of death and martyrdom conjured up in my mind by the mere mention of the word "crusade." Conducting a crusade may be the most natural display of Christian faith for a Baptist. For the Jew, however, such language evokes an entirely different response. It reminds him of the slaughter and suffering of his ancestors over the centuries.

In another instance, I overheard a Christian minister ask a friend who had haggled with a merchant over the price of an item in a Jerusalem marketplace whether he had "jewed him down." Knowing the minister as I do, I am certain that his comment did not reflect a deep-seated, unconscious contempt for Jews, because it was not the least bit characteristic of him to associate Jews in particular with cheating or haggling. Rather, I believe it came from a complete unawareness of the derivations and implications of his remark. We will have to be patient with one another as we become more aware of the full extent of our words and sensitive to how they will be received by members of another community.

Catholic thinker Ed Flannery tells in his book *The Anguish of the Jews* of his shock in learning that the associations most Jews have with the crucifix and the cross are radically different from those of Christians. What for him was an object of love and reconciliation was for Jews a symbol of fear and revulsion, a reminder of their past persecution and suffering under Christianity.

Christians are also surprised to learn that Jews tend to lump all non-Jews together as Christians without recognizing that not only are Christians not monolithic, but unlike the Jewish condition, they are not born into their faith. Contrary to the predominant Jewish impression, all non-Jews are not Christians. Moreover, some are only nominally Christian.

A further source of difficulty in dialogue is the fact that even fundamental entities and terms such as *the Bible* have different nuances for Christians than they have for Jews. The term *Old Testament*, for example, implies the existence of a "new" one, something Jews do not acknowledge. It has become common, therefore, for Jews and many Christians to refer to it as "the Hebrew Bible." The same is true with regard to designations such as B.C. and A.D., which define time in Christological terms and are not acceptable to most Jews. Instead they use B.C.E. (Before the Common Era) and C.E. (for Common Era).

However, potential areas of agreement between the two communities should be explored and should lead to joint efforts. Such issues as religious liberty, crime, hunger, the family, the aged, as well as more theologically oriented themes such as the dignity of man, God's love for man, and the centrality of Scripture, can all provide fruitful ground for dialogue and, hopefully, coordinated action. Even when there is a clash in views, conversations should continue, perhaps especially then. Both groups should try, at least, to understand what is motivating each other's positions. And while genuine dialogue asks that both Christians and Jews be open to modifying their positions, it does not call for them to bend or accommodate their views to the point where they compromise their integrity and threaten their individual identities in the process. For at the heart of true dialogue is the commitment to respect its parameters.

For centuries, the preeminent Christian view was that Jesus came to the world to bring mankind the possibility of salvation and eternal life. Without a belief in him, man could not reach the Father or be freed from the shackles of sin. What this viewpoint meant for Judaism, which gave birth to Christianity, is that, with the dawn of the new Christian faith, Judaism ceased to exist and was instead displaced by a triumphalist Christianity. Thus, in the new scheme of things, Christians became the new "people of God"; the Hebrew Bible or Tanakh became the "Old Testament," and Christianity became the exclusive *ortho doxo* system through which one could achieve proper living and relationship with God.

Paul in Romans 9–11, on the other hand, seemed to rail against such theological hubris and usurpation when he declared that God's promises to Israel are irrevocable. He warns Jesus' followers not to become haughty with their newfound spiritual possession, for the root supports the branch, not the branch the root. Tragically, Paul's warning was not heeded. For centuries, Christians adopted this "displacement theology," as it has come to be known, casting Judaism aside as though it died on the cross along with Jesus.

The situation today is not much better. While all Christian seminaries teach about Judaism in the biblical period, those that teach about Jewish life after the first century are few and far between. Voltaire and the historian Arnold Toynbee reflected this triumphalist spirit best when they characterized Judaism as a relic, a "fossil religion," with no relevance or instructive purpose today.

What are the forces underlying such a condescending and arrogant theology? Are they Oedipal in their origins? A rebellion against one's Jewish parentage? Are they part of an attempt to form one's own distinct identity by denying one's parent's legitimacy? Whatever their origin, this exclusivist theology led to the Marcian movement, which, in the patristic period of the early church, attempted to eliminate all vestiges of Christianity's Jewish roots—including the Hebrew Bible (*aka* Old Testament). Ultimately, the church rejected Marcian's view, though not entirely. Indeed, it continued to belittle and degrade the Jewish faith along with the practitioners of that faith. They insisted there is no salvation outside the church, and there is no coming to the Father except through the Son.

For centuries, Christianity effectively denied its Jewish roots and rejected its heritage, to Christians' own detriment as well as to that of the Jewish people. The fact that Jesus was a Jew was buried under the rubble of polemic and fratricide. For centuries, Jews suffered oppression and persecution at the hands of followers of Christ—and in his name—for the sin of rejecting the Christian faith. That this displacement theology, which reduced the Jew and his faith to "pariah" status, led to violence against Jews over the centuries is clear. What haunts us today is the realization that it also may have created the groundwork and context in which the Holocaust was spawned.

In recent decades, there has been a dramatic change in the church's relationship with the Jewish people and also with Christians' awareness of the Jewish roots of their own faith. Christians (and Jews, for that matter) are just beginning to come to grips with the fact that Jesus was a Jew and that they cannot be truly Christian without drawing sustenance from their Jewish roots. Put differently, Christians cannot begin to comprehend Jesus the Christ without first confronting Jesus the Jew of Nazareth.

This movement to recover Christianity's roots in Judaism comes precisely at the time that the interfaith and ecumenical movements have become important forces in American life. We live today in a pluralistic American society in which it is both inevitable and advantageous that we learn of one another—who the other truly is, not as we have come to stereotype them—and gain greater insight into one another's respective lives of faith.

This book is my attempt to find common ground between Christians and Jews and teach greater understanding of the Jewish roots of the Christian faith. It brings to the fore the ancient wisdom of Judaism both before and after the rise of Christianity.

One of my favorite verses in the Tanakh (Hebrew Bible) is "He has showed you, O man, what is good; and what does the LORD require of you but to do justice, and to love kindness, and to walk humbly with your God?" (Micah 6:8). *How Firm a Foundation* gives the reader, Christian and Jew alike, the gift of Jewish wisdom over the centuries. More specifically, it teaches them how they can best fulfill Micah's pithy dictum.

It is my hope and prayer that this book might mark the beginning of our common search not only for wisdom but also for how we might better uplift our souls and walk in the straight path, deepening our bonds of love with one another and strengthening our relationship with God and devotion to him.

Christians owe the Jewish people a debt of gratitude—for giving them their God, their Bible, and the way to achieve salvation. In this book, I try to share another gift—the vision and wisdom of Judaism—with all who wish to partake. Now Christians (and Jews) can recover that dimension of holiness and Jewish spirituality described in our classical sources which had been buried and lost to Christians for centuries under the rubble of polemic. It is a gift we Jews gladly share with others and hopefully study ourselves so that we might all merit spiritual renewal and holiness in our lives. Indeed, for Jews, there is no greater good deed and commandment than to study Torah, God's blueprint of how we ought to lead our lives in the here and now of this world. And so, let those who thirst for knowledge of the Lord and eagerly await the day when "when the earth shall be full of the knowledge of the LORD as the waters cover the sea" (Isa. 11:9), come and imbibe from the wisdom of Judaism.

My primary objective in writing this book is to provide Christians and Jews with a resource from which they can glean a better understanding of and appreciation for Jews and Judaism. It is also a primer for dialogue, one that I hope will advance the cause of Jewish-Christian relations. Telling the story of the Jewish people—their faith and experiences—has been a most humbling experience. Although I have tried to make it as comprehensive as possible, it is necessarily limited. I had to be ruthlessly selective in what to include and exclude. Even those themes that are treated merit much greater elaboration, as each could easily constitute a book in itself.

This book is written unabashedly from a traditional (Orthodox) point of view. It strives to convey the essential unity of the Jewish people—their shared memories, values, ideals, and experiences—and to outline my conception of Jewish authenticity, although it also tries to respect the diversity of Jewish expressions. I hope that the reader will see in it the reflection of a person for whom religion and spirituality are not only static entities but ones of dynamic growth, as well. Parts of this book may even appear as apologetics. Certainly my goal is to present a favorable image of Jews and their faith. But I also have tried to avoid idealizing either.

It is extremely difficult for people standing outside a system to peek in and fully grasp what is going on. They may even find it impossible to appreciate all that the system means to the person experiencing it from "within." A Jewish story is told of a musician who was playing for a wedding celebration at a local inn and whose music so enthralled the gathering that they all began to dance. At that very same moment a deaf man happened to pass by. As he looked into the window and saw them jumping wildly up and down, he muttered, "Madmen, all madmen," and proceeded to go on his way. Indeed, only those who hear the music can truly appreciate its sweet melody.

This book, with all its limitations, hopes to provide Christians and Jews with a glimpse into the Jewish world. It seeks to serve as a window through which the reader might come to view the Jew, understand his faith, and learn of that which brings him joy and pain.

It seems to me that much of the understanding Christians have of Jews arises from a knowledge of biblical history from the time of Adam to the times of Jesus and the rise of Christianity. In contrast, this book attempts to portray the *living* Jew and to convey his experiences over the past two millennia.

When a Gentile came to the great Rabbi Hillel (who was roughly a contemporary of Jesus) and asked him to explain all of Judaism while standing on one foot, Hillel responded by paraphrasing the biblical verse "love thy neighbor as thyself" and said, "What is hurtful to you do not do unto others." The essence of Judaism today is captured, as it always has been, by that biblical phrase.

In writing this book I felt an awesome sense of responsibility, knowing that my words might influence many Christians' views of my people and my faith. I often felt as if whatever I wrote would be inadequate to the task. For this reason, I ask that all the limitations inherent in this book be attributed to me, and not to the people and tradition I am attempting to portray. I write with great reservation and trepidation, but in the spirit of the rabbis who, acknowledging the enormity of such challenges, stated, "Not upon you is the requirement to complete the job. But neither are you free from beginning it entirely."

It was in working with the Christian community that I came to realize the pressing need for such a comprehensive handbook on Jews and Judaism. The book is intended for a wide range of Christian readers—clergy, academicians, and laypeople alike. At the same time, I know it will be of benefit to those Jews seeking a deeper understanding of their own faith, as well. Indeed, as the late Abraham J. Heschel wrote, "Faith must precede interfaith." My deepest prayer is that it create greater harmony and understanding between Christians and Jews, two groups of people who have been estranged from each other for too long; my most profound hope is that it be a source of blessing and enrichment to both communities.

Who are these people, "Israel," the Jews, I try here to portray? They are a unique people, a sanctified people, pragmatists, and idealists. They are realists who draw inspiration from their past, meaning from their present, and hope for their future. They are a chosen people and a choosing people—doubters, questioners, and even quarrelers with God. Indeed, they are the seed of Abraham!

Jews are a battered people—shattered, traumatized, and martyred—whose lives often remain threatened and insecure. They are a tenacious, stubborn lot—a stiff-necked people—committed to bearing testimony, despite adversity, to the existence and oneness of God and to the fact that the world has yet to be redeemed; they are both instruments of God's will and actors on the stage of history; they are a people who feel God's spirit moving in their lives and in the world, but who question his absence, too. They are a group that refuses to despair or to allow their will to survive to be consumed; they are a covenanted people composed of mystics and rationalists, Orthodox and Reform, even "culturalists." They are a people who not only pray, dream, and yearn for Messiah and the world's salvation, but also insist on actively preparing the world for his coming by alleviating human suffering in the here and now; they are a people who thirst for peace but who have had to engage in war to survive.

Who are these people, Israel, the Jews? They are God's witnesses in the world. They bear testimony to his presence and love even at times of his concealment. They are "a people who dwellest alone," but one who seeks to be a source of blessing for all humankind. They are, as Abraham Heschel wrote, "a spiritual order in which the human and the ultimate, the natural and the holy enter a lasting covenant, in which kinship with

God is not an aspiration but a reality of destiny." They are the sons and daughters of Abraham and Sarah, Isaac and Rebekah, Jacob, Rachel, and Leah—they have struggled with both God and man—and they have overcome. They *are forever, "Israel"*!

According to the Bible, when God spoke to Moses his voice was heard from between two cherubic figures that rested atop the tabernacle. The figures faced each other with hands uplifted to God and outstretched toward each other. Only when we Christians and Jews are willing to "dialogue" with one another, in its etymological sense of "to speak through," and to face each other with hands outstretched toward God as well as toward one another will *either* of us hear the voice of God speaking to us "from between" the cherubs.

This book is my way of stretching out my hands in friendship toward my Christian neighbors with the hope that they, in turn, will extend their hands lovingly toward the Jewish people, my faith community. I believe very deeply that through such a relationship both will be blessed and that within such a fellowship both will come to hear the voice of God.

> *Praise the LORD, all nations!*
> *Extol him, all peoples!*
> *For great is his steadfast love toward us;*
> *and the faithfulness of the LORD endures forever.*
>
> (Psalm 117)

> *May the LORD open up my lips,*
> *May the words of my mouth be pleasing,*
> *and the meditation of my heart before thee,*
> *May my mouth sing his praises . . .*
> *the LORD is my rock and redeemer.*

> *May the LORD give strength unto his people;*
> *May he bless his people with shalom, peace.*

4 SIVAN, erev Shavuot, 5757
June 9, 1997

ABBREVIATIONS

A.Z. . . . . .Avodah Zarah
B.T. . . . . .Babylonian Talmud
B. . . . . .Bava
B.C.E. . . . . .Before the Common Era
Ber. . . . . .Berakhot
Bik. . . . . .Bikkurim
C.E. . . . . .Common Era
Git. . . . . .Gittin
Hag. . . . . .Hagigah
Hul. . . . . .Hullin
Kidd. . . . . .Kiddushin
Meg. . . . . .Megillah
Men. . . . . .Menahot
Rab. . . . . .Rabbah
Sanh. . . . . .Sanhedrin
Shab. . . . . .Shabbat
Shev. . . . . .Shevuot
Suk. . . . . .Sukkot
T.Y. . . . . .Talmud Yerushalmi
Y.S. . . . . .Yalkut Shimoni
Yev. . . . . .Yevamot

Part 1

JEWS AND JUDAISM

⊳─┤◆⟩─O─⟨◆├─┤◄

Chapter 1

FOUNDATIONS OF
JEWISH BELIEF

Torah

To speak of the Jew and his faith is to focus on the quintessential dimension of that faith, Torah. It is the Torah that brings solace, inner strength, and spiritual fulfillment to the Jew during times of joy, security, and prosperity, as well as during periods of wandering, suffering, and adversity. It is the Torah that guides the Jew's path, shapes his character, and links him with ultimacy. The Torah is the lens through which the Jew perceives life and reality; it is that which unites him indissolubly with his fellow Jew. The Torah is the very lifeblood of the Jewish people.

The term *Torah* has a variety of connotations. Etymologically, it means "teachings," not "law," as it is so often mistranslated. In its broadest sense, Torah means "correct" or "properly Jewish," as in "leading a Torah way of life." More narrowly, it refers to all Jewish religious writings, including the Hebrew Scriptures, Talmud, *responsa* literature, rabbinic commentaries, and others. The term is most generally used, however, in reference to the Bible or written scriptures that Jews refer to as the *Tanakh* and Christians refer to as the Hebrew Bible or Old Testament. In its narrowest sense, the term *Torah* refers to the five books of Moses, or *Pentateuch*.

The traditional view of the Torah in its narrowest sense is that it is the embodiment of God's word par excellence; the *sine qua non* of our knowledge of God and of the divine will for man. Although given to the people of Israel at a particular juncture in history, it is, nevertheless, eternally valid and authoritative. Everything there is to know about life, claim the rabbis, can be derived from the Torah. "Turn it around and inside out and everything is in it." As the psalmist declared, "the law [Torah] of the LORD is perfect, reviving the soul" (Ps. 19:7). Without the Torah man has precious little knowledge of God and the divine intent, nor of the means by which he might link up with them.

The Torah is divine in the sense that every word and letter—even the designs or "crowns" on top of the letters as they appear written in the parchment scrolls—are believed to have been revealed by God. The rabbis regarded the concept of *torah mishamayim,* or "torah from heaven" (i.e., its divinity), as one of the most central of all Jewish affirmations. (The term *the rabbis* is used throughout this book in reference to the collective body of rabbis through the centuries, but particularly those in the Talmudic Period. See below.) They tell a *midrash* (a homiletic story) of how Moses sought reassurance from God that all his efforts in bringing the children of Israel out of Egypt and giving them the Torah would not be in vain and that the Torah would continue to be studied and practiced long after him.

God, according to the midrash, took Moses in a time machine centuries ahead to the second century C.E. (Jews often do not use the acronyms "B.C." and "A.D.," which implicitly define time in terms of the birth and death of Jesus. Rather, they refer to these periods of time as "B.C.E.," or "before the Common Era," and "C.E.," or "Common Era.") There Moses sat in the talmudic academy of the great sage and Torah scholar Rabbi Akiva, who was deriving laws exegetically from the crowns on top of the Torah letters. The *Talmud,* or oral tradition, states that Moses was so confused by Rabbi Akiva's intricate discourse that he could not even recognize that the rabbi was commenting on the same Torah he had brought down from

Sinai! Moses was shocked and filled with grief. Finally, a student asked Rabbi Akiva how he derived a particular law from the Torah text. He responded, "It is a law to Moses from Sinai" that was passed down (orally) through the generations. At that, concludes the talmudic story, Moses became reassured that God's Torah, the very same one revealed to him at Sinai, would remain forever with the people of Israel and would, in fact, be studied intensively and applied to daily life long after he died (B. T., Men. 29b).

The Torah is written on parchment and tied together in a scroll. It is the holiest ritual object in Judaism in that it contains both the name and message of God. The Torah is to be treated with utmost reverence and respect, not lightly or frivolously. It may not be desecrated or defiled. Indeed, there are numerous laws pertaining to the sanctity with which we are to treat the Torah. Scrolls that are old or torn, for example, may not be discarded but must be buried in the earth like human beings. If a Torah scroll accidentally falls, a fast day is decreed for all those who saw it drop. (Charity may be given in lieu of the fast.) If a printed Torah text drops, we kiss it as a sign of our respect. The meticulous care involved in writing a Torah scroll, letter by letter (writing a scroll takes, on the average, one full year), is another reflection of its sacredness in the eyes of Jews.

How did God reveal his word through the Torah? Did he "dictate" it verbatim to Moses on Sinai? Was Moses "inspired" to write it down? Was it all written by man and then sanctioned retroactively by God? These and many other explanations are proffered as to how God actually communicated his will to man. In whatever way traditionalists understand the mechanics of the Sinai theophany, however, they all regard the Torah as we have it today as the primary source of our knowledge of God's word to man, and indeed, of God himself. It is, in the words of the Jewish liturgy, "given to the children of Israel from the mouth of God through the hand of Moses."

God is not a physical being mortal man can ever come to fully know, nor can we expect to completely comprehend his immutable ways. Even Moses, the greatest of all prophets who talked with God "face to face" (Exod. 33:11), was allowed to "see" only God's "back" (Exod. 33:20, 23). (These, as well as other instances in which the Torah describes God's physical attributes, were considered by the rabbis to be anthropomorphisms, written in that manner since "the Torah speaks in language man can understand.") But if the Torah is, in a very real sense, God's word, we can come as close as humanly possible to "knowing" God himself by studying its content. The term "to know" in biblical Hebrew—*ladaat*—is often used in the Greek sense connoting not only cognitive and speculative knowledge, but unification and attachment as well, as in the verse, "Now Adam *knew* Eve his wife" (Gen. 4:1, emphasis added). This principle guided Maimonides (1135–1204), whose opening words in his magnum opus, *Mishneh Torah,* are, "The foundation of foundations and pillar of wisdom is to *know* that there is a God. . . ." It is the Torah that enables us to truly know God and to unite with him as much as humanly possible.

By immersing ourselves in the sacred act of Torah study, we can come to better understand both the content and source of that divine word. For this reason Jewish education, and particularly *Talmud Torah,* or "study of the Torah," is one of the most important *mitzvot,* "religious duties," in all of Judaism. The Talmud states that good deeds such as honoring parents, acting kindly toward strangers, visiting the sick, attending the dead, devotion in prayer, and bringing peace among people are all important, but that "the study of Torah excels them all." (See B. T., Shab. 127a.) Its supreme importance lies in the fact that, in the words of the rabbis, "an ignorant person cannot be pious." Daily, the Jew links his love for God with his love for God's Torah. He prays, "With an eternal love hast thou loved thy people, the house of Israel; Torah, commandments, good deeds, and laws hast thou imparted to us. Therefore, O Lord our God, when we lie down and when we rise up, we will ponder thy laws and rejoice in the words of thy Torah and commandments. For they are our lives and the length of our days and upon them will we meditate day and night" (from the Jewish prayer book). The study of the Torah is the Jew's loftiest spiritual pursuit.

In Judaism, the intellectual and the spiritual are inseparable; the heart *and* the mind must be applied in the service of God. Even Jewish prayer and devotion are interlocked with Torah study. For this reason, a portion of the Bible is read publicly in synagogue each Shabbat (Sabbath) so that over the course of a year the entire five books of the Torah will have been completed and everyone who attended prayer services will have heard and studied it. (This emphasis on Torah study may also have contributed to the fact that Jews historically have been a highly literate people.)

Traditional Judaism affirms that the Torah is not only God's revealed word to man, but it also has been passed on to us from generation to generation without error. This doctrine of inerrancy underlies the traditional Jewish hermeneutic which derives laws and theological concepts from each word (and, at times, from each letter) in the Torah. The validity of this exegetical method rests upon the belief that every word in the Torah as we have it today is divine, without error, and consequently, imparted to man for an express purpose. (The possibility of error is, indeed, reduced since Torah scribes must be pious individuals who work slowly and meticulously in the arduous task of transcribing each letter of the Torah onto the scroll parchment. If a scribe makes even the slightest mistake in writing the name of God, for example, he must undergo ritual acts of purification.) Seen from this perspective, the Torah cannot be redundant, can have no missing words, nor can it contain mistakes since God would not repeat or contradict himself without reason. Biblical critics, of course, might disagree. It remains left to man to interpret such textual "irregularities" through the use of the oral tradition (see below). Thus, for example, the threefold repetition of the phrase "you shall not boil a kid in its mother's milk" (Exod. 23:19, 34:26; Deut. 14:21) was explained by the rabbis as a threefold prohibition against cooking meat and milk together, eating them together, or deriving any benefit from such a mixture.

The Torah constitutes the primary component of the Jewish "written tradition," which also includes the *Neviim* (prophets) and *Ketuvim* (writings comprising the Scrolls of Esther, Psalms, Song of Songs, Ecclesiastes, Job, Ruth, Lamentations, and Proverbs, as well as the Books of Daniel, Ezra, Nehemiah, and Chronicles). This written tradition, more widely known by its acronym, *Tanakh (T* for *Torah, N* for *Neviim, K* for *Ketuvim),* came to a close roughly after 586 B.C.E. with the destruction of the first temple and end of the prophetic period (Ezra and Nehemiah are considered the last prophets). It was not canonized, however, until after the first century C.E. Christians generally refer to the Tanakh, or written tradition, as the Old Testament, although many, in deference to Jewish sensitivities, have come to use the term *Hebrew Bible* since *Old* Testament implies the existence of a *New* Testament, something that Jews deny.

The Jewish hermeneutical treatment of the Torah is fundamentally different from that of the rest of the Tanakh (Bible). For while all other holy writ in the Tanakh (i.e., the prophets and writings) are sacred and divine, none carries the same authoritative force as the Torah, wherein every word is regarded as divine and inerrant and, consequently, is to be interpreted by man. In the case of the rest of Scripture, only the concepts are sacred and divine. Laws cannot be derived exegetically from every word or letter.

While the Jewish view of the inerrancy of the Torah suggests that its every word is from God, portions, such as the Genesis account of the Garden of Eden, can legitimately be interpreted allegorically rather than literally. In contrast, a conservative Christian view of inerrancy might not suggest that each and every word and letter of the Torah is to be interpreted exegetically (much like the Jewish view of the rest of Scripture), although it would be inclined to claim that they are to be understood literally. In Judaism, the Torah, which is inerrant, is interpreted through the eyes of the rabbis and oral tradition (see below), which at times treat certain portions allegorically, though always as the embodiment of the word of God.

Biblical authority, which serves as the foundation for traditional Jewish authority as a whole, is premised on the belief that the Torah was "revealed"—however one understands that term—by God. The Sinai theophany was a unique moment in human history: "For ask now of the days that are past, which were before you, since the day that God created man upon the earth, and ask from one end of heaven to the other, whether such a great thing as this has ever happened or was ever heard of. Did any people ever hear the voice of a god speaking out of the midst of the fire, as you have heard, and still live?" (Deut. 4:32-33). The Torah is the repository of divine truth and is, therefore, binding and authoritative upon humanity: "Keep them and do them [i.e., the statutes of the Torah]; for that will be your wisdom and your understanding in the sight of the peoples, who, when they hear all these statutes, will say, 'Surely this great nation is a wise and understanding people'" (Deut. 4:6).

Unlike most other faiths that are founded upon the revelatory experiences of an individual, Judaism was born out of a divine revelation to a collective people. For while the Torah was written by Moses, the Sinai theophany was experienced by the entire Jewish people (see Exod. 20:19). There is a midrash that suggests that the whole world, including all the animals and birds, heard God speaking the Ten Commandments, and another claiming that the souls of all Jews not yet born at the time were also present then at Sinai (see Deut. 5:3 upon which this idea is based).

The very concluding phrase in the Torah, "in the sight of all Israel" (Deut. 34:12), points to the centrality of this concept within Judaism. By addressing the people of Israel collectively and directly, God sought to teach them that Moses was his trusted servant and that all that he would speak and write in God's name would equally be his word (see Exod. 19:9). In other words, Moses' position of authority as transcriber of the word of God was vindicated by God's having revealed himself to the community of Israel and publicly endorsing Moses as such. According to the midrash, Moses' stature became so great and his voice so authoritative, God feared that the Jews might come to regard him as divine. For this reason, states the midrash, God told Moses to "go down" the mountain (Exod. 19:21) so that the people would see that he was really human. Only then did God begin speaking the first of the Ten Commandments, declaring, "I am the LORD your God" (Exod. 20:2). Moreover, lest Moses become deified posthumously by Israel and his gravesite turned into a venerated place of worship, God did not disclose its location "to this day" (Deut. 34:6). For while man can be godly, only God is God.

While revelation presumes a revealing God, it also presumes a receiver, man. Indeed, in many respects, the question of how we hear and interpret God's word is of far greater importance than that of how God revealed it. For although man may acknowledge the Torah as the repository of divinely revealed wisdom and truth, he can also distort and abuse that word. Man has the power to mold the Torah into either a holy Bible or an instrument for idolatry.

The partnership of God and man as revealer-receiver is exemplified by two verses in the Torah's account of revelation, "And the LORD came down upon Mount Sinai" (Exod. 19:20) and "And Moses went up to God" (Exod. 19:3). It is at the point of encounter between God and man when, in Martin Buber's terminology, the "I" meets the eternal "Thou" that genuine revelation takes place. God makes himself immanent by moving "down the mountain" and meeting man halfway. In Christian terms, this is his act of grace. On the other hand, man, his copartner, elevates himself and spiritually goes "up the mountain" to greet the Lord. The midrash states that if man initiates even a slight movement toward God and creates an opening in his heart the size of a needle, God will respond magnanimously by enlarging it so that even chariots could pass through.

While affirming man's need for divine grace, the rabbis insisted that the initiative for this turning and reconciliation must come from man who is eminently capable of uplifting himself and initiating such a return. Man must open up his heart to God, repent of his sins, and observe the laws of the Torah (see the section on the High Holy Days in chapter 4). The Hasidic expression "Where is God? Wherever we let him in" is a reflection of the Jewish conviction that man possesses the ability to initiate a movement toward God who, through his love and grace, responds a thousandfold. For Judaism maintains that man is a dignified being, created with free will and an innately pure soul (see chapter 2).

In contrast, the predominant Christian view is that man is shackled by his sinfulness and incapable of self-regeneration. It is God, through an act of love and grace, who initiates the movement toward man. While Judaism and Christianity indeed differ on this matter, their differences are often grossly exaggerated and very much misunderstood. Certainly, Judaism professes that it is not man's works, observance of the law, or merit *alone* that bring him closer to God, but God's love and act of grace in response to his initiative, despite man's unworthiness, as well. Daily, the Jew recites in his morning prayers, "Not out of our righteousness do we appeal to you, but because we rely on your mercy. What are we? What value are our lives? Our righteousness? . . ." And while Christianity, indeed, emphasizes God's initiative of grace in spite of man's sinfulness, it, too, regards man's deeds and works as essential. "Not every one who says to me, 'Lord, Lord,' shall enter the kingdom of heaven, but he who does the will of my Father who is in heaven" (Matt. 7:21).

Clearly, while traditional Jews and conservative Christians may share much in common on the fundamental question of the divinity and inerrancy of Scripture (at least, the Old Testament or Hebrew Bible portion of it), differences abound regarding how we exegetically interpret that divine message and relate it to our life of faith. The differences become especially pronounced when we consider the question of the oral tradition.

The Oral Tradition

There are Christians who maintain that Judaism came to an end as a viable religion after the coming of Jesus and was then displaced by Christianity. Some also claim that the overwhelming Jewish rejection of Jesus (who, after all, came to bring the message of salvation to them) resulted in their being cut off from the divine covenantal olive tree and in the Gentiles' being grafted on in their place (see Rom. 11). Indeed, there are even those who maintain that God has cast away the Jews as a punishment for killing Jesus (see Matt. 21:39, 43). Christians, according to this line of thinking, supplanted the Jews as the true (spiritual) descendants of Abraham (see Rom. 9:6-9) and as the new covenantal people of God. This point of view, which treats Jews and Judaism as fossils of the past (to use the English historian Arnold Toynbee's expression), is quite prevalent among Christians, despite the fact that the Christian Bible itself seems to regard the Jews' election and belovedness as eternally valid since "the gifts and the call of God are irrevocable" (Rom. 11:29; see also Rom. 9:4-5; 11:1-2).

Such New Testament passages attesting to the continued vitality of the Jewish people and those passages in the Hebrew Bible affirming the eternal nature of Israel's covenant contradict Christian claims that Jews no longer remain God's "chosen people" and that their Jewish faith has ceased to be valid. Rarely do Christian seminaries teach about Jews or Judaism, for example, and those that do, generally treat them only up until the first century C.E. There are few (if any) evangelical institutions, in particular, offering courses or lecture series on the subject of Jews, Judaism, or Jewish-Christian relations *after* the time of Jesus. It is as if the entire Jewish story from the time of Abraham on came to a halt with the coming of Jesus. It is as if Jews and Judaism became totally (and triumphantly) displaced covenantally by Christians and Christianity.

Such subtle, and often unconsciously distorted, approaches to history and theology reinforce the prevalent Christian view that Jews can achieve fulfillment only through Christianity.

Jews, however, maintain that they were never cut off from God's promises and that their covenant with their Father was never displaced. Jews insist that they continue to serve as God's witnesses in this world—as Jews even after Jesus. In the words of the Bible, "Yet for all that, when they are in the land of their enemies, I will not spurn them, neither will I abhor them so as to destroy them utterly and break my covenant with them; for I am the LORD their God" (Lev. 26:44). The past two millennia of Jewish history are regarded as a direct, unabridged continuation of the first two thousand years before Jesus and, needless to say, are treated as equally valid and compelling. Using the Pauline analogy described in Romans 11, Jews would characterize themselves diagrammatically like this:

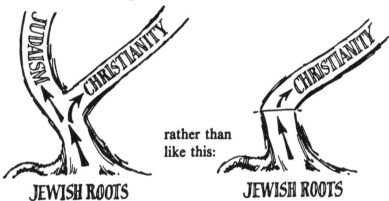

There exists among Christians a widespread lack of awareness of the fact that Jewish life, scholarship, and religious expression flourished, rather than diminished or abruptly ended, after the time of Jesus. Indeed, the first five centuries of the Common Era were, in many respects, the most religiously creative and culturally productive years Jews have ever had. Much of the very foundation on which Jewish life as it has been understood and practiced ever since the first century was established then. To better appreciate how Judaism developed in its own right after the time of Jesus, and by extension, how the Jew conducts his religious life today, it is important that one be aware of one of the most significant aspects of Jewish life and faith over the centuries: the oral tradition.

Of the various Jewish groups in existence at the time of Jesus, only the Pharisees collectively survived the destruction of the second temple in 70 C.E. (The followers of Jesus, who also survived, did so in the form of what later became a new religion, Christianity.) This was largely due to the fact that the principal modes of Pharisaic spiritual life and expression—the synagogue, rabbi, prayer, Torah study—were not entirely dependent on the existence of the Jerusalem temple, but were extremely versatile and adaptable to the new Jewish condition of exile and to the traumatic loss of the temple and Jewish sovereignty. The synagogue became the Jews' "miniature, transportable temple," accompanying them into exile. Moreover, claimed the Pharisees, the *Shekhinah,* or "Divine Presence," went into exile along with them. By the end of the second century, Pharisaic Judaism had become normative Judaism; its overall theology and religious institutions continue to be valid and compelling for Jews today.

One of the central ingredients of Pharisaic doctrine was the affirmation that already from the time of Moses and Sinai there was an oral tradition elucidating and accompanying the written one. This oral tradition, or at least the hermeneutical framework from which it evolved, was believed also to have been revealed by God to Moses (see, for example, Exod. 18:20; Deut. 5:28) and was expounded upon and applied by rabbinic scholars from generation to generation. The Torah states, for example, that on the holiday of *Sukkot* we are to take the fruit of "a beautiful tree" and dwell in a *sukkah,* or "hut." It was left to the oral tradition, however, to clarify the meaning of the written word and to explain what it referred to. The cryptic references of the Torah, therefore, seem to presume and to prove the existence of an oral tradition expounding upon the written one. Thus, the oral tradition injects into the written tradition both content and relevance, thereby enabling the Jew to use it as a guide for his daily life. It was to remain fluid, and resilient to change and adaptation in light of the conditions of the times. The oral tradition was God's word and continuing revelation both to man and *through* him.

Within a century or so before the Common Era one component of that oral tradition, *midrash* (homiletic literature that often used allegory to illuminate the moral teachings of the Torah and constituted the "sermons" of the time), came to be written down. Jesus, in all likelihood, was quite familiar with this rich body of Jewish literature, and many scholars maintain that he drew heavily from it, as well. Midrashic material continued to develop well into the Common Era and, indeed, is still written today. The overwhelming majority of the oral tradition, particularly the vast legal tradition, was not committed to writing but instead to memory by "scribes." It was carefully transmitted orally from rabbi to student from generation to generation and was studied in the various seminaries and talmudic academies of Palestine and Babylonia, which served as the main centers of Jewish learning during the first few centuries.

The decentralization and dispersion of Jews to different parts of the world, and the overwhelming amount of material that had accumulated as part of the oral tradition by the third century, contributed to the growing fear that aspects of that tradition would become distorted or forgotten. It was these conditions that finally prompted Rabbi Yehudah ha-Nasi (Judah the Prince) of Palestine to commit a skeletal outline of the oral tradition to writing (circa 250 C.E.). The *Mishnah,* meaning "teachings," as it came to be known, was written entirely in Hebrew. It is a concise commentary on the Tanakh, or written tradition, and was transmitted orally from generation to generation until finally written down in the third century. For example, it clarifies the concept of *lex talionis* ("an eye for an eye"), which the oral tradition had always understood as meaning that the *value* of the eye be ascertained and paid, not that the eye itself actually be removed. The Mishnah, therefore, codifies the meaning and intent of the Torah in light of the generations-old oral tradition.

Although written in Palestine, the Mishnah was accepted as authoritative by the prominent Torah academies in Babylonia, as well. And while Rabbi Judah was the one to compile and edit it, it was Rabbi Hillel, another Pharisee, whose views became most often cited in it and whose legal decisions became its cornerstone. Hillel moved from Babylonia to Israel around 30 B.C.E. and lived there at the time of Jesus. He was a patient, loving, and generous human being, a tolerant individual, always seeking to help the outcasts of society. Whether or not he and Jesus ever met is uncertain. They did, however, share many qualities such as a gentle temperament and a strong moral sense. Even some statements attributed to them are similar. Unlike Jesus, however, whose later followers parted with Judaism and the Jewish community and founded a new religion, Christianity, Hillel and his students remained within the ideological Jewish fold and constituted the mainstay for the preservation of Judaism.

Another prominent and well-respected Pharisaic Torah scholar of the time, Shammai, opposed Hillel's views on a variety of legal matters. Both Hillel and Shammai had large followings of Torah students, although in almost every instance in which they differed, the law was decided in Hillel's favor, which usually was the more lenient position.

The Talmud tells the story of a pagan who once came to Shammai asking to learn the entire Torah while standing on one foot (i.e., in a few minutes). Shammai considered the request so brazen and foolhardy he threw the pagan out. The pagan then went to the home of Hillel who welcomed him and patiently responded, "What is hurtful to you do not do unto others." He added that the rest of the Torah was commentary and said, "Go study it!" The striking similarities between Jesus' and Hillel's congenial, irenic dispositions and the fact that both insisted that the essence of the Torah lies in the biblical commandment to "love your neighbor as yourself" (Lev. 19:18) are, in all likelihood, more than coincidental. This supports the view that Jesus, like Hillel, came out of the Pharisaic tradition, which was more open to the masses and more tolerant and democratic than other Jewish groups at the time.

The skeletal outline of the oral tradition provided by the Mishnah, however, soon became insufficient to meet the needs of the Jewish people. By the fifth century there had developed an extensive body of unwritten rabbinic commentaries on the abbreviated Mishnah, stemming from the discussions that had taken place in the major Torah academies during the intervening years. Fearful lest this too be forgotten or distorted, Rabbis Ravina and Ashi of Babylonia decided to compile the material and commit it to script. They wrote in Aramaic, the spoken language of the time, and completed their work sometime in the early part of the fifth century. The *Gemara*, as it came to be called, is a direct and far more extensive commentary on the Mishnah, which itself is an abbreviated commentary on the Tanakh. A separate Gemara commentary on the Mishnah was written in Jerusalem in Palestine, although it is very similar to the one compiled in Babylonia.

Rabbis living at the time of the Mishnah are called *tannaim,* and the period (roughly 70–250 C.E.) is referred to as *tannaitic.* Rabbis living later on at the time of the Gemara are referred to as *amoraim,* and the period (roughly 250–450 C.E.) is referred to as *amoraic.* The Mishnah, along with its commentary, the Gemara, are together referred to as the *Talmud.* The span of those few centuries (roughly 70–450 C.E.) is often called the "Rabbinic" or "Talmudic" Period.

The Talmud is divided into tractates, each dealing with a different subject matter. Together they comprise hundreds of pages of text. The Jerusalem Talmud, comprising the Mishnah as well as the Gemara commentary edited in Palestine, never achieved the same prestige and authority that the Babylonian Talmud did. For the religious stature of the Babylonian Jewish community waxed greatly between 300–500 C.E., while the influence of the Palestinian Jewish community waned. Today, Jews study the Babylonian Talmud almost to the exclusion of the Jerusalem one.

In summary, the oral tradition, one of the principal Pharisaic contributions to the survival of Jewish life after the destruction of the temple, revolves around the written tradition, or Tanakh. It comprises the Talmud and Midrash, as well as *responsa* literature (i.e., questions and answers pertaining to law that arose over the centuries and that continue to be written today). The traditional belief dating back at least as far as the time of the Pharisees is that the principles, and perhaps even the content of this oral tradition, while written down in the first few centuries of the Common Era, were actually imparted by God at Sinai. Accordingly, the oral tradition is treated as constituting the word of God just as the written Tanakh does. Jesus, in all likelihood, was intricately familiar with the oral tradition since it was studied then in the synagogues. In all likelihood, he also participated in the discussions of the law and oral Torah that took place in the academies at the time. However, he seems to have been particularly influenced by the rabbinic *midrashim,* many of which are strikingly similar to his parables.

Religious Authority

While the Torah was revealed by God, the interpretation of that Torah, the oral tradition, is "revealed" (in its etymological sense of "uncovered") by man. It is man who assumes the prominent role of final arbiter of God's will and intent. The Talmud tells a homiletic story of a disagreement that arose between Rabbi Eliezer and other rabbinic sages of his time concerning whether or not a particular stove was kosher and could be used (see B. T. B. Metzia 59b). The standard rule in *halakhah,* or Jewish law then operative, was that such questions were to be resolved by a majority rabbinic vote. (This is based on Exod. 23:2.)

Rabbi Eliezer was so convinced that the stove was kosher, however, that although he differed with the majority of other rabbis, he resorted to miracles in order to prove that he was correct. "If the law is like me," Rabbi Eliezer exclaimed, "let the tree outside move." Lo and behold, the tree became uproot-ed and moved twenty yards away. The rabbis did not change their opinion. Rabbi Eliezer, according to the talmudic story, then called upon the roof of the academy to tilt, and lo and behold, it tilted! The rabbis stood aghast but continued to maintain that the law was according to the majority and that the stove was not kosher. Rabbi Eliezer then said, "Let the river change its course and flow downhill if I am correct," and the river changed its course! The rabbis in the academy still did not budge from their positions. Finally, Rabbi Eliezer appealed to God himself to disclose who was correct, and behold, a miracle occurred—a voice from heaven loudly proclaimed that Rabbi Eliezer was, in fact, correct and that the stove was kosher! At that, continues the talmudic story the rabbis turned to the heav-enly voice and, invoking the verse from Scripture that "it [the Torah] is not in heaven" (Deut. 30:12), declared (in para-phrase), "God, you already gave us the Torah at Sinai and we, therefore, no longer take heed of such revelatory voices. Did not you yourself write in the Torah that the law is determined by the majority?"

The story concludes with a depiction of God as being pleased with the rabbis and amused by their argument. God declared, "My children are correct, they have beaten me" (i.e., at my own game).

This delightful talmudic story provides a powerful insight into the Jewish concept of religious authority. God revealed himself and gave his Torah to Israel on Mount Sinai. It is now the rabbis' right and obligation to interpret that divine word according to the proper hermeneutical principles of the oral tra-dition that God himself ordained. Biblical authority rests not with God, but with the rabbis who were given that authority by him. "If any case arises requiring decision . . . any case within your towns which is too difficult for you, then you shall arise and go . . . to the . . . priests, and to the judge who is in office in those days, you shall consult them, and they shall declare to you the decision. Then you shall do according to what they declare to you . . . and you shall be careful to do according to all that they direct you" (Deut. 17:8-10).

God has spoken. The people of Israel possess the written and oral traditions, the divinely sanctioned tools by which they are to interpret God's will. And so, even though the stove in question in the above story may, in fact, have been kosher as Rabbi Eliezer claimed, God "admitted" that the rabbis were correct and that his law was to be determined now by man on the basis of the scriptural guidelines, which state that the majority rules. Even God cannot (i.e., would not) contradict his own word as revealed to man in the Torah.

Moreover, even if the Sanhedrin (the highest rabbinic court before 70 C.E.) accidentally selected the wrong day as the beginning of the new month, God nevertheless "sanctions" the decree since man, in his finitude, is the final arbiter of the divine word (see B. T., Ber. 19b). While today the months of the Jewish year are determined by a set lunar calendar, in ancient times scouts were sent out to view the new moon. In the event of cloudy or inclement weather, they might not have seen the new moon and their calculations could have been wrong by as much as one or two days. This could have thrown the entire holiday season off schedule so that Passover, for example, which is supposed to be celebrated on the fourteenth of the Hebrew month of Nisan, would have been observed on what actually was the fifteenth or sixteenth of Nisan.

According to the same principle, one who declares himself to be a prophet but who violates the laws of the Torah or proclaims something contrary to it is declared a fraud (Deut. 13:1-6). It is a heresy to suggest that the laws of Shabbat, for example, are no longer valid and are to be permanently suspended, since that would run counter to the divine word as revealed in the Torah. This idea is instructive for the question of how Jews view Jesus. For God, according to this principle, would not reveal a "new testament" that contradicted elements of his previous one as the New Testament appears to do, especially on the issue of the validity of Jewish law.

The question of divorce provides another good illustration of Jewish exegesis and religious authority in action, particularly since the outcome in this instance diverged from that adopted by Christianity. At the beginning of the Common Era there were two schools of Jewish thought on the subject of divorce, both deriving their views from the biblical phrase that states, "When a man takes a wife and marries her, if then she finds no favor in his eyes because he has found some indecency [in Hebrew, *ervat davar*] in her, [then] he writes her a bill of divorce . . ." (Deut. 24:1). The school of Shammai, which was conservative on most issues, focused on the word *ervah,* or "indecency" (the term is difficult to translate but clearly has a sexual connotation), and claimed that the Torah permitted divorce only in the event that the wife had committed adultery. The school of Hillel, on the other hand, focused on the word *davar,* which Hillel interpreted not as "something" but "anything," and insisted that the Torah allowed a man to divorce his wife for almost any reason. In all likelihood, Jesus, who was probably familiar with the different rabbinic views on this matter, accepted Shammai's conservative one, while later Judaism opted for the liberal position advocated by Hillel (see chapter 5).

Jews and Christians would be inclined to differ also in the very manner in which they read the portions of Scripture they share. Since the Torah is not the sole source of authority for Jews but rather is understood through the eyes of the far more elaborate oral tradition, traditional Jews would be inclined to study scriptures along with the many commentaries that were written over the centuries, some of which are, in fact, printed alongside standard versions of the Bible. And while Jews may offer their own insights into the biblical text (provided they do not conflict with the Talmud or traditional principles of Jewish exegesis), they would be inclined to ground them in the rabbinic commentaries. Christians, on the other hand, and Evangelicals in particular, believe that their reading of the Bible is guided by the Holy Spirit. They, therefore, tend to read the biblical text directly, in and of itself, rather than through the lens of a vast body of earlier commentary literature.

Judaism professes that prophecy ceased after the destruction of the first temple in 586 B.C.E. and that man, today, cannot speak authoritatively as if guided by a "divine holy spirit," or *ruach hakodesh*. As the talmudic story cited earlier indicates, we do not even heed "divine voices" or miracles that either bypass or conflict with traditional laws and hermeneutics. Jews are, therefore, highly critical and suspicious of those claiming to have received special divine messages urging them to speak or act in a particular manner, or informing them personally of future events. There are Christians, in contrast, who speak "prophetically" on issues of major significance, claiming, for example, to have had a divine revelation informing them when the next Mideast war or global catastrophe might occur. Some even insist that they had such revelatory experiences about trivial matters, such as God telling them to go out and buy flowers for their wives. Usually such Christians preface the divulgence of their private revelation with the phrase: "God told me. . . ." While such statements are sometimes intended to be taken figuratively, often they are meant quite literally. Jews invariably cringe when they hear such statements and instinctively ask where are the checks and balances that might prevent one from abusing and manipulating the word of God. For them and their faith, prophecy has come to a halt. To believe that they can discern God's will today directly, without recourse to Torah, Talmud, tradition, and other such factors, is to rely too much upon human nature, which is heavily influenced by the evil inclination toward sin.

By what authority should people claiming to be especially privy to God's message and speaking absolutely in his name be believed? And who should be believed when a variety of Christian preachers, all speaking in the name of God and the Bible, claim conflicting revelatory experiences? What constraints does the Christian tradition impose to protect itself from the potential abuse of those claiming to speak in God's name but who simply may be psychologically unbalanced or merely seeking power? What, in short, are the limits of legitimate interpretations of the word of God, and by what process does one arrive at those limits? Catholics claim that an ecclesiastical, hierarchical system headed by a pope, coupled with factors such as community, canon law, and tradition, establishes the boundaries for orthodox exegesis. Protestants, and Evangelicals in particular, claim that the Bible as interpreted through the aid of the Holy Spirit serves as the proper vehicle for discerning God's will, although Jews are rather skeptical of relying on such factors today, as the story of Rabbi Eliezer's stove indicates.

In Judaism, it is the oral tradition as developed through the centuries and as codified in the Talmud and by later rabbinic commentators that colors the Jews' understanding of the written word and delineates its content. The Bible, God's written word to man, is to be understood through the prism of the oral Torah, which is both divinely revealed and humanly created in response to God's revelatory initiative. (In the Hasidic and mystical traditions, this twofold dimension of Jewish authority is often described as "black fire" and "white fire." God imparts his word to man not only through "black fire," the portion of the Torah scroll written in ink, but also through "white fire," the oral Torah, symbolized by the white parchment space surrounding the imprinted letters of the Torah. Both are equally God's word.) To be sure, Jewish interpretations of the Bible often differ, at times radically. Yet there always exists a commonly accepted, biblically rooted process by which biblical exegesis is conducted and through which the decision as to orthopraxy, proper action, is reached. Once determined, those decisions are deemed binding upon the community and true to God's intent. They may not, however, conflict with earlier rabbinic decisions with which all decrees must be reconciled.

Judaism maintains that there is a diminution of religious authority with each successive generation, as we get further and further away from the Sinai revelation. The Torah is, therefore, more authoritative than the Prophets, which is more authoritative than the Mishnah, which is more authoritative than the Gemara, and so on. For the same reason, an *amora*, or rabbi living in the time of the Gemara, may not disagree with the legal decisions arrived at in the tannaitic period of the Mishnah, nor may a rabbi today disagree with a decision made by the Gemara.

Following the destruction of the temple, the demise of the Sanhedrin, and the redaction of the Talmud, Jewish law no longer was determined on the basis of rabbinic majority. Instead, a handful of rabbinic scholars in each generation became viewed as authorities on Jewish law by virtue of their piety and scholarship of earlier codes and commentaries, upon which even they must base their pronouncements. When electricity was discovered, for example, the question arose for the first time whether or not it constituted "fire" and was prohibited from being ignited on Shabbat in light of the Torah edict, "You shall kindle no fire in all your habitations on the sabbath day" (Exod. 35:3). After studying the combustion principle of electricity as well as related legal precedents, the vast majority of orthodox rabbinic authorities determined that electricity, in fact, operated on the same principles as fire and was, therefore, not to be turned on and off on Shabbat. This view became accepted by Orthodox Jews.

The *Shulchan Arukh,* or Code of Jewish law, written in the sixteenth century by Rabbi Joseph Caro, remains the principal codification for Orthodox Jews today. When differences regarding the law arise among rabbinic authorities, the accepted rule is to follow one's own rabbi.

Religious decisions for Conservative Jews today (see chapter 8) are determined also on the basis of traditional codes, although they inject into the decision-making process the additional stipulation that the outcome reflect the response of the totality of the peoplehood and community of Israel and that the given practice also find broad acceptance by that community.

For while the people of Israel may not be prophets, states the Talmud, they are the sons and daughters of prophets and their intuitive collective consciousness helps determine what is authoritative. Moreover, the rabbis maintained that a decision should not be made that would be too difficult for the community to bear. Thus, while both the written and oral traditions are authoritative in Conservative Judaism as they are in Orthodoxy, the views of the masses, which tend to be more lenient, play a far greater role in the Conservative determination of the law than they do in Orthodoxy. For these and other reasons, Orthodoxy's legal decisions are almost always more stringent and demanding than are Conservatives'. In Jewish life today, the Orthodox are the Jewish conservatives (see chapter 8).

Religious authority for Reform Jews, the third major Jewish denomination, is determined by the individual who, after confronting the ancient Jewish tradition, arrives at an autonomous decision as to his own personal practices. It is the individual, ideally informed by past Jewish traditions and writings, who determines the intent of God's word, not the rabbis as in Orthodoxy or the community as in Conservative Judaism. Modalities of conservative Christians' religious authority, for example, appear to be most closely akin to those of Reform Judaism, though their views on the authority of the Bible would be more closely linked with those of Orthodoxy.

The novel (and controversial) question of whether or not women may be ordained as rabbis is instructive in shedding light on the process by which the various Jewish denominations arrive at their legal decisions today. Orthodox rabbinic authorities, finding not only no precedent in Jewish law allowing such a practice, but finding sources expressly prohibiting it, have categorically denied women the right to become rabbis. Indeed, the issue is still so remote sociologically and halachically (i.e., legally), that it is rarely ever raised, let alone debated, in Orthodoxy.

Reform Judaism, on the other hand, approaches the issue from a more historical and sociological perspective, with a decidedly liberal approach to the sources or with a flat rejection of their binding authority, and permits the ordination of women. Indeed, there are many female Reform rabbis today. Finally, the Conservative movement, which takes seriously into account the views of Conservative Jews at large and employs a more liberal approach to the traditional written and oral sources than would Orthodoxy, remains divided on the issue, with liberal Conservatives favoring the ordination of women and conservative Conservatives opposing it. Only in 1983 did the Conservative movement decide to ordain women.

It is evident that Jews have not had a centralized and universally accepted system of religious authority for many centuries. There is no one person or rabbinical group today that can speak authoritatively for all Jews—even for all Orthodox Jews. Even the State of Israel has two Orthodox chief rabbis, each with his own following, who often differ with each other on questions of religious law. Moreover, many Orthodox Jews follow neither! With the exception of the dynastic Hasidic community where authority is passed on by lineage, rabbinic authority is derived from a rabbi's piety and scholarship of Torah, Talmud, Shulchan Arukh, and other Jewish sources.

Law

Throughout the centuries, the rabbis, in their role as interpreters of God's Torah and conveyors of the oral tradition, often extended the biblical law by establishing *gzerot,* or "fences," around it, so that the core law itself would be less likely to become violated (see Mishnah, Avot 3:13). The dietary laws, for example, were embellished by the rabbis to the point where today traditional Jews use separate dishes and tablecloths for dairy and meat. They even wait a few hours after eating meat before drinking milk or eating milk products. These and other such extensions of the dietary laws (see chapter 5, section on *kashrut)* are all, nevertheless, based on the core biblical prohibition against cooking a kid in its mother's milk.

Christians at times speak of the "burden" of the law upon the Jews, particularly how it places them in bondage and blinds them to the true message of Christ and how their obedience to it petrifies and perverts both the word and will of God (see, for example, Acts 15:10). Judaism, however, understands the *love* of God as the willingness to accept upon oneself the "yoke of the kingdom of God." For when seen from within, this yoke or burden is one that the observant Jew accepts willingly, out of abiding love and immeasurable joy. He regards the Torah and its laws as God's precious gift to Israel, as the concrete manifestation of his goodness and love for his people. The law purifies him, ennobles his spirit, and sanctifies his daily life (see below, *mitzvah*). It gives form to his quest for moral living. Observing God's law is the Jew's way of responding to the divine revelatory initiative that imparted that law. Far from the negative impressions some Christians (and Jews) have of Jewish law, often stemming from the way it was depicted and contrasted with Christian love and grace over the centuries, the observant Jew regards it as a way of life linking him with the divine, a vehicle enabling him to fulfill God's will, and a means for bringing him ever closer to the spiritual realm. Instead of bondage, the law represents true freedom. Rather than a burden, it is the Jew's greatest delight.

Judaism is a spiritual and moral system rooted in law, a "covenantal nomism," as E. P. Sanders has described it.[1] As in any legal system, however, the danger exists that man might become so engrossed in obeying the detail and minutiae of the law as to lose perspective of its overall primary purpose. Similarly, he might confuse the means by which he tries to reach God with the transcendent, infinite God himself. The repeated practice of law or ritual can, admittedly, also lead to its trivialization, mechanization, and routinization. Jewish observance of the law has often been denigrated for these and other such reasons and contrasted with Christianity which, it is suggested, supplanted law with love, human merit with God's grace, and works with faith.

Such pat dichotomies are actually byproducts of the historic polemic between Judaism and Christianity. In reality, there will always exist a creative tension in both traditions between man's actions and God's grace, between human merit and God's gift of love, between obedience to law and spontaneity, between righteousness through faith and righteousness through works. Indeed, the phenomenon of law is quite evident in Christianity, while that of love is most central in Judaism. Jesus, in the Book of Matthew, for example, clearly states that he did not come to abolish even one iota of the law but to fulfill it (see Matt. 5:17). And of course, Jesus' primary command to love one's neighbor as oneself (Matt. 22:37-40) was taken from the Hebrew Bible (Lev. 19:18) and reaffirmed as the quintessence of Judaism by the Talmud later on (see, for example, B. T., Shab. 31a). Judaism maintains that the dangers inherent in an ethical legal system that concretizes and directs human emotions toward God are far less threatening than those present in a subjective, open-ended system calling for "love" but not objectifying or systematizing those human emotions into a legal framework. For this reason, the rabbis state, "Greater is he who is commanded and observes [the law] than he who is not commanded and observes." Moreover, while the Jew is called upon to observe the law, he is also obligated to go "beyond the letter of the law" and to observe its "spirit" as well.

There are a myriad of situations prompting different kinds of moral responses that the average person may not be able to discern and for which he needs direction. The sixth of the Ten Commandments, for example, is "thou shalt not murder." What is involved in the prohibition of "murder"? Killing in self-defense? Striking first? Maiming someone who dies later from related causes? Killing inadvertently? Therapeutic abortions? There are countless circumstances arising daily wherein our response is to be determined on the basis of the core biblical phrase, "Thou shalt not murder." The Talmud even derives the prohibition against embarrassing someone in public or speaking evil about others from this phrase, since such behavior "murders" their reputation and kills their human dignity. Jewish law, which is grounded in the Bible, sheds light on all such issues and guides the person through the ethical maze that often besets him.

It should be noted that the King James Version of the Bible (mis)translated this commandment as "Thou shalt not *kill*," instead of *murder*. Even today Christians often cite this verse and interpret it as barring killing of any kind. Actually, there are two distinct and separate Hebrew words for the act of taking a human life—*hereg*, meaning "killing," and *ritzicha*, meaning "murder." The word used in both instances in which the Torah cites the sixth commandment (see Exod. and Deut.) is *ritzicha*, "murder."

There is a fundamental moral and biblical distinction between the act of "killing," which may be justified, and "murder," which is not. Man is permitted to *kill* in order to save himself from being *murdered* (i.e., in self-defense). It is the latter that the Torah in the sixth commandment prohibits, and for this reason, Judaism does not subscribe to a strictly pacifist view.

From a Jewish perspective, Christianity lost much of this original distinction due to its mistranslation of the Hebrew Torah text and due to its lack of an oral tradition. This prohibition of the sixth commandment, with all its meanings and applications, is but one example of the need for a judicious legal framework to guide one's actions. Such a framework, despite its shortcomings, was regarded by the rabbis as far better than the absence of any such one.

Jewish *halakhah*, or "law," is the code of Jewish religious life applied to daily exigences. It is similar to the American jurisprudence system in that both base themselves on a core constitution, supplemented by dockets of legal discussion that developed through the years, which interpreted and applied the words of the basic constitution to the varying circumstances of life.

The midrash tells that before giving the Torah to the people of Israel, God first offered it to all of the other nations of the world who invariably asked what was contained in it. When they heard of the many laws that would be required of them should they accept the Torah, they all decided to reject it. But, when God finally offered the Torah to Israel, suggests the midrash, their response was "everything God tells us, we shall *do* and we shall *listen*" (Exod. 24:7). The rabbis note that the order should have been reversed—first one listens, then one acts. Rather, the Jewish people loved God so dearly and trusted in him so completely that they were willing to accept his Torah and observe its laws even before learning what that commitment entailed.

At Sinai the Jews had a revelatory experience wherein they encountered a commanding God who unfolded his will for man. That was itself sufficient reason to accept his word unquestioningly. Such is the Jewish love for God's word and commitment to it. The Torah is a tree of life, an eternal heritage to be passed on from generation to generation. It is that which gives depth and meaning to the Jew's life (Deut. 6:1-4). The Torah is God's precious gift to Israel so that she might truly live (Deut. 5:30–33).

Prophecy

Judaism maintains that God not only revealed himself to Moses and the people of Israel at Sinai but that he also revealed himself at times to other select individuals—prophets—until after the destruction of the first temple (in 586 B.C.E.) when prophecy came to an end. Thereafter, states the Talmud, prophecy was given only to fools and children! The Jewish view of prophecy is strikingly similar to the Christian one as presented in 2 Peter 1:20-21 in affirming that it involves the bestowal of the divine spirit upon an individual, prompting him to speak out on God's behalf.

Unlike the case of Moses and the Torah, however, the revelations recorded in the prophetic Books were general ones, not verbatim "dictations" (see above). Thus, while the themes that Isaiah, for example, treated were, in fact, conveyed to him by God, the precise words he used were his own. They, therefore, differ stylistically from those used by Jeremiah, Ezekiel, or any of the other prophets. The principal mission of the prophets was to present God's message to the people and only secondarily to predict future events.

There are different levels of prophecy. Moses reached the highest rung humanly possible in that he spoke with God "face to face" (Deut. 34:10). All the other prophets, on the other hand, received their revelations through dreams or visions while in a hypnotic state (see Maimonides' *Mishneh Torah* for a description of the different levels of prophecy).

While the prophets spoke out on a host of ethical issues and often harshly admonished the people of Israel for not obeying God's word, their rebuke was premised in the conviction that Israel's covenant with God was never broken nor invalidated. The prophets, speaking from "within the family," often took liberties in saying things that, if said by an "outsider," would be outrageously offensive. In all likelihood, they also deliberately exaggerated the degree of Israel's iniquity in order to make their point as sharply as possible. Their message was, unfortunately, interpreted by Christians as a warning to Israel to repent of their sins lest they become despised and rejected by God, cut off from his covenant, and replaced by others (i.e., Christians) as his people. Early Christianity, in particular, viewed the Jews' exile and the destruction of the second temple as proof of Jewish sinfulness and of the fact that the Jews were being punished by God for having rejected their prophets, including Jesus, and were being replaced as God's people. Yet, unlike Amos or Hosea who castigated Israel for her sinfulness, but who did so from *within* the Jewish community as brothers motivated by a deep love and an abiding attachment to their people, the diatribes directed against the Jews over the centuries by Christians were from *outside* of that faith community. Far from being motivated by love, more often than not they stemmed from feelings of intolerance and contempt. As Bible scholar Pinchas Lapide has noted, when the prophetic tradition of censuring and reprimanding Israel was "somewhat abruptly transplanted into the language, thought, and lifestyle of Gentile-Hellenism, the compassionate sorrow of Jesus, as he placed himself in the succession of the prophets, hardened into a self-righteous reassurance in the church. Admonition was misconstrued into condemnation and well-meaning diatribes became words of stern divine judgment."[2]

Covenant

Judaism rests upon the fundamental proposition that Israel and God are eternally linked covenantally. "You stand this day all of you before the LORD your God . . . [to] enter into the sworn covenant of the LORD your God, which the LORD your God makes with you this day" (Deut. 29:10, 12). This *berit*, or "covenant," is an everlasting one, binding God with all future generations of Israel, as well. "Nor is it with you only that I make this sworn covenant, but with him who is not here with us this day as well as with him who stands here with us this day before the LORD our God" (Deut. 29:14-15).

Covenants were commonly made in the ancient Near East. They served as contracts or formal agreements between two parties, usually between kings or between kings and his subjects. The Jews transformed this concept entirely, however, by insisting that it also represented the modality of the relationship between God and his people, Israel. The specific format of covenantal agreements, such as the need for witnesses (in the biblical scheme, heaven and earth), the means by which they are sealed (e.g., the rainbow or circumcision), as well as the nature of the stipulations of the agreements themselves (e.g., if one party to the agreement acts properly then the other will reward him accordingly), remained essentially the same.

The first covenant described in the Torah was that between God and Noah, entered into after the flood. As part of his agreement, God promised never again to destroy the earth, while Noah, for his part, promised to observe basic moral, or "natural," law. The rabbis deduced seven commandments from the Torah, all of which are incumbent upon the sons of Noah and their future descendants—in other words, upon all humankind, always. These included the prohibitions against murder, theft, cruelty to animals, worshiping idols, blaspheming God, engaging in sundry illicit sexual relationships, as well as the positive command to set up a system of justice so that society would be ruled fairly (see B. T., Sanh. 57a and Gen. 9:1-9).

The Noahite covenantal agreement is not limited to Jews (since Noah himself was not a Jew) but is universal in nature and extends to all people. It represents the moral and religious expectations Judaism has of the non-Jew. In the Jewish view, the non-Jew who abides by these seven commandments merits salvation. He need not convert to Judaism to gain a place in the eternal "world to come," the Jewish term for the afterlife. This divine-human covenantal relationship and agreement was symbolically sealed by the appearance of the rainbow (see Gen. 9:12-17).

The second covenant described in the Torah was between God and Abraham, the first Jew, in which God promised him descendants and also to make him into the father of a great nation. God, moreover, promised Abraham that he would be his God and the God of his descendants, and that he would give them the land of Canaan as an eternal possession. "And I will establish my covenant between me and you and your descendants after you throughout their generations for an everlasting covenant, to be God to you and to your descendants after you. And I will give to you, and to your descendants after you, the land of your sojournings, all the land of Canaan, for an everlasting possession; and I will be their God" (Gen. 17:7-9). Abraham, as part of his agreement, promised to believe in God and to act justly and righteously before him (Gen. 17:11). In contrast with the Noahite covenant, the Abrahamic one is particularistic in nature; it applies only to Abraham and his descendants, the Jews.

The next covenant, which is regarded by Judaism as a culmination of the Abrahamic one rather than as an entirely new one, was made between God and the entire people of Israel at Sinai. As part of their agreement, Israel promised to obey God's Torah and commandments, while God promised to bless them and reward them for their deeds. "'See, I have set before you this day life and good, death and evil. If you obey the commandments of the LORD your God which I command you this day, by loving the LORD your God, by walking in his ways, and by keeping his commandments . . . then . . . the LORD your God will bless you. . . . But if your heart turns away, and you will not hear, but are drawn away to worship other gods and serve them, I declare to you this day, that you shall perish. . . . I call heaven and earth to witness against you this day, that I have set before you life and death, blessing and curse; therefore choose life, that you and your descendants may live" (Deut. 30:15-19). The symbol of the Sinaitic covenant is the Torah, which is also the repository of our knowledge of the content and stipulations of that eternal agreement.

The Abrahamic-Sinaitic covenantal agreement presumes both God's reaching out to Israel as well as Israel's acceptance of him. For if Israel is "the chosen" people, she is also "the choosing" people in that she chose to accept God as Lord. Revelation, God's movement toward man, represents only one part of the covenantal foundation. The act of *mitzvah* (i.e., Israel's commitment to obey God's commandments, see below) represents the human response to God's revelatory initiative and constitutes the other part of that agreement. They are to be a "light to the nations" (Isa. 42:6), a source of blessing to the world (Gen. 12:2–3).

It is essential to point out that Jewish chosenness does not imply Jewish superiority. God has a special relationship with Israel deriving from Abraham and Sinai, but he remains the God of the universe and of all people. His covenant with the descendants of Noah remains in force: "You shall be my own possession among *all* peoples; for *all* the earth is mine" (Exod. 19:5, emphasis added). As a result of that special relationship, however, Jews are also called upon to act especially ethically and responsibly. They are to serve as God's witnesses in the world through their testimony and actions. Furthermore, in the end of days this special covenant will be extended to all people (see, for example, Isa. 2:1-5; 56:1-8). God is Lord of the universe, not just of Israel. He seeks out all his creatures so that they might follow him and obey his word.

It should also be noted that although one is born into the covenanted Jewish community, Gentiles can enter this particularistic Abrahamic-Sinaitic covenant, too, through conversion. Jewish chosenness, in other words, does not imply absolute exclusivity. However, Judaism does not proselytize or seek out such conversions since Gentiles are already linked covenantally with God through the Noahite covenant. The Talmud even claims that a Gentile who acts according to the ethics of the Torah is as holy as the high priest (B.T., A.Z. 3a). Thus, a Gentile who abides by the seven Noahite commandments merits salvation and "a place in the world to come" *without* having to accept Judaism, while Jews are called upon to observe the laws emanating from the Abrahamic-Sinaitic covenant in order to attain that same salvation.

While the covenant is essentially a formalized, legal agreement, the relationship between God and Israel is rooted in love and cannot be reduced to mere legalisms. God so loved Israel that he gave them his Torah, while Israel's love for God was so overwhelming they blindly agreed to follow his law. Jewish tradition often portrayed the covenantal relationship between God and Israel as analogous to the institution of marriage which, likewise, is established through vows and legalities but whose underpinnings are love and commitment. The prophet Hosea described God as saying to Israel, "I will betroth you to me for ever; I will betroth you to me in righteousness and in justice, in steadfast love, and in mercy. I will betroth you to me in faithfulness; and you shall know the LORD" (Hos. 2:19-20). Jeremiah, too, affirmed this link of love, "Thus says the LORD: . . . 'I have loved you with an everlasting love; therefore I have continued my faithfulness to you'" (Jer. 31:2-3).

Daily the Jew affirms in his prayers, "With an everlasting love thou hast loved the House of Israel—thou has taught us Torah, Mitzvot. . . . Blessed are thou, O Lord, who lovest thy people, Israel." This prayer is then immediately followed by the *Shema:* "Hear, O Israel, the Lord our God, the Lord is One. Thou shalt love the Lord your God with all your heart, with all your soul, with all your might . . ." (i.e., Deut. 6:4-10). The links between God and Israel may have indeed been formalized through a covenant that demanded loyalty and commitment from the parties. They remain rooted, however, in a mutually abiding love.

As mentioned earlier, the covenant is an eternal, everlasting pact, binding God with all future generations of Israel, too: "Nor is it with you only that I make this sworn covenant, but with him who is not here with us this day as well as with him who stands here with us this day before the LORD our God" (Deut. 29:14-15). The rabbis deduced from this verse that the souls of all Jews who ever lived and who *would* ever live stood at that moment at Sinai and heard the resounding voice of God speaking to them (see B. T., Shev. 39a).

Preserving the generational links on the chain of Jewish tradition is one of the most powerful driving forces for Jews and a key mandate for their survival. The covenant is not a marginal aspect of the Jews' lives; it is embodied in their very flesh and being. This is symbolized by the rite of circumcision which marks their entrance into the covenant (see chapter 5). The Jew renews his commitment to the covenant daily by observing God's mitzvot, and linking himself to the chain of Jewish life and tradition. He reaffirms it constantly through covenantal living. And while God's covenant with Israel can undergo strain and tension, it can *never* be broken. It is an eternal covenant rooted in mutual love and commitment, and remaining in effect for all times, all generations, and under all conditions. On Sinai, infinity met finitude, God encountered man, and the Divine Revealer entered into a covenant with a willing receiver, Israel. From then on they are bonded together eternally.

The covenant is not only instructive for Israel, one party to the agreement, but also binds God and involves him in the life and destiny of his partner, Israel. For this reason, Abraham felt justified in arguing with God over the injustice of wanting to destroy Sodom, and similarly, Hasidic masters brazenly confronted God when they felt that he was not fulfilling his part of the covenantal agreement. In our day, we have witnessed the most serious challenge ever to the existence of the covenant—the Holocaust. As Elie Wiesel, Holocaust survivor, author, and struggler with God, has written, "The Jewish people entered into a covenant with God. We were to protect His Torah and He in turn assumes responsibility for Israel's presence in the world." But while God sent the Jews on a mission to redeem the world, quipped Wiesel, he "failed to tell us it was a suicide mission!"[3] The very existence of the covenant and of the covenantal people was placed in jeopardy by the Holocaust. And yet, the depth of Jewish commitment to Judaism, to the State of Israel, and to Jews worldwide, indeed to life itself, is powerful evidence of their willingness to reaffirm the validity of the covenant anew.

The covenant has undergone repeated testing by fire at various times in Jewish history. And yet the people of Israel, God's covenantal community, have remained faithful to it. They have willingly renewed covenantal living even in our own day, despite what appears to be God's greatest breach of the agreement thus far. 'You are my witnesses,' says the LORD, 'I am God'" (Isa. 43:12). This divine promise and Jewish conviction remains as valid and compelling today as it has ever been.

Mitzvah

"For this commandment [*mitzvah*] which I command you this day is not too hard for you, neither is it far off. . . . But the word is very near you; it is in your mouth and in your heart, so that you can do it" (Deut. 30:11, 14). "Then he [Moses] took the book of the covenant, and read it in the hearing of the people; and they said, 'All that the LORD has spoken we will do, and we will be obedient'" (Exod. 24:7).

Israel responds to God's covenantal love and imparted will through mitzvah. The Hebrew term mitzvah (plural, *mitzvot*) means much more than just law, commandment, or good deed. By performing an act of *mitzvah* the Jew attests to the continued vitality and force of the covenant as a whole on his life. His very acceptance of the Lordship of God necessarily involves his adherence to God's mitzvah, as well. For inherent in the Jew's obligation to abide by the word of God is his duty to observe the responsibilities and commitments put forth therein. The mitzvot are concretized and applied to everyday life situations through the system of *halakhah*, or Jewish law, literally meaning "the way to walk" as in *tao* in Chinese culture. Halakhah transforms the sublime concepts of covenant and encounter with God into daily realities by regulating virtually every aspect of the Jew's life. God has an abiding love for his people, Israel, and because of that love, he gave them Torah and mitzvot.

The mitzvot sanctify the Jew's life and imbue it with transcendent meaning and content. Daily the Jew prays, "For they [the mitzvot] are our lives and the length of our days and upon them we will meditate day and night." The mitzvot are the vehicles by which Israel is transformed into a kingdom of priests and a holy nation; they are the divinely ordained tools enabling her to emulate God's ways *(imitatio dei)* and to become holy—"You shall be holy for I the Lord your God am holy." Through them we become cleansed and purified. As the Jew recites in his weekly Sabbath prayers, "Our God and God of our fathers, sanctify us in thy commandments [mitzvot] and make thy Torah our portion, satisfy us with thy goodness and bring us to rejoice with thy salvation; and purify our hearts so that we might worship thee in truth. . . ." All blessings, therefore, begin with the words, "Blessed are you, O Lord our God, King of the universe who has sanctified us with your mitzvot and commanded us to . . ." (the specific mitzvah is mentioned). The mitzvot elevate, sanctify, and ennoble man. Indeed, the only reason the Torah was revealed, claim the rabbis, was "for the purpose of purifying human beings" (Gen. Rab. 44). The mitzvot shape the human character, mold his personality, and color his worldview. The concept of mitzvah is not foreign to man but "is in your mouth and in your heart, so that you can do it" (Deut. 30:14). In the words of the blessing recited over the public reading of the Torah, "Blessed art thou, O Lord our God, King of the universe who has given us his Torah which is truth and who has planted eternal life within us thereby. Blessed art thou, O Lord, giver of the Torah."

"In Judaism," writes Martin Buber,

> one need only note how many everyday actions are introduced by a blessing to recognize how deep the hallowing reaches into what is in itself unhallowed. One not only blesses God every morning on awakening because He has allowed one to awaken, but also when one begins to use a new house or piece of clothing or tool, because one has been preserved in life to this hour. Thus, the simple fact of continued earthly existence is sanctified at each occasion that offers itself. . . . The separation between the [profane and the holy] realms is only a provisional one. . . . In the Messianic world all shall be holy. . . . The profane is now regarded as a preliminary stage of the holy; it is the not-yet-hallowed. Human life is destined to be hallowed in its natural form. "God dwells where man lets Him in!" The hallowing of man means this "letting in." Basically the holy in our world is what is open to God as the profane is what is closed off from Him, and hallowing is the event of opening out. . . .[4]

On Sinai, Israel encountered a loving, commanding God who, out of his profound concern for man, revealed his will to him. Mitzvot provide man with the opportunity to transform his every action into a means of relating with transcendence and ultimacy.

They are not merely objects of intellectual speculation or metaphysical cognition. Nor is their function only, as Rousseau believed, to restrain man, to establish order in society, and to create a social contract among people, although these admittedly form part of it. The Talmud even states that "if not for the fear of the laws of the land, people would swallow each other up alive." The concept of mitzvah, however, goes well beyond such definitions of "law" and is far more profound and engaging. As the late Rabbi Abraham J. Heschel so eloquently wrote, "Religion without mitzvot is an experience without the power of expression, a sense of mystery without the power of sanctification; a question without an answer. Without the Torah we have only deeds that dream of God; with the Torah we have mitzvot that utter God in acts."[5]

For this reason, Judaism is far more concerned and precise when it comes to questions of deeds and actions than it is, for example, with those of speculative theology. As Heschel wrote,

> We must not try to read chapters in the Bible dealing with the event at Sinai, as if they were texts in systematic theology. Its intention is to celebrate the mystery, to introduce us to it rather than to penetrate or to explain it. . . .
>
> A Hasid, it is told, after listening to the discourse of one who lectured to him about the lofty concept of God according to the philosophers, said: "If God were the way you imagine Him, I would not believe in Him." However subtle and noble our concepts may be, as soon as they become descriptive, namely, definite, they confine Him and force Him into the triteness of our minds. Never is our mind so inadequate as in trying to describe God. The same applies to the idea of revelation. When defined, described, it completely eludes us. . . .
>
> The dogmatic theologian who tries to understand the act of revelation in terms of his own generalizations takes himself too seriously and is guilty of over-simplification. Revelation is a mystery for which reason has no concepts. To ignore its mysterious nature is an oversight of fatal consequences. Out of the darkness came the voice

of Moses; and out of the darkness comes the word to us. The issue is baffling.

And if you ask: What was it like when the people stood at Sinai, hearing God's voice? the answer will be: Like no other event in the history of man. There are countless legends, myths, reports, but none of them tell of a whole people witnessing an event such as Sinai.[6]

The concept of mitzvah flows logically from the belief in a Supreme Being who loves man and is concerned for his welfare. The mitzvot are God's blueprints of how man ought to lead his life and imbue it with divine purpose and content. They enable man to sanctify life and to advance the dawning of the *malkhut shamayim,* or "heavenly kingdom," on earth. Man, through his performance of mitzvot, can actually help bring the Messiah! The Jewish mystical tradition, in fact, claims that mitzvot even metaphysically "fix" the world and affect the spiritual composition of the universe as a whole. Man's observance of even the smallest and most trivial mitzvah—when performed with the proper intent and commitment—advances the redemption of the world.

As Heschel noted,

We have never been the same since the day on which the voice of God overwhelmed us at Sinai. . . . Something unprecedented happened. God revealed His name to us, and we are named after Him. "And all the peoples of the earth shall see that the Lord's name is proclaimed over you" (Deut. 28:10). . . . If other religions may be characterized as a relation between man and God, Judaism must be described as a relation between man with Torah and God. The Jew is never alone in the fact of God; the Torah is always with him. A Jew without the Torah is obsolete. The Torah is not the wisdom but the destiny of Israel, not our literature but our essence. It is said to have come into being neither by way of speculation nor by way of poetic inspiration, but by way of prophecy or revelation.[7]

The significance of the concepts of Torah, the oral tradition, law, prophecy, covenant, and mitzvah cannot be overestimated. They constitute the very building blocks of the Jewish faith, the fundamentals of Jewish living. They are the means through which God imparts his will to his children, Israel, and the ways in which Israel responds in love to his beckoning call.

Chapter 2

JEWISH PATHS
TO SANCTIFICATION

The Jewish View of Humankind

"Then the LORD God formed man of dust from the ground, and breathed into his nostrils the breath of life; and man became a living being" (Gen. 2:7).

The Torah describes man as having been created "of dust from the ground." Indeed, his very name, "Adam," derived from the Hebrew word *adamah,* meaning "ground," and reflective of his essence, symbolizes man's earthly, material, and insignificant state of being. Abraham expressed a similar anthropology when he exclaimed, "I am but dust and ashes." This deprecating view of man, in fact, constitutes the central motif of an entire book of the Bible, Ecclesiastes. Later rabbinic literature and theology also endorsed the concept, and even introduced it into the daily liturgy. Each morning the Jew declares, "What are we, what value our lives . . . for everything is like nothingness in your eyes," and on the Day of Atonement he recites a prayer beginning with the words, "What is man that thou should even think of him?"

The Mishnah, too, affirms the insignificance of man. "Consider these three things and you will not come to sin: know from whence you came, where you are going, and before whom you will in the future have to give an accounting of your deeds. From whence you came? From a foul smelling drop. Where are you going? To a place of dirt, insects, and worms.

And before whom will you in the future have to give an accounting for your deeds? Before the King of Kings, the Holy One, blessed be He."

Another rabbinic commentary asks why God created man on the sixth day and not earlier. Its answer is this: to teach him the lesson of humility, for even the lowly insect (which was created on the fifth day) preceded man in the order of creation. This derogatory anthropology was so well entrenched in rabbinic thought that a disagreement arose among the talmudic rabbis whether or not it was better for man to have even been created in the first place, considering his unworthy character. Amazingly, their conclusion was that it would have been better had man, in fact, *not* been created, but "now that man has been created, let him examine his deeds." In short, an array of Jewish sources presents a portrait of man as a frail, finite, and corporeal being of no greater intrinsic significance than any other living creature. In the words of the daily liturgy, "The advantage of man over the beast is nothing, for all is vanity."

The same Genesis verse cited above from the Torah, however, continues by saying, ". . . and [God] breathed into his [man's] nostrils the breath of life." The rabbis derive from this portion of the verse that man is not only a physical being fashioned from the dust of the earth, but also a creature imbued with a divine soul. Man is an "inspired" being, in its etymological sense of "breathed into" by God. He is of infinite value for he possesses a part of the divine himself.

The psalms, for example, extol man's greatness, affirming that God "made him [man] little less than God" (Ps.8:5). In fact, according to the midrash, when God created man the heavenly angels were so overwhelmed and awed by man's divine soul and creative abilities that they mistook him for another god and began praising and worshiping him! Man is unique among all of God's creation, for only he was created *bitzelem elokim,* "in the image of God," with the awesome power either to preserve and fulfill the world or to destroy it.

Man was of such immense worth that the rabbis characterized him as a copartner with God himself in the creation of the world. God *needs* man to assist him in the task of building and completing the world. For this reason it was Adam, not God, who named the animals (see Gen. 2:20) and who demonstrated thereby his ability to capture their essence, to exert mastery over them, and to complete their creation. Man is commanded to conquer the earth, to subdue nature, and to rule over all of creation (see Gen. 1:28-29).

Through the rite of circumcision, the Jew also shows that man must "fix" and complete *all* of God's creation, including his very own self. "Why was man created singly (instead of in a community)?" asks the Talmud. To teach us the tremendous value of human life, that "he who destroys even one soul is as if he destroyed the entire world" (B. T., Sanh. 37a). For had Adam died, the entire world and all humankind would, in fact, have come to an abrupt end. The entire body of rabbinic thought pertaining to human life issues, such as abortion, euthanasia, suicide, and so on, is premised on this cardinal Jewish doctrine of the dignity, worth, and absolute value of humankind.

The Jewish view of the nature of man is rounded out by the final words of the above Torah passage, ". . . and behold, man became a *nefesh chaya.*" The Hebrew word *nefesh* means "spirit," while *chaya*, which is derived from the root *chai* meaning "life," is the generic term for "animal" or "creature." Man, in the Jewish view, is a unique being in that only he comprises a dual nature of both spirit and animal, both *nefesh* and *chaya*. He is both physical vessel and spiritual being, both dust from the earth and a divinely inspired creature. He is of inestimable significance and insignificance at the same time. Only man embodies both earthly and divine characteristics which are combined together in such a unique and majestic manner.

In the Jewish view, man's soul is derived from God who is pure and good. Man is, therefore, likewise inherently pure and good. This is alluded to in the Torah, claim the rabbis, which states only after man's creation on the sixth day that, "God saw everything that he had made, and behold, it was *very* good" (Gen. 1:31, emphasis added). Daily the Jew recites the following prayer upon awakening: "O God, the soul which you have implanted in me is a pure one—you created it, you molded it, you breathed it into me, and you will some day take it away from me. . . ."

Man is intrinsically pure since he was created by God, the embodiment of absolute purity and goodness. Moreover, since materialism and finitude were rarely treated as evils per se, the fact that man comprises a physical as well as a spiritual component rarely deterred the rabbis from regarding him as innately pure. The radical dualistic approach to life, which viewed the material world as evil and the spiritual and aesthetic realms as good, filtered into Western thought predominantly through Greek rather than Jewish influence (although Jews were certainly not immune to its influences, either).

This Jewish view of the nature of humankind stands in sharp contrast with the classical Christian one that suggests that as a result of Adam's sin, all future generations of man became tainted with Original Sin. In the Jewish view, sin is a human action, not a condition. In the dominant Christian view, however, man is so caught up in his sinfulness that he lacks the ability for self-regeneration. God, therefore, sent his only begotten Son into the world to die for man's sins so that those believing in him might be saved. (While the dichotomy between the Christian and Jewish conceptions of sins is real, it is often exaggerated.[1]) Rabbi Heschel described the differences between Judaism and Christianity on this fundamental issue in the following manner:

> Christianity starts with one idea about man; Judaism with another. The idea that Judaism starts with is that man is created in the likeness of God. You do not have to go far, according to Judaism, to discover that it is possible to bring forth the divine within you and the divine in other men. There is always the opportunity to

do a mitzvah. It is with that opportunity that I begin as a Jew. Christianity begins with the basic assumption that man is essentially depraved and sinful—that left to himself he can do nothing. He has to be saved. He is involved in evil. This is not the Jewish way of thinking. The first question of Christianity is: "What do you do for the salvation of your soul?" I have never thought of salvation. It is not a Jewish problem. My problem is what mitzvah can I do next. Am I going to say a blessing? Am I going to be kind to another person? Am I going to study Torah? How am I going to honor the Sabbath? These are my problems. The central issue in Judaism is the mitzvah, the sacred act. And it is the greatness of man that he can do a mitzvah. How great we are that we can fulfill the will of God! But Christianity starts with the idea that man is never able to fulfill the will of God. All he has to do, essentially, is to wait for salvation. Here we have two different ways—the classical Jewish way, the way of the Bible and the rabbis, and the other way. I have profound respect for Christianity and Christian theology. Christianity is one way and Judaism is another.[2]

The question of whether evil, in fact, exists or is just perceived as such by man, has been debated among the rabbis for centuries. The problem they faced was that if evil *does* exist, how could it have been created by God since evil cannot stem from pure goodness? And if evil exists and God did *not* create it, then one must assume the autonomous, ontological status of the devil who is a being coequal with God, something that Judaism has utterly rejected. It was this dilemma that prompted many rabbis to claim that evil and Satan as ontological forces do not, in fact, exist, but are only perceived as such by man. Perhaps for this reason the Talmud ruled that we are to recite the blessing, "Blessed art thou, the true judge," even upon hearing bad tidings. For while bad news may appear to man

as evil, it must be regarded as in some way serving a greater
providential purpose, which in the long run may even be for
man's benefit.

Although the rabbis regarded man as intrinsically pure, they
readily acknowledged that he is in possession of both "a good
and a bad inclination"—a *yetzer ha-tov* and a *yetzer ha-ra*. Man
has the potential for doing great evil as well as good, as God
himself "realized" (see Gen. 6:5). His disposition toward evil
may even be stronger than his one for good. Nevertheless,
man, in the Jewish view, remains innately pure. Moreover,
insisted the rabbis, man has in his possession an effective antidote to the seductive power of the evil inclination—the study
and practice of Torah. Man, according to the Talmud, is not
only required to direct his good inclination toward God, but
his bad one as well. For the Torah states, "You shall love the
LORD your God with *all your heart*" (Deut. 6:5, emphasis
added), in Hebrew, *bichol livovcha,* which is a plural form
implying two hearts. From this the rabbis derived that we are
to love God not only with our "good heart" or inclination but
with our evil impulses as well, for even they have the potential
for becoming good (see B. T., Ber. 9:5). Therefore, while man
was created inherently pure, he lives in a state of potentiality,
capable of doing great good or evil.

Underlying this doctrine is the presumption that man was
also created with the ability to *choose* between good and evil.
Indeed, the entire Torah is predicated on the notion that man
possesses free will and that his actions are not predestined.
Concepts such as law, covenant, and reward and punishment,
which are all rooted in human choice and an act of will, would
otherwise not be at all valid.

The Jewish mystical tradition explained the doctrine of
free will by first examining how the physical world was able
to come about since God is omnipresent and "occupies" all
space. It resolved this dilemma by introducing the concept of
tzimtzum, meaning divine "shrinking" or "limitation." God created the world, suggest the Jewish mystics, by first "shrinking"

himself, so to speak, and then creating the material world within the vacuum that remained. Similarly, God restrains himself from wielding his overwhelming power and from controlling man's destiny, and allows man's free will to fill the power void instead.

The Jewish View of the World

The Jewish view of the physical world is that it, too, is intrinsically good, as indicated by the biblical pronouncement after each day of creation: "And God saw that it was good." Man has the privilege and, indeed, obligation to derive pleasure from the material world and to avail himself of its goodness. He should neither deny himself such pleasure nor radically dichotomize the world into spirit versus matter or sacred versus profane. Rather, as both Martin Buber and early twentieth century Zionist leader Rabbi Kook suggested, man should view life as comprising the realms of the holy and the "not yet" holy. Everything in the world, they maintained, was created with the potential for becoming an object of sanctity, otherwise God would not have created it. Nothing in creation can be intrinsically or unalterably profane. Like man, the material world exists in a state of potentiality, capable of being used as a source for good or for bad.

As a result of this positive worldview, rather than denying material pleasure as the early Christian Church tended to do, Rabbinic Judaism affirmed its essential value, provided it was consecrated and "blessed" (see Mark 14:22, which combines both the Jewish and Christian aspects). The act of blessing in Judaism does not bestow a new state of holiness unto an object, as with the blessing and consecration of the communion bread in many Christian traditions. Rather, through the act of blessing in Judaism, man gratefully acknowledges that all of his material benefits derive from God. The blessing "entitles" man to partake of pleasure; it does not metaphysically transfer holiness to the object itself. This doctrine is fundamentally different from a Calvinist one, for example, which goes one major step further and claims that being blessed with material goods is itself a sure sign of one's election in the eyes of God. Such a view is utterly rejected by Judaism.

A further implication of this Jewish ethos is that asceticism rarely became accepted as a Jewish ideal. In fact, according to the rabbis, the reason the Nazirite brought a sin offering upon completion of his vow to abstain from drinking wine and cutting his hair was because he sought to attain spiritual union with God *apart* from the community and this-worldly pleasures, rather than *through* them. Similarly, acts of material self-denial and renunciation, such as fasting, are categorically prohibited on Shabbat and other festivals. Instead, the Jew is to partake of pleasures such as eating, drinking, dressing well, and engaging in sexual relations with his spouse. Man is to partake of this-worldly blessings, not to renounce them, though he is called upon to bless them and acknowledge them as God's gifts. The New Testament injunction to sell all of one's possessions and distribute them to the poor since "it is easier for a camel to go through the eye of a needle than for a rich man to enter the kingdom of God" (Luke 18:25) is most unrabbinic. The spiritual ideal in Judaism is attained through sanctified participation in God's creation, not through acts of denial and deprivation. Life is to be lived in its entirety. "In the future [world]," declares the Jerusalem Talmud, "every person will have to give an account for every pleasure in this world which he did *not* partake of."

This-worldly pleasures can be consecrated on two different levels. Sexual relations, for example, can be sanctified through the institution of marriage as a means of procreating the earth and fulfilling the commandment to be fruitful and multiply (see Gen. 1:28). A second level of sanctification lies in the fact that sexual relations in the context of marriage bring man and woman closer together and alleviate their existential fears and loneliness (see Gen. 2:18). That these two dimensions of sexuality are truly distinct can be seen from the fact that a woman who is either already pregnant or who cannot bear children may nevertheless engage in sexual relations with her spouse although no new procreation is possible. In terms of the first level of biblical sexuality, procreation has already been achieved. In terms of the second, it is still possible to provide comfort and companionship to each other. Humankind is called upon to consecrate pleasure on both levels.

Similarly, the Jew recites a blessing to sanctify his act of eating and drinking. Drinking alcoholic beverages (in moderation), for example, is entirely permissible in Judaism, though a blessing is to be recited before and after drinking them as with all other foods and drinks. However, these pleasures, too, can be consecrated on a second, more profound level when they are used to elevate the festive Shabbat meal and to enhance the Shabbat joy. Fasting can also be accompanied by a second level of consecration when one not only abstains from eating but actively engages in feeding the hungry, clothing the naked, and setting the oppressed free (see Isa. 58:6-8).

Judaism is not a faith system serving as one compartment of life, separate and apart from all others. It is a way of life that embraces the totality of existence and forms the root of all the Jew's commitments. Judaism should impact all of a Jew's actions and sensibilities. It is his window to the ultimate and his gateway to salvation. The Jew's every step in life should be taken "Jewishly"; no area should be devoid of a Jewish insight and response. For this reason, when the Talmud sought a biblical citation expressing the foundation of all Judaism, it chose the phrase "In *all* thy ways acknowledge him [God] . . ." (see B. T., Ber. 63a). For this reason also, blessings are recited over some of the most mundane actions, such as upon seeing lightning or hearing thunder, and even after using the washroom. For it is man's daily routine—eating, sleeping, working, and so on—that is most in need of sanctification. Judaism's claim is upon man in his entirety. It spills over into all facets of life and does not leave any part exempt from divine penetration. In the words of the psalmist, "I keep the LORD always before me" (Ps. 16:8). Even fundamental, other-worldly Jewish doctrines, such as salvation, are secondary to the principal task engaging man, which is to sanctify life and redeem this world in the here and now. Indeed, the Talmud states that the first question man is asked upon entering the next world after death is the mundane one of whether he was honorable in the conduct of his everyday business (see B. T., Shab. 31a).

One of the persistent charges directed against Jews in the Middle Ages was that they were an extremely carnal people. And since carnality was equated with evil, the stereotype emerged that Jews were the incarnation of the devil and embodiment of the demonic. Although, of course, false and pernicious, such perceptions did accurately pinpoint the fact that salvation for the Jew is attained precisely through creation and that Jewish spirituality is indeed rooted in earthliness and materialism. Pleasure, in the Jewish view, can express religious value; material enjoyment can become a positive source for spirituality. Judaism insists that the physical world is an aid, not an obstacle, in man's path toward salvation. It professes the value of sanctified materialism.

As a result of this positive worldview and anthropology, Jews tend to place less theological emphasis than Christians on other-worldly matters such as heaven and hell, life after death, Messiah, resurrection of the dead, salvation, and so on. Indeed, these and other such compelling tenets fundamental to both the Christian and Jewish faiths were rarely addressed by the rabbis (or the Torah for that matter) with any degree of explicitness or specificity. Instead, Judaism stressed the obligation upon the Jew to devote his religious energies to sanctifying this-worldly objects and pursuits. For while this world is, indeed, but a corridor to the next, that world to come can only be entered into if our deeds are meritorious while we inhabit this one. The Torah, in the Jewish view, is a blueprint of how we ought to lead our lives and achieve salvation in the here and now more than it is an account of other-worldly dogmas. It affirms a spirituality of worldly participation and sanctification.

This Jewish approach to spirituality is also characteristic of Judaism's understanding of salvation which, likewise, must involve the physical as well as spiritual realms—God's kingdom in heaven and on earth. Largely because both of these dimensions of the redemptive promise remained unfulfilled, Jews have rejected the many pseudo-messiahs who arose throughout history. The Jewish preoccupation (or, perhaps, messianic obsession) with social justice concerns, such as aiding the poor and oppressed, probably stems from the rich cultural, religious, and prophetic heritage that bids Jews to sanctify and redeem this world in the here and now, not to escape it or to become preoccupied with other-worldly pursuits. In Judaism, the Exodus and Sinai events became paradigmatic of what constitutes salvation in the messianic era, with the former pointing to the nature of man's physical redemption and the latter to his spiritual deliverance. Both were events taking place in history, not transcending it. Jews, therefore, tend to view the Christian concept of salvation as involving the interiorization and spiritualization of redemption. They reject Jesus as the Messiah, in part, because *both* dimensions of the messianic promise, the spiritual and physical redemption of the world, were not fulfilled by him. And while the Christian starting point is generally the Augustinian question of "Are you saved?" the Jewish one is essentially "Have you sanctified your life and the world and thereby tried to bring Messiah?"

Invariably, the rabbis understood the Garden of Eden account allegorically as paradigmatic of the ideal state of universal man in his relationship with God, his fellow man, and creation itself. It represents the state of the world in its completeness. The story sets forth the condition of universal man in a nonstructured, uncomplicated world devoid of religious structures and symbols and transcending all religious dogmas and institutions. It is the story of universal man pre-Sinai and pre-Calvary, the universal God Creator of all things, and the ideal relationship between the two. Man's role in this ideal state is to acknowledge and worship his Creator—*leovdah ulshomrah,* meaning "to work and preserve it," with the term "it" here referring not only to the earthly garden but to God's word and will as well. The Garden of Eden represents the fulfilled state of both man and the world in the messianic age.

Such a paradigmatic worldview is intended to be affirmed by non-Jews as well as by Jews. It represents Judaism's vision for all humankind. Universal man has a vocation to build the earth and to participate in this garden. He is to be fruitful and multiply, to conquer and subdue nature and unravel its mysteries, and to work by the sweat of his brow. (That man is to labor vigorously was not understood by the rabbis so much as a curse as it was a part of the same biblical Garden of Eden ideal. For work can bring dignity to the spirit and nobility to the soul. Adam's "curse" was that despite his toil, the ground would not bear fruit but only thistles and shrubs.) All humankind serve as God's copartners in the majestic task of building and completing the creation of the world; all were placed on earth "to work and preserve" the "garden" and to be loyal to God's word.

Participating in material pleasure and other this-worldly pursuits, particularly in the most carnal and profane of them, in order to sanctify and redeem the world and, as the mystical tradition suggests, to salvage the divine sparks inherent in all things, admittedly involves great risk. It is easy to forget the religious impulses and sensibilities serving at the very center of such a worldview that call for such participation in the first place. One can become so engrossed with materialism as to lose sight of the very obligation to consecrate it. Conversely, members of religious traditions that give less sanction to materialism and this-worldly pursuits run the risk of ignoring history and turning their backs on the physical needs of their fellow human beings. Judaism and Christianity can, therefore, genuinely complement each other by reminding one another of the need to strike a proper balance between man's materialistic and spiritual pursuits. If Jews, due to the emphasis in their theology, become overly preoccupied with materialism, and if Christians, because of the stress of theirs, become obsessed with other-worldly concerns, then ideally they should interrelate and create a comfortable relationship in which they help one another modify their actions and theologies by reminding each other of the second dimension of the biblical dialectic.

While man should participate in this world and help shape his physical environment, he does not have the ecological license to abuse that privilege by plundering or destroying the earth. Man's responsibility is to work and *preserve* this garden, earth. Just as the Shabbat bears testimony to God as the true Creator and ultimate source of human creativity, so *shemittah* (the Sabbatical year, every seventh year) and *yovel* (the Jubilee year, every fiftieth), during which times the land must lie fallow, serve as reminders that while man may conquer the earth and subdue nature, they, too, are the Lord's, and man is but their caretaker.

Similarly, while man may exert mastery over the animal kingdom, he is forbidden to abuse that privilege. Indeed, one of the only mitzvot for which the Torah promises a reward of longevity to those who fulfill it is the commandment not to take birds' eggs from their nest while the mother hovers over them but to send the mother away first. The intention of this mitzvah, in all likelihood, is not only to demonstrate concern for the feelings of the mother bird, but perhaps even more important, to tame man's exploitative impulses. For while Judaism permits man to engage in this-worldly pursuits, it insists that he be aware of the limits and potential abuses of his power. The story of the Tower of Babel in which man tried to build an edifice reaching the sky so that he could dethrone God often was understood allegorically as teaching this profound message of the potential abuses of man's creative abilities and exploitative impulses. Universal man has a dialectical vocation in life to work and preserve this garden, earth. While he may reap the world's benefits, he also bears the responsibility of preventing that privilege from ever becoming abused.

This Jewish worldview lends itself to adaptation by a variety of different economic systems, none of which can be regarded as exclusively "God's way." The socialist model, for example, can readily be incorporated into a Jewish ethos. Jews, in fact, have been very attracted to socialist principles, as evidenced by their early involvement in Soviet communism and the founding of *kibbutzim* in Israel and workers' unions in America. But while the socialist economic theory may in principle be compatible with biblical teachings, it can also be perverted as it was in the Soviet case, where it was accompanied by human suffering, oppression, and the deprivation of fundamental freedoms and rights. As Christians such as Karl Barth and Dietrich Bonhoeffer have warned, *everything* in life has the potential for becoming a source for idolatry, even sound and just economic principles.

A capitalist economic model can also be incorporated into the biblical ethos provided it takes sufficient care of the needs and dignity of the poor, aged, homeless, and less fortunate through acts of charity, taxes, or other such means. Material possessions, as has been pointed out, are not inherently evil, but rather exist as potential forces for the benefit or detriment of man and his worship of God. Like socialism, capitalism can also be abused and fail biblical standards. For capitalism to be sanctioned by Judaism it must take sufficient note of the needs and dignity of others and have as its central ingredient acts of *tzedakah.*

The English term *charity* is an inadequate translation of the Hebrew word *tzedakah,* which stems from the root *tzedek* meaning "justice." Giving tzedakah is not an act of mercy that goes beyond the call of duty or the letter of the law. It is an act of justice that is required and expected of us. It is rooted in the conviction that wealth is ultimately God's, given to man as a trust with the stipulation that he share it with those less fortunate. We are duly obligated to help our fellow man who is equally deserving of a life of dignity free from want. Indeed, even the manner in which we give tzedakah must reflect these principles. "Better no giving at all," states the Talmud, "than the giving which humiliates" (B. T., Hag. 5a).

And while giving charity anonymously is, of course, a very noble gesture, "the eighth and most meritorious degree of

charity," writes Maimonides, "is to anticipate charity by preventing poverty, namely . . . by teaching a person a trade, or
putting them in a business so that they may earn an honest liveli-
hood and not be forced to the dreadful alternative of holding out
a hand for charity" *(Mishneh Torah,* Matnot Aniyim 10:7).

The Torah also states that instead of hardening our hearts
and closing our hands from helping the needy we ought to
"give to him freely, and your heart shall not be grudging when
you give to him; because for this the LORD your God will bless
you in all your work and in all that you undertake" (Deut.
15:10). According to the Talmud, even those who are themselves sustained by charity are obligated to give it to others. The
centrality of the mitzvah of tzedakah in the Jewish heritage
probably accounts for the fact that Jews tend to be an extremely
philanthropic people.

The question of which particular economic system is religiously acceptable is therefore secondary, in the Jewish view, to
the role it must play in alleviating human need and in promot-
ing both the welfare and dignity of individuals. Moreover,
beyond the particular economic system which is selected we are
to recall that "man does not live by bread alone, but that man
lives by everything that proceeds out of the mouth of the LORD"
(Deut. 8:3).

It is likely that Jesus, too, shared in this integrated and
holistic Jewish worldview of participation and blessing (see, for
example, Mark 14:22-24). His command to render unto Caesar
that which is Caesar's (i.e., the political realm), however,
appears to contradict the traditional Jewish view that Caesar's
world is also God's world and that politics, too, must be
imbued with religious value (see also Gal. 5:16). Moreover,
Christianity was greatly influenced by Hellenistic and Gnostic
thought and, later, by Augustinian thought, which radically
dichotomized the physical and spiritual realms. As the church
developed, a number of Jewish concepts such as Messiah and
salvation, as well as rituals and regulations such as circumcision,
the Passover meal sacraments, and kosher rules, all originally

rooted in the physical realm, were severed from their materialistic base and incorporated by Christianity in their spiritualized form only. Judaism, on the other hand, continued to insist that such phenomena not be completely interiorized but that they retain their this-worldly as well as spiritual characteristics. In Judaism, divergent elements of life are to be synthesized into a creative whole. To abandon either dimension of the spiritual-material dialectical formula is to depart from the traditional Jewish view of spirituality, wholeness, and holiness.

Ironically, the rabbis also insisted that even though he properly may bring together both dimensions of life, the Jew, nevertheless, cannot hope ever to attain fully the ideals of wholeness and completeness in this pre-messianic era, so long as the prophecies of world peace are not fulfilled. This is, in fact, alluded to by the Hebrew word for "wholeness," *shlemuth*, which is derived from the root *shalom*, or "peace," and which presumes its existence. For this reason, God told King David that he could not build the holy temple since he was a man of war but that his son, *Shlomo* (Solomon), whose name is derived from the root *shalom* and reflective of it, would build it since he lived at a time of peace. In the Jewish view, human completeness and total spiritual fulfillment remain elusive until the coming of the Messiah and the dawn of world peace.

The rabbis reinforced this idea through a variety of means. For example, they instituted the custom of the groom breaking a glass at the wedding ceremony to show that the couple's joy remains incomplete so long as the Messiah has not come to bring redemption to Israel and the world. This ritual, which is still practiced at Jewish marriage ceremonies today, originated in light of the pledge made by the Babylonian Jews during the first exile: "If I forget you, O Jerusalem, let my right hand wither! Let my tongue cleave to the roof of my mouth, if I do not remember you, if I *do not set Jerusalem above my highest joy!*" (Ps. 137:5-6, emphasis added). At marriage, the moment of a couple's greatest personal joy, when all their sins are forgiven and they become whole and fulfilled, they are to remember that, in fact, neither their joy nor their spirituality is truly complete so long as the collective Jewish condition and state of humankind remain unredeemed, as they inevitably do before the coming of Messiah.

Largely for the same reason, the rabbis prohibited the playing of musical instruments on Shabbat, even though they were played in the temple. (The introduction of the organ into Reform Shabbat prayer services was, therefore, a very controversial departure from tradition. See chapter 8.) The Jew remains unfulfilled and incomplete even in his moments of prayer and religious devotion. Precisely at those times when we believe that we are truly complete and fulfilled, such as on the Shabbat and at our marriage, we are reminded that, in fact, we are not. Only in messianic times, note the rabbis, will the various solemn and mournful fast days in the Jewish calendar be transformed into festivals of happiness and rejoicing; only then will we be capable of feeling true wholeness, complete joy, and total spiritual fulfillment.

It remains man's obligation to narrow the gap between the presently fractured reality and that represented by the messianic ideal. Man is not to stop dreaming, longing, and actively striving to bring the Messiah. In fact, Hasidism, which draws heavily from the mystical tradition, suggests that not only man, but the world itself is incomplete before the coming of Messiah and that it is man's duty to "fix" or "repair" the world by redeeming the divine sparks of holiness inherent in all things.

This doctrine of *tikkun olam,* or "fixing the world," has become widely accepted in recent years, even among non-Hasidic Jews. It presumes the unfulfilled character, albeit inherent goodness, of the world today, as well as man's ability to complete it and make it whole. To a large degree it is man, through his actions, who can either bring the Messiah and age of redemption or delay their arrival. According to the midrash, the Messiah waits in heaven, eager to enter the world as soon as all people become either righteous (i.e., as a reward) or sinners (i.e., when redemption from a source outside of man becomes necessary to fulfill God's covenant and promise of redemption). In either case, it is man's actions that can bring the Messiah, complete the world, and redeem the universe. God *needs* man, his copartner in the building of this earth, to achieve these goals.

The people of Israel are to bring about the world's redemption by serving as "a kingdom of priests and a holy nation" (Exod. 19:6). At first glance, these two roles appear contradictory since the priests in ancient times were the teachers who served among the people, while holiness, in Hebrew, implies separateness and apartness. In fact, the very mission of the Jewish people is both universal and particularistic. They are to serve both as teachers to the world and as a holy people unto themselves. Israel is, on the one hand, a people that dwells alone (see Num. 23:9), and on the other hand, a nation that is to strive for *shalom* and *shlemuth,* "wholeness and completeness," within herself and with the entire world.

The Jew is to strive toward the ideals of personal growth, fulfillment, and holiness by engaging in prayer, Torah study, and the practice of mitzvot. Judaism, of course, sanctions man's quest for spirituality and *devekut* (meaning "attachment" or "union with God") and is even amenable to the highly personalized, Kierkegaardian concept of spirituality, or to spiritual exercises such as meditation and the liberation of inner consciousness. The Jew is reminded, however, that these practices remain insufficient for bringing about his total spiritual fulfillment. For the Jew's personal completeness is inexorably linked with that of the Jewish people as a whole and with the redemption of all humankind. As long as the world remains unredeemed—spiritually and physically—the Jew must feel deficient both in his spiritual achievements as well as in his moments of personal joy.

This idea sheds light on one of the most fundamental differences between Judaism and Christianity—the Christian belief that the Messiah has come and the Jewish insistence that he has not. Judaism affirms the inevitable incompleteness of a personalized salvation and individualized holiness so long as they are not indissolubly linked with the messianic redemption of Israel and the world. Christianity, on the other hand, affirms that the Messiah *has* come and that the individual *can* achieve spiritual completion and fulfillment now by accepting Jesus as his personal Savior and Redeemer.

The Jewish mission is to bring about the completeness and fulfillment of both man and the world—to bring the Messiah! The continued existence of evil and suffering in the world and the ongoing mystery of the survival of the Jewish people bear eloquent testimony that the Jewish mission is not yet complete—the world has yet to be fully redeemed.

Chapter 3

THE SABBATH:
A DAY OF SANCTIFIED TIME

Of all the holidays in the Jewish year, the weekly Sabbath is the most cherished and beloved. Conveying its grandeur and significance in the life of the observant Jew is a most formidable task, perhaps one inevitably doomed to failure. For Shabbat is ineffable. It cannot be fully grasped or explicated through words alone. It must be experienced to be fully appreciated and understood. As the psalmist wrote of God, "*Taamu uroo ki tov hashem,*" "O taste and see that the LORD is good" (Ps. 34:8), so too, the Shabbat. And just as it is impossible to describe the beauty of a sunset to one who has never seen it, so one cannot fully convey the import and majesty that the Shabbat has for the observant Jew to one who has never experienced it. He is in love with the Shabbat queen, and love, too, cannot be completely expressed, nor can its spiritual warmth and cleansing power ever be fully conveyed. Intellect alone will not suffice in unlocking its mysteries and hidden spiritual treasures, nor can it fully grasp the significance of that day. Indeed, we do not "grasp" the Shabbat as much as it grips us.

Shabbat Significance
Of the many contributions Judaism has made to humanity through its two great daughter religions, Christianity and Islam, the Shabbat is perhaps the most important. Its significance in Jewish life and theology cannot be overstated. There is

more Jewish literature—legal, mystical, and homiletic—on this subject than on any other. The Shabbat is the only ritual mentioned in the Ten Commandments. It is described by the rabbis as *shekulah kineged kol hamitzvot,* "of equal import to all the rest of the commandments put together." Those who observe the Shabbat are regarded as if they had observed the entire Torah, while those who desecrate it are viewed as having violated the entire Torah (see Exod. Rab. 25:12). The Shabbat is personified in rabbinic literature as a majestic queen, a radiant bride, and a heavenly jewel. It is the only act of creation that was sanctified and hallowed by God (Gen. 2:3).

The noted modern Jewish essayist and Zionist philosopher Achad Haam once wrote, "One can say without exaggeration that more than Israel has kept the Sabbath, the Sabbath has kept and preserved Israel."[1] Novelist Herman Wouk was also enamored with the Shabbat. He once described it as "the point where many Jews leave the Jewish tradition and where many enter it." Indeed, when the rabbis sought to describe what life would be like in the messianic age, they invoked the Shabbat as their point of reference, describing that time as days *shekulo Shabbat,* meaning "when it is always Shabbat" (i.e., when the beauty and tranquillity of the Shabbat are felt constantly). The Shabbat enables the Jew to experience a foretaste of the world to come, a return to his ideal state in the Garden of Eden. The rabbis say that those who observe the Shabbat are imbued with a *neshama yeterah,* or "additional soul," which enters them at sunset on Friday evening and departs from them on Saturday after sundown, enabling them to experience a "double" measure of joy and spirituality. The weekly Shabbat uplifts the spirit of the tormented Jew and enables him to transcend his life of drudgery and to feel physically and spiritually refreshed, able to confront another week. The Shabbat offers Jews the promise of redemption: "If Israel were to keep two Sabbaths . . . they would immediately be redeemed" (B. T., Shab. 118b).

While the Shabbat has been universally acclaimed, it also, unfortunately, often has been grossly misunderstood. It is commonly believed that the Shabbat is observed in order to replenish our physical strength and to enable us to work more energetically and productively during the coming week. Even Philo, the first century C.E. Alexandrian Jewish philosopher, apologetically invoked this argument as his defense against Greek charges that Jews observed the Shabbat out of laziness. Actually, instead of treating the Shabbat as the beginning of the week or as that which facilitated greater productivity in subsequent days, the rabbis insisted that it be viewed as the culmination of the week and zenith of living. For this reason there are no Hebrew names for the days of the week. Instead, they are known by the number of days remaining until the Shabbat. Thus, Sunday is *yom rishon beshabbat*, or "the first day toward Shabbat," Monday is *yom shainee beshabbat*, or "the second day toward Shabbat," and so on, until finally the acme, the day of Shabbat, is reached.

The Jew's entire week is lived in anticipation of the Shabbat. Everything points to it; everything leads to it. And while it is certainly true that the Shabbat rejuvenates man's spirits, replenishes his physical strength, and revitalizes him so that he is able to face another work week, the deeper meaning of the Shabbat is that it is observed not for the sake of the rest of the week, but that the rest of the week is the prologue for the arrival of Shabbat. So too, the purpose of letting the land lie fallow in the *shemittah* (every seventh) and Jubilee years was not so much in order that it should become more fertile and reap greater harvests in subsequent years, but to demonstrate that ultimately the earth is the Lord's and man is but its caretaker. Shabbat is a unique institution, fundamentally different from all other days of the week. It is the epitome of sanctified living. It is, as Heschel described it, "an island in time."

Shabbat Observance

Like all other Jewish holidays, Shabbat begins at sundown, in this case, on Friday evening. (In the Jewish calendar, the day begins at sunset. This is derived from the fact that the Genesis account of creation states, "and there was *evening* and there was *morning*," indicating that the day follows the night.) There is an atmosphere of excitement and anticipation on Friday—the house is cleaned, candlesticks are polished, Sabbath delicacies are bought and prepared (cooking is prohibited on Shabbat), and the Sabbath table is set. As sundown draws closer, we wash up, put on our finest clothes, and get ready to welcome the Shabbat. We recite our Shabbat prayers and then partake of a festive Shabbat meal. The preparation and anticipation of the momentous, beloved day forms an essential ingredient of its endearment to us. Similarly, God demanded that the Jewish people prepare themselves physically and emotionally before receiving the Torah at Mount Sinai (see Exod. 19:10).

We are to undergo a spiritual preparation, as well, before entering into the Shabbat. This is derived from the verse, "Six days you shall labor, and do *all* your work" (Exod. 20:9, emphasis added). How, ask the rabbis, can a person complete *all* his work in the course of the six days of the week? Rather, we must *feel* as if all our work has been completed. We are to greet the Shabbat queen in a spirit of openness, anticipation, and tranquillity, without thoughts of what has yet to be done burdening us. We create such a meditative mood by setting aside our money, dismissing thoughts of business from our minds, and directing our hearts to God. We immerse ourselves in Torah study, prayer, and fellowship.

The Shabbat is formally welcomed at sunset with the woman's lighting of the candles. It is customary to light one candle for each member of the household. In Judaism, the family and the home are the primary vehicles for Shabbat spirituality and, by extension, for Jewish values as a whole. Traditional Shabbat songs are sung, the father blesses his children, and he then extols his wife's virtues and declares his love and appreciation for her by reciting the "woman of valor" prayer (Prov. 31:10-31). The *kiddush,* or "sanctification," is recited over a full cup of wine symbolizing the joy of the day, and a blessing of *ha-motzi* is made over the special *Shabbat challah,* or

"Sabbath bread." Two whole loaves are used, symbolizing the double portion of manna the Jews received in the desert on Fridays as they were not permitted to collect it on Shabbat. We eat a festive meal, chant songs of praise to God, study Torah, and recite the *birkat ha-mazon,* or "grace after meals." There are no distractions—driving a car and using the phone or any form of electricity are all prohibited on Shabbat for the Orthodox Jew. The central theological motif of the evening is the celebration of God's creation. The evening is spent in warmth and meditation, fellowship and harmony, wonder and awe, as we marvel over the miracle of God's creation.

On Shabbat morning we attend prayer services at synagogue where, in addition to the liturgy, a weekly portion from the Torah and prophets is read. Following the services families return home to eat their second festive meal. (The rituals at this meal are essentially the same as those on Friday evening.) They spend the afternoon relaxing, studying Torah, and sharing with family and friends. As sunset and the close of Shabbat draw nearer, it is customary to study the *Pirkei Avot,* or the Ethics of the Fathers section of the Mishnah. The afternoon service, *Minhah,* is recited, and the third and final Shabbat meal is eaten. The central theme of this concluding portion of the Shabbat is redemption. If we have truly partaken of the Shabbat experience, we have now reached our spiritual acme— a foretaste of the messianic world. We yearn and long for Messiah and redemption. To show our sorrow and spiritual loss with the passing of the Shabbat, we extend it for one additional hour after sunset.

The Shabbat is formally concluded with *Maariv,* the evening prayer service. We conduct the *havdalah,* or "separation ceremony," in which we reaffirm our belief in the coming of Messiah, the redemption of the world, and our obligation to sanctify life and imbue it with holiness. We light a long braided candle, drink from an overflowing cup of wine, and smell the fragrance of spices as we chant the prayer, "Be not afraid, my servant Jacob, for I, the Lord, am with you." The light of the candle symbolizes the eternal, divine spirit in man ("the Lord is our Light and Redeemer"); the spices refresh our soul and dispel the emptiness and sadness we feel at the conclusion of Shabbat (for we have now lost our "extra soul"); and the overflowing cup of wine symbolizes our uncontainable optimism and hope for the coming week.

Shabbat Laws

Shabbat laws are divided into positive and negative categories, based on the fact that the Torah describes the Shabbat differently in the two biblical accounts of the Ten Commandments. The first account states, "zakhor *et yom hashabbat*" (Exod. 20:8), "*remember* the sabbath day," a term that has a positive connotation in Hebrew and refers to the positive commandments, while the second states, "shamor *et yom hashabbat*" (Deut. 5: 12), "*observe* the sabbath day," conveying a negative connotation and alluding to the negative commandments. The reason for the switch in terms, claim the rabbis, is that when God proclaimed the Ten Commandments, he actually spoke both words, *shamor* and *zakhor,* together—something man cannot grasp—in order to teach man that he is to sanctify the Shabbat by observing both its positive and negative commandments. While the Jew is to observe the various prohibitions of the day, such as abstaining from lighting fire and engaging in business, he must also rejoice in the spirit of the Shabbat by observing its positive dimensions such as studying Torah, praying, eating the festive meals, and engaging in fellowship with family and friends.

There are thirty-nine basic categories of "creative work" prohibited on Shabbat from which all of the more specific laws are derived. These include the prohibitions against kindling a fire (Exod. 35:3); ploughing, harvesting, and reaping (Exod. 34:21); gathering wood (Num. 15:32-35); baking and cooking (Exod. 16:22-23); buying and selling (Neh. 13:15-17) (see further Mishnah, Shab. 2:2). The prohibited categories were refined and applied to countless circumstances arising over the centuries, to the point that today they constitute an extensive body of *responsa* literature.

There is a great deal of ignorance and misunderstanding, even among Jews, about the Shabbat laws. It often needs to be pointed out, for example, that all of the Shabbat laws are suspended in life-threatening situations (B. T., Shab. 132a). We are duly obligated to "violate" the Shabbat to help someone who is dangerously ill. Also, we may not be "overly pious" and refuse to accept help that involves a violation of the law. It is better for man to violate one Shabbat, say the rabbis, in order that he might live and be able to observe many more. For God gave the Torah and its commandments to man so that he shall *live* by them (Lev. 18:5), from which the rabbis infer "and not die by them."

"How do we know that the duty of saving life supersedes the Sabbath?" asks the Talmud. Rabbi Jonathan ben Joseph said, "It is written in the Scriptures 'You shall keep the sabbath, because it is holy *for you*' (Exod. 31:14, emphasis added). This implies that the sabbath is committed to you, not you to the sabbath" (see B. T., Yoma 85). The similarity between these ideas and Jesus' rebuke of the Pharisees that man was not made for the Sabbath but the Sabbath for man (see Matt. 12:8; Mark 2:27) is striking. It reflects Jesus' keen awareness of, and probably entrenchment in, the pharisaic tradition, which affirmed the oral as well as written traditions and the sanctity of man over the Shabbat.

Shabbat laws, stringent though they may be, are a reflection of God's love and concern for man. They are the tools given us with which we create a spiritually meaningful, uplifting environment. They are instruments of *life* and are therefore suspended if that life is threatened. There are, however, three cardinal sins—murder, idolatry, and engaging in illicit sexual relationships—for which Jews are indeed commanded to sacrifice their lives rather than transgress the laws (see B. T., Sanh. 74a). During periods of *shemad* when a government attempts to force Jews en masse to publicly abandon their faith, the Jew is also commanded to give up his life even for the most minor transgression. Jewish history is, unfortunately, replete with such scenarios.

Shabbat Theology

There are two principal motifs underlying the observance of Shabbat, both of which are derived from the Bible and affirmed in the *kiddush,* or the act of sanctification over wine: (1) *zekher leyitziat mitzraim,* in commemoration of the Exodus from Egypt; and (2) *zekher lemaaseh bereshit,* in commemoration of God's creation of the world.

Exodus motif. "You shall remember that you were a servant in the land of Egypt, and the LORD your God brought you out thence . . . therefore the LORD your God commanded you to keep the sabbath day" (Deut. 5:15).

On Shabbat we recall our slavery and exodus from Egypt in order that we might acknowledge the true nature of freedom, which is freedom from servitude to man and acceptance of servitude to God. For this reason, the Torah states, "You shall not do any work, you, or your son, or your daughter, your manservant, or your maidservant, or your cattle, or the sojourner who is within your gates." (Exod. 20:10). Everyone and everything is to feel free, at least for this one day, in order that they might embrace something more ultimate in their lives. Man can be his own taskmaster when he enslaves himself to non-ultimate things that bring no tranquillity to the mind, body, and soul. The Talmud, therefore, declared that the genuinely free person is one who engages in the study and practice of Torah. Moses expressed this same concept of freedom when he pleaded with Pharaoh in the name of God to "let my people go, *that they may serve me*" (Exod. 8:20, emphasis added). For freedom from slavery is only true freedom if it leads to the acceptance of servitude to God.

By recalling the exodus motif on Shabbat we are reminded of the true nature of slavery and freedom, and of our duty to bring religious purpose and meaning into our lives. The

Shabbat bids us never to despair from redemption, even though we may be living in the midst of slavery or suffering. It also reminds us that should we, in fact, be free, we are obligated to work toward extending that condition of freedom to all those living in bondage. We ought never to become so accepting of this world or complacent with our role in it that we stop hoping, believing, and actively working toward its ultimate redemption.

Creation motif. "Thus the heavens and the earth were finished, and all the host of them. And on the seventh day God finished his work which he had done, and he rested on the seventh day from all his work which he had done. So God blessed the seventh day and hallowed it, because on it God rested from all his work which he had done in creation" (Gen. 2:1-3; see also Exod. 31:17; 20:11). The thrust of this motif is that just as God stopped creating on the seventh day, so man should cease from creating.

One of the most prevalent misconceptions about the Shabbat is that the Bible forbids man from working on that day. No wonder that many Shabbat prohibitions such as lighting a fire or cooking are viewed as antiquated, since today they involve little effort and cannot be considered "work." Actually, what the Torah prohibits is *milekhet machashevet*, "creative work" (see Exod. 35:33). For six days man is permitted and even *commanded* to work and subdue nature and to fulfill his role as copartner with God in the building of the earth. (The rabbis understood the Torah verse, "Six days you shall labor . . ." [Exod. 20:9] as an obligation and commandment.) The danger exists, however, that as a result of man's profound intelligence and creative abilities, he might come to forget the true Creator, the source of his creative power.

"The function of the Sabbath," writes Mordecai Kaplan, the founder of Reconstructionism, "is to prohibit man from engaging in work that in any way alters the environment, so that he should not delude himself into the belief that he is complete master of his destiny."[2] Man can easily neglect the transcendence in life, the ultimate God, and come to believe that *he is* God—or at least, that he does not need a God. This is symbolized by the story of the Tower of Babel. The act of building a tower reaching the sky represents man's attempt to dethrone God, to rid himself of divine sovereignty, and to put in its place man's creative genius. By refraining from creative activities in the physical universe one day each week, man acknowledges God as the true Creator of all things, including his very own implanted ability to create. In ceasing from controlling nature he gives testimony that the world is ultimately not his to dominate, nor is nature his to manipulate. Rather, the earth is the Lord's. God is the ultimate source of being, creation, and human creativity. Man is to recognize that he is not God, although he is created in his image and likeness. Only God is Lord. The concluding words of the High Holy Day service, the holiest time in the Jewish year, are, "God is the Lord." We recite this verse seven times as a reminder that while man should aspire to be godly, he must not become so arrogant either in his material or spiritual acquisitions as to believe he is God.

For one day in seven we live on "an island in time" where time itself is suspended and we cease to be enslaved by it. In its place we embrace eternity. For the sense of awe, wonder, and rapture with life can only be grasped if we stop and think about the grandeur of the eternity in time. Only then can we recharge our spiritual batteries, give direction to our lives, and return to the ideals we have set for ourselves. As Heschel has noted, "The world has our hands, but our soul belongs to someone else. Six days a week we seek to dominate the world, on the seventh day we try to dominate the self."[3]

The creation theme underlies the "why" of many Shabbat laws, such as the prohibition against building, lighting a fire, sewing, and so on, and also explains why the rabbis regarded Shabbat as of equal importance to the rest of the Torah. By observing the Shabbat the Jew gives testimony to the sovereignty of God and to man's finitude and creatureliness under him. "We renounce on this day," writes Dayan Grunfeld, "every exercise of intelligent, purposeful control of natural objects and forces. We cease from every act of human power in order to proclaim God as the source of all power."[4]

The exodus motif invariably leads us toward activism in reminding us to pursue true freedom and liberation for all people everywhere. The creation motif, on the other hand, leads us to reflection and soul-searching insofar as it beckons us to stop and reflect upon God as the ultimate source of freedom and creativity. By recalling these two motifs on Shabbat, man is reminded of God's immanence in history in the form of redemptive power (as evidenced by the Exodus), and God's transcendence beyond history (as demonstrated by the Creation). These motifs of exodus and creation underlie the Jewish ethos, which combines activism with pacifism, and worldly pursuits with spiritual ones. They are axiomatic to all Jewish life and faith. No other commandment encompasses these motifs quite to the extent that the Shabbat does.

The Shabbat is an eternal sign of God's creation of the world and covenant with man (Exod. 31:17). It embodies the ideal synthesis of the physical and spiritual realms of life. Fasting and mourning are strictly forbidden on Shabbat, while eating, drinking, wearing fine clothes, and engaging in sexual relations with one's spouse are all mitzvot or good deeds. We are to experience the Shabbat in our *entirety*, and to live life and to enjoy creation in its completeness.

Former Soviet dissident Alexander Solzhenitsyn raised a number of critical concerns about Western society in his famous Harvard commencement address, although none as important as those relating to matters of the spirit. "Society appears to have little defense against the abyss of human decadence," Solzhenitsyn said. He attributed the moral decay to the prevailing Western view of the world first born during the Renaissance, a view that he referred to as "nationalistic humanism," which regards man "as the center of everything that exists. . . ." Modern Western civilization, in his view, is based on the dangerous trend to worship man and his material needs. While Solzhenitsyn was quick to acknowledge that Western man has been enriched by such a worldview, he insisted that "we have lost the concept of a Supreme Complete Entity which used to restrain our passions and our irresponsibility. We have placed too much hope in political and social reforms, only to find out that we were being deprived of our most precious possession—our spiritual life."

Solzhenitsyn concluded his address by challenging some of the very foundations of Western society:

> Even if we are spared destruction by war, our lives will have to change if we want to save life from self-destruction. We cannot avoid revising the fundamental definitions of human life and human society. Is it true that man is above everything? Is there no Superior Spirit above him? Is it right that man's life and society's activities have to be determined by material expansion in the first place? Is it permissible to promote such expansion to the detriment of our spiritual integrity? . . . If the world has not come to its end, it has approached a major turn in history, equal in importance to the turn from the Middle Ages to the Renaissance. It will exact from us a spiritual upsurge. We shall have to rise to a new height of vision, to a new level of life where our physical nature will not be cursed as in the Middle Ages, but even more importantly, our spiritual being will not be trampled upon as in the Modern Era.[5]

It is precisely these concerns and characteristics of our time, that point to man's desperate need for the Shabbat today. Through it, we can reaffirm the centrality of the family, the home, and the synagogue in our lives. In observing the Shabbat, the Jew bears testimony to the existence of a Supreme Being, one who loves humankind and is concerned for his welfare. The Shabbat can give to a society searching for its soul the essential building blocks with which it can become reinvigorated and transformed into one with a deep moral character, strong spiritual backbone, and profound sense of justice, community, and fellowship.

No wonder that the Shabbat is described by the rabbis as equal to all the other mitzvot in the Torah. It brings together under its overarching canopy virtually every Jewish value— warmth, spirituality, sanctified materialism, family, community, prayer, love, Torah study, song, ritual, longing for Messiah, and covenant. Those who truly observe the Shabbat, states the liturgy, call it "a day of delight." They are amply rewarded for their observance. In the words of the prophets, "If you turn back your foot from the sabbath, from doing your pleasure on my holy day, and call the sabbath a delight and the holy day of the LORD honorable . . . then you shall take delight in the LORD, and I will make you ride upon the heights of the earth; I will feed you with the heritage of Jacob your father, for the mouth of the LORD has spoken" (Isa. 58:13-14).

Chapter 4

FESTIVALS OF THE JEWISH YEAR

The Jewish calendar is replete with holidays, each bearing its own distinctive historical and theological motif. The major festivals can be divided into two categories—the Pilgrim Holidays of Passover, Pentecost, and Tabernacles when Jews in ancient times would visit the temple in Jerusalem to celebrate, and the High Holy Days comprising Rosh Hashanah and Yom Kippur. The minor festivals include Purim and Hanukkah. Two of the more significant fast days are Tisha b'Av and Shivah Asar b'Tammuz. Since the Jewish calendar is a lunar rather than a solar one, the holidays always fall on a different date in the Jewish calendar than they do in our standard Western calendar. A lunar year has 354 days whereas the solar one, which is based on one revolution around the sun, has 365½ days, making a difference of 11½ days. The Jewish calendar is, therefore, adjusted seven times every nineteen years by adding an extra month, Adar II. The festivals give meaning and character to the Jewish year. They attest to the fact that history is infused with divine purpose. In the Jewish view, events do not occur at random nor in isolation from one another, but instead they form part of an unfolding divine plan leading to the world's ultimate redemption. The holidays compose sanctified time. They provide Jews with an opportunity to break through their mundane, humdrum lives and to inject into them spiritually rich, uplifting customs and rituals.

The holidays are also the primary vehicles for transmitting the Jewish heritage to the children, the next generation.

"The holidays are the jewels on the crown of Judaism. They add beauty to the life of a people whose vocation is to proclaim the sovereignty of God. . . . He [man] desists from labor and soars through heart and mind to spheres of spiritual delight. He breaks the bonds of time as he relives experiences of ages past and envisions with the prophets the end of days."[1] The holidays are spiritual way stations dotting the Jewish calendar, invigorating the Jew's soul, and sanctifying his life.

THE PILGRIM HOLIDAYS

Pesach (Passover)

The holiday of Pesach commemorates the seminal event in Jewish history—the Exodus of the people of Israel from Egyptian bondage. It was at that particular juncture some three thousand years ago that the national Jewish identity was truly shaped. From this primal event some of the most profound affirmations ever to be made by the Jewish people were drawn. Most notable among those propositions was the notion that God is present in human lives, that he hears the cries of the suffering and tormented, and that he intervenes in history to deliver man from affliction and to redeem him from oppression.

Israel's redemption from Egypt is proffered by the Torah as a rationale for a variety of mitzvot such as the dietary laws (see Lev. 11), the observance of Shabbat (see chapter 3), and even for ethical imperatives such as the duty to love the convert, the stranger, the widow, and the orphan. Daily the Jew fulfills the mitzvah, to "remember the day when you came out of the land of Egypt *all the days of your life*" (Deut. 16:3, emphasis added), by recalling the Exodus in his morning and evening prayers, in grace after meals, as he wears his *tallit,* or "prayer shawl," and by virtue of the fact that the Torah account of the Exodus is the one that is included in the *tefillin,* or "phylacteries," that are worn daily. Because of the significance of Pesach in the life and experience of the Jewish people, the Hebrew month in which it falls, Nisan, is described by the Torah as the first month of the Jewish year (see Exod. 12:2).

The events marked by Pesach are well known to both Christians and Jews alike (see Exod. 1–15). Joseph's brothers and their families moved to Egypt because of the famine in Canaan and lived there freely. Many years later a "new" pharaoh arose who enslaved the Israelites and brought upon them great suffering. The Jews cried out to God to save them and to redeem them from their oppression. God heard their entreaties and sent Moses to Pharaoh with the message to "let my people go." When Pharaoh repeatedly refused, God brought ten plagues upon the Egyptians. After the devastation of the final plague, Pharaoh ordered the Israelites to leave (although he later changed his mind again and pursued them into the desert). Before leaving, however, the Jews were told by God to sacrifice a lamb, one of the many Egyptian gods, and to eat it hastily. They were also instructed to sprinkle the lamb's blood on the doorposts of their homes as a public demonstration of their faith in God and of the impotence of the Egyptian deity. The angel of death, seeing the blood on the doors of the Jewish homes, *pasach,* or "passed over," them and spared the children inside; only the Egyptian first-born were smitten.

The Jews were so rushed to leave that they did not have time to bake bread. Instead, they made *matzah,* a simple mixture of wheat and water in the form of a flat wafer that bakes quickly. When they arrived at the Red Sea, the Jews' situation appeared hopeless. Having reneged on his decision to let them go, Pharaoh sent his army behind them; in front of them was the impassable sea. The Torah tells how the children of Israel cried out to God to save them, and God, hearing their plea, said to Moses, "Why do you cry to me? Tell the people of Israel to go forward" (Exod. 14:15). The Jews faithfully entered the sea. Miraculously, the waters parted, and they walked across on dry land. When the Jews reached the safety of the shore on the other side, the waters of the sea returned to their normal state, drowning the Egyptians who were in pursuit.

The Torah tells us to mark this entire series of events by celebrating the Pesach festival and recalling our salvation from Egyptian oppression. We retell the story and symbolically relive the events. We are to feel as if *we ourselves* were just delivered from Egyptian bondage. Judaism maintains that God's act of liberation was not a onetime-only event, but an ongoing and often repeated one. In the words of the *Haggadah* (see below), "For God did not redeem our ancestors alone, but us, as well."

The Torah refers to the holiday as *Chag ha-Matzot,* or "Festival of the Unleavened Bread," although it is more generally known as *Chag ha-Pesach,* or "Festival of Passover." In a fascinating Hasidic commentary on the different nomenclatures for the holiday, Rabbi Levi Yitzchak of Berditchev noted that God and the Jewish people refer to it with the name that best expresses each other's greatness and loving kindness. God, in the Torah, called the holiday "the festival of matzot" to highlight the fact that Israel had such a deep, abiding trust in him that they were willing even to leave the security and comfort of their homes in Egypt and to enter into the dry, barren desert. The Jews, on the other hand, refer to the holiday as *Pesach,* stressing God's goodness and act of love in passing over their homes and sparing their first-born.

The holiday is celebrated in the Diaspora (i.e., outside the land of Israel) by Orthodox and Conservative Jews for eight days and by Reform Jews for seven days (in Israel, seven) beginning on the fourteenth of Nissan, which occurs in the spring. Work is prohibited on the first two and the last two days (in Israel, on the first and last days only).

Matzah and chametz. Pesach dietary laws are stringent and complex; fulfilling them requires extensive preparation and meticulous adherence to detail.

> This day shall be for you a memorial day, and you shall keep it as a feast to the LORD; throughout your generations you shall observe it as an ordinance for

ever. Seven days you shall eat unleavened bread; on the first day you shall put away leaven out of your houses, for if any one eats what is leavened, from the first day until the seventh day, that person shall be cut off from Israel. On the first day you shall hold a holy assembly, and on the seventh day a holy assembly; no work shall be done on those days; but what every one must eat, that only may be prepared by you. And you shall observe the feast of unleavened bread, for on this very day I brought your hosts out of the land of Egypt: therefore you shall observe this day, throughout your generations, as an ordinance for ever. In the first month, on the fourteenth day of the month at evening, you shall eat unleavened bread, and so until the twenty-first day of the month at evening. For seven days no leaven shall be found in your houses; for if any one eats what is leavened, that person shall be cut off from the congregation of Israel, whether he is a sojourner or a native of the land. You shall eat nothing leavened; in all your dwellings you shall eat unleavened bread (Exod. 12:14-20; see also Exod. 13:10; Deut. 16:1-8).

Matzah is the only form of grain produce that may be eaten throughout the holiday, although we are obligated to eat it only on the first night. It is the antithesis of *chametz,* or "leavened grain" (such as bread), which is prohibited from being eaten and even from being in one's possession for the entire duration of the holiday (see verses above). Since even the most minute amount of chametz is prohibited from being in our possession, we meticulously clean the house before the holiday, searching for chametz in every nook and cranny. (Some people begin cleaning months in advance!) We set aside (or, through a special procedure, make *kosher for Pesach*) the utensils used during the course of the year that absorbed chametz and use others reserved for Passover that never came into contact with chametz. (Observant Jews, therefore, have at least four sets of dishes, silverware, and pots and pans—one for dairy, one for meat, one for Passover dairy, and one for Passover meat. See chapter 5, section on dietary laws.)

On the evening before Passover we conduct the *bedikat chametz*, or "searching for leaven" ceremony, in which the family slowly and methodically goes around the house with a candle searching for chametz a final time. Following the ceremony we relinquish ownership over any chametz that may accidentally still be in our possession, and we declare it as valueless, like "the dust of the earth." Whatever chametz is left over or found by the morning before Pesach is burned. From that time on, chametz may neither be eaten nor be in our possession. It should be evident that observant Jews take the biblical edict not to eat any leaven nor to have it in their possession on Pesach very seriously. Food products that are under rabbinic supervision and that contain no traces of chametz are stamped with the words "Kosher for Passover" (or sometimes simply "KP"). This assures the observant consumer that they may be eaten on the holiday.

Viewed from the outside, such arduous practices and obsession for detail may seem overly stringent, legalistic, and antiquated. For the Jew who takes tradition and the word of God seriously, however, fulfilling a mitzvah is an "all out" affair, especially in this instance where the Torah considers it so serious a matter that it prescribes the most severe punishment of all for its transgression—*koret,* or "being cut off from one's people" (in the world to come). For such a Jew, obedience to God and his word follows naturally from his love for him and from his strong ties to previous generations who also lived by that tradition.

Pesach is one of the most beautiful and meaningful of all Jewish holidays. Families come together in a spirit of warmth, fellowship, and devotion to God; respect for tradition permeates the atmosphere. Far from detracting from this spirit, the laws and customs of the holiday enhance it.

Fast of the first-born. All first-born males are obligated to fast on the day before Pesach as a sign of gratitude to God for sparing the Jewish first-born in the final plague in Egypt. Since it is a minor fast day, however, the fast is suspended for joyous occasions such as completing the study of a tractate of Talmud. For the joy of learning Torah outweighs the obligation of the first-born to fast. It is, therefore, customary for synagogues to arrange a *siyyum* in which the final page of a talmudic tractate is studied publicly, after which the entire congregation is invited to join in the *seudat mitzvah* or "feast of mitzvah."

The Seder. On the first two evenings of Pesach a special ritualized feast, the *Seder,* is conducted in the home. It is here, at the family Seder, that the essential dimensions of the holiday are celebrated. The Seder is marked by an abundance of ancient customs and rituals, feasting, prayer, joy, and warm hospitality. We are obligated to share our Seder meal, not only with family, but with others as well. In fact, we begin the Seder by declaring, "Let all who are hungry come eat with us."

Seder, meaning "order of service," refers to the order of ceremonies performed at the festive meal. The text containing the readings and ceremonies of the Seder is called the *Haggadah,* meaning "the telling" or "narration." Actually, the Seder is more a forum for retelling the story of Pesach than it is a worship service. For the primary mitzvah of the Pesach holiday is to tell the story of God's redemption of our forebears from Egyptian bondage. "And you shall tell your son on that day, 'It is because of what the LORD did for me when I came out of Egypt. . . .' You shall therefore keep this ordinance at its appointed time from year to year" (Exod. 13:8, 10; see also Exod. 12:26; 13:14; Deut. 6:20). The Seder is the Jews' instrument for fulfilling this obligation. The rabbis note that the Torah deliberately used the first person expression "what the Eternal One did for *me*" to indicate that the primary mitzvah of the holiday is not only to tell the story of the Exodus, but to reenact it. We are to feel as if *we ourselves* experienced the pain of slavery and joy of liberation. In the words of the Haggadah, "In each generation a person must feel as if he himself just came out of Egypt."

Since the Torah stresses the obligation to teach our children about the Exodus so that it will never be forgotten, the Seder was organized to heighten their inquisitiveness and sustain their interest. We begin the telling of the Exodus story with "the four questions," or *mah nishtanah,* in which the youngest child, curious as to the many different ritual objects and customs surrounding him, asks, "Why is this night different from all other nights of the year?" Only after the child raises these questions in Socratic manner and shows his eagerness to learn more about the holiday does the family then proceed to recount the story of the Exodus. Three matzot are placed in front of the Seder leader, two and a half of which are eaten, and one half of which is hidden until the conclusion of the Seder when the children customarily search for it and receive a present for finding it. This gimmick was instituted to sustain the children's interest and to keep them awake for the duration of the Seder.

Like all other holiday meals, the Seder begins with the *kiddush,* or "blessing of sanctification over wine." Unlike all others, however, we drink four cups of wine (or grape juice) during the course of the Seder to symbolize our trust in God's fourfold promise of redemption: "And I will *bring you out* from under the burdens of the Egyptians, and I will *deliver you* from their bondage, and I will *redeem you* with an outstretched arm and with great acts of judgment, and I will *take you* for my people, and I will be your God" (Exod. 6:6-7, emphasis added).

It is also customary to pour a fifth cup of wine representing the fifth form and stage of God's promise of redemption: "And I will *bring you into the land* . . . [and] give it to you for a possession" (Exod. 6:8, emphasis added). For centuries Jews have poured, but not drunk from, this fifth cup to symbolize that God's promise for their return to their homeland remains unfulfilled. It came to be called "Elijah's cup" since, according to tradition, it is the prophet Elijah who will usher in the Messiah and the ingathering of the Jewish people into the land of Israel. Ever since the miracle of the birth of the State of Israel in 1948, however, there are some Jews who drink from this fifth cup as an affirmation that Israel marks the beginning of that redemptive period.

More recently, another custom has taken root in which an empty chair, matzah, or cup of wine is set aside as a symbol of the incompleteness of our own joy and freedom so long as our fellow Jews in the countries of the former Soviet Union and elsewhere are not free to celebrate. It is "reserved" for those still living in bondage, for those who are not able to practice their ancestral faith freely. It is also customary to recite a meditation as a reminder to all assembled of the continuing struggle of the Jews in Russia for religious freedom. With the fall of the Soviet Union and communist repression of Jews in 1989, many no longer recite this meditation. The following is an example of one such meditation:

> This matzah, which we set aside as a symbol of hope for the Jews of the Soviet Union, reminds us of the indestructible links that exist between us.
>
> As we observe this festival of freedom, we recall that Soviet Jews are not free to leave without harassment; to learn of their past; to pass on their religious traditions; to learn the language of their fathers; to train teachers and rabbis of future generations.
>
> We remember the scores who sought to live as Jews and struggled to leave for Israel—the land of our fathers—but now languish in Soviet Union. Their struggle against their oppressors goes on. They will not be forgotten.
>
> We will stand with them in their struggle until the light of freedom and redemption shines forth.

As we drink the wine, we recline slightly, as was the manner of Roman emperors, to demonstrate our freedom on this day. Even if we live under conditions of oppression, and are not in fact physically free, we are to *feel* as if we were. Pesach reminds us that true freedom also involves the inner, spiritual realm. It cannot be externally denied, nor can a condition of slavery and servitude be outwardly imposed. The physically oppressed must also recline and feel like emperors on Pesach night. According to the Talmud, those who are poor must even sell their clothes or borrow money if necessary to buy wine for the four cups! Nothing must stand in the way of fulfilling the mitzvah of feeling free on this holiday. (I have often marveled at how it was humanly possible for Jews living in concentration camps and the Warsaw Ghetto during the Holocaust to fulfill this mitzvah of "feeling free" on Pesach. And yet, the amazing testimony to the power of God's spirit moving within humankind is that many Jews *did* find the spiritual strength and courage to fulfill it, despite their wretched conditions.)

Passover bids us to affirm the indissoluble link between slavery and redemption, between our tribulations and our joys. To lose sight of either dimension of this dialectic, or of the tension that affirming both necessarily involves, is to miss the mark. We are neither to be fixated and obsessed with past suffering nor overly and unrealistically optimistic about the future. For this reason, explain the rabbis, we begin the Seder with deprecating remarks of how our ancestors were once slaves in Egypt, but conclude it by praising God for delivering us from our suffering. Passover bids us to remember the good and the bad, our joys and our tribulations, our past suffering and our hopes for the world's future redemption.

More and more Christians are conducting Seders today and celebrating the Passover holiday in their own way, motivated by a desire to reclaim the Jewish roots of their Christian faith and the Jewishness of Jesus. Certainly, the links between suffering and joy, and death and resurrection, are not foreign to them. Christians, like Jews, affirm that darkness will be followed by light, oppression by redemption, and death by resurrection.

Since Pesach generally falls around Easter time when Christians are telling *their* story of the crucifixion, there is often a heightened Christian interest in Jewish ritual during this season. While today this is of positive value, in the Middle Ages, and even as late as the early twentieth century in Eastern

Europe, it had negative repercussions. For example, "blood libel" charges (i.e., that Jews killed Christian children and used their blood for the matzah) were often leveled. Thousands of Jews were slaughtered, and at times entire Jewish communities were wiped out, in most cases by peasant masses, as a result of that terrible, malicious libel. Lest we believe that such accusations are absurd, preposterous, and inconceivable in modern times, it should be noted that there was a blood libel raised in 1928—in New York State.[2] The irony and absurdity of it all—as if it were not ridiculous enough in itself—is that Jews are biblically *prohibited* from eating blood (see chapter 5, section on Kosher).

Prayers of *hallel*, or "thanksgiving," taken from the Psalms, are chanted at the Seder meal and throughout the Pesach festival. It is customary, however, to omit a few psalms on the last six days of the holiday, to symbolize the incompleteness of our joy and the fact that we mourn the loss of the Egyptians who drowned in the Red Sea. According to the Talmud, when the heavenly angels saw that the Egyptians drowned and the people of Israel were saved, they became so jubilant they began to sing songs of praise to God for his mighty triumph. God, however, was angered by their songs and exclaimed, "My creatures are drowning in the sea and you sing songs of praise?" (B. T., Meg. 10b). For the same reason, it is also customary to spill off a drop of wine from our full cups as we recount each of the ten plagues. For an overflowing cup of wine is a sign of complete joy and we seek to demonstrate that our gladness is diminished by the fate of the Egyptians who perished in the course of our salvation. Although we were delivered from the Egyptian oppressors, we reaffirm the injunction "Do not rejoice when your enemy falls" (Prov. 24:17).

Other Seder rituals include our eating *maror* (bitter herbs, e.g., horseradish) as a reminder of the bitterness of slavery and as a way of "re-experiencing" that pain, not just cognitively "knowing about it." We also eat *charoset*, a mixture of chopped nuts, apples, cinnamon, and wine, into which we dip the maror, to symbolize the mortar mixed by our Israelite ancestors. The maror and charoset remind us how "they [the Egyptians] . . , made their lives bitter with hard service, in mortar and brick, and in all kinds of work in the field; in all their work they made them serve with rigor" (Exod. 1:13).

Another ritual item that is placed on the Seder plate and exhibited (though not eaten) is the *zroa,* or "roasted shankbone," representing the paschal lamb that was sacrificed and eaten during the time of the temple. With the destruction of the temple, it became prohibited to offer sacrifices such as the paschal lamb, since the Torah prescribes that "you may not offer the passover sacrifice within any of your towns which the LORD your God gives you; but at the place which the LORD your God will choose, to make his name dwell in it, there you shall offer the passover sacrifice, in the evening at the going down of the sun, at the time you came out of Egypt. And you shall boil it and eat it at the place which the LORD your God will choose; and in the morning you shall turn and go to your tents" (Deut. 16:5-7). Accordingly, the zroa is only shown, not eaten. The Seder reaches its crescendo as everyone gathered at the table proclaims, *"lishanah ha-baah b'Yerushalayim!"*—"next year in Jerusalem!"

The Pesach festival bears eloquent testimony that God hears the cries of the oppressed and redeems man. "And the people of Israel groaned under their bondage, and cried out for help, and their cry under bondage came up to God. And God heard their groaning, and God remembered his covenant with Abraham, with Isaac, and with Jacob" (Exod. 2:23-24). Curiously, although Moses was the key figure in the exodus drama, his name is not mentioned even once in the entire Seder service. For we are not to confuse Moses, the divine instrument of God's salvation, with God himself. It was God who heard Israel's cries. It was he who interceded in history to redeem them.

The Seder is rich with beautiful rituals and liturgy. Its quintessence is perhaps best expressed by its concluding reading: "Our Passover service is completed. We have reverently repeated its ordered tradition. With songs of praise we have called upon the name of God. May he who broke Pharaoh's yoke forever shatter all fetters of oppression, and hasten the day when war will be no more. Soon may he bring redemption to all mankind—freed from violence and from wrong, and united in an eternal covenant of brotherhood."

In addition to recalling their exodus from Egypt long ago, Jews are also urged to actively pursue freedom for all those to whom it is presently denied. That is the meaning of the biblical command to love the stranger since you were once strangers in Egypt and can best understand their hearts. And while bringing about man's spiritual freedom and redemption is, of course, a significant part of the Jewish mission, Judaism regards the poor, the hungry, and the oppressed as equally enslaved and also in need of redemption, albeit of a materialistic kind. True freedom and redemption, in the Jewish view, involve both spiritual and physical liberation. For this reason, we link Pesach, the holiday marking our physical liberation from Egypt, with Shavuot, the holiday commemorating the giving of the Torah at Sinai and marking our spiritual birth as a people, by counting the days of the *omer* in between (see below, Shavuot section). Jews are commanded to take an active part in extending freedom—both physical and spiritual—to all people.

The first of the Ten Commandments is, "I am the LORD your God, who brought you out of the land of Egypt, out of the house of bondage" (Exod. 20:2). Would it not have been more appropriate, ask the rabbis, for the Torah to have described God at that historic juncture as the Lord "who created heaven and earth"? Rather, they answer, the Torah wishes to teach us that God is not merely some abstract idea or object of philosophical speculation. Nor is he only an utterly transcendent "power" or divine "force." The God of Israel is a God who hears the cries of "all who call upon him, . . . who call upon him in truth" (Ps. 145:18). He is a God who cares deeply about humankind—so much so that he intervenes in human history to liberate them. It is this message of a loving, caring, and personal God, one who is immanent in history, that Israel, his holy people, are to carry to all humankind. At the same time, however, it was this very concept, one of the most fundamental in all of Judaism, which was so radically challenged in our own day by the events of the Holocaust (see chapter 6).

Shavuot (Pentecost)

The holiday of Shavuot is known by a number of different names, each reflecting a particular agricultural or historic motif:

Shavuot, or "Feast of Weeks," since it is celebrated seven complete weeks after the holiday of Passover (see Deut. 16:9-10).

Pentecost, meaning "fifty" in Greek, since it occurs on the fiftieth day after Passover.

Zman Mattan Toratainu, or "Season of the Giving of our Torah," because the festival commemorates God's giving of the Torah to Moses and the people of Israel at Mount Sinai.

Chag ha-Bikkurim, or "Festival of the First Fruits," since the first produce was brought to the temple on this day (see Num. 28:26).

Chag ha-Katzir, or "Festival of the Harvest," celebrating the harvest season and temple offering of the two loaves of bread and first wheat (see Exod. 23:16).

Atzeret, meaning "assembly" or "conclusion," since the festival marks the conclusion of the Passover season.

"You shall bring from your dwellings two loaves of bread to be waved, made of two tenths of an ephah; they shall be of fine flour, they shall be baked with leaven, as first fruits to the LORD" (Lev. 23:17). In ancient times sheaves of barley were brought to the temple each day, beginning on Passover, until Shavuot, the beginning of the harvesting period fifty days later. Farmers looked forward to Shavuot with great excitement and anticipation. When it finally arrived, they would bring their *bikkurim,* or "first fruit," to the temple in Jerusalem amidst great pomp and ceremony. They rejoiced before God and thanked him for their material blessings. As the Talmud (Mishnah, Bik. 3:1-8) describes it: "When a farmer saw a beautiful fruit ripening on his trees, he tied a ribbon around it, setting it aside as an offering. . . . In accordance with the ordinance of the Torah, he placed all the fruit in a basket and brought it to the temple." As the farmers neared Jerusalem, the people of the city would come out to greet them, and led by a flutist, they all proceeded together, amidst song and dance, to the temple mount. There the pilgrims held the baskets of fruit and together with the priest proclaimed, "'A wandering Aramean was my father; and he went down into Egypt . . . and the LORD brought us out of Egypt . . . into this place and gave us this land, a land flowing with milk and honey. And behold, now I bring the first of the fruit of the ground, which thou, O LORD, hast given me'" (Deut. 26:5, 8-10).

The Torah bids us to reenact the joy and anticipation the farmers experienced during the harvest season by linking the spring harvest festival of Passover with the summer agricultural one of Shavuot. We fulfill this duty by counting the days of *omer,* or "measures of grain," offered in the temple ". . . from the time you first put the sickle to the standing grain. Then you shall keep the feast of weeks to the LORD . . . as the LORD your God blesses you" (Deut. 16:9-10).

With the destruction of the second temple and the forced separation of the Jewish people from their land, the centrality of the agricultural harvest motif diminished. Instead, the theme of the anniversary of the Sinai revelation and the giving of the Torah achieved dominance. Although the Torah itself does not offer this rationale, a computation based on the narrative shows that the revelation on Mount Sinai took place exactly fifty days after the Exodus from Egypt, which is the same day as Shavuot (see Exod. 19). In other words, seven weeks after leaving Egypt the Jews came to the foot of Mount Sinai where they received the Torah. The holiday is called *zman mattan toratainu,* or "season of the giving of our Torah," to commemorate that theophany and root experience of the Jewish people. Moreover, just as farmers in temple days counted the days from Pesach until the harvest holiday of Shavuot with great excitement and anticipation, so we today demonstrate our love for God and devotion to his word by counting the days in between Pesach and Shavuot when we received the Torah.

Just as a groom longingly awaits the time when he can live with his bride, so, explain the Jewish mystics, we count the days until we can greet our beloved, the Torah. By counting the forty-nine days between Pesach and Shavuot and linking them thereby, the Jew declares that man does not attain complete freedom through physical liberation alone. The Exodus from Egypt was incomplete without a spiritual redemption. The agricultural motif of bringing the barley omer to the temple for each of the forty-nine days between Pesach and Shavuot was, in short, infused with the new meaning of linking our physical liberation with our spiritual freedom and birth as a people.

That we are to strive toward a higher spiritual purpose in life was actually expressed by Moses, as well, when he declared to Pharaoh, "Let my people go, that they may serve me." For the ultimate purpose of the Jews' freedom and salvation lies in that they are then able to serve God. The Exodus was incomplete without Israel's acceptance of the Torah. In the Jewish view, true freedom is servitude to God. It was for this reason also that a Hebrew slave who insisted on remaining with his master after six years of servitude was to have his ear pierced (Exod. 21:5-6). For it was that same ear, explain the rabbis, that heard God declare at Sinai, "Ye are my servants," that now wishes to remain a servant to man. In the words of the Mishnah, "A truly free man is one who engages in the study and practice of Torah." This is derived by the rabbis from an exegetical play on words. The Torah states that the Ten Commandments were written by God *charut,* meaning "imprinted" on the tablets. Do not read *charut,* say the rabbis, but *chairut,* meaning "freedom," for a truly free person is one who engages in the study and practice of the Torah.

Finally, Shavuot reminds us that we are to strive for spiritual growth all year round. Why, ask the Hasidic rabbis, is the holiday referred to as "the season of the *giving* of Torah" instead of as "the season of our *receiving* the Torah"? For although it was *given* to our forefathers at Sinai on that specific date, we are to *receive* it everywhere, always.

Shavuot observance. Shavuot is celebrated for two days in the Diaspora (except for Reform Jews who celebrate only one day), and for one day in Israel. Unlike all other Jewish holidays, it has no specific rituals or symbols associated with it, although it does have a rich assortment of special customs and liturgies. Synagogues are decorated with flowers and foliage as a reminder that Shavuot was first and foremost an agricultural harvest festival and that today, too, we are to feel indebted to God for our material blessings. Reform congregations traditionally conduct their confirmation ceremonies on Shavuot, as an affirmation that the holiday marks the Jews' acceptance of God's Torah not just in ancient times, but today as well. Orthodox Jews commonly study Torah and Talmud throughout the entire first night of Shavuot until dawn, to show their acceptance of God's word and also to spiritually prepare themselves for the reading of the Ten Commandments which takes place at morning services.

Prior to the reading of the Torah on the first day of Shavuot we chant the *Akdamot,* a beautiful poem written in Aramaic in the eleventh century. *Akdamot,* meaning "introduction," prepares the congregation for the Torah reading of the Sinai revelation and for our own "reenactment" of the Jews' acceptance of Torah at Sinai. The poem glorifies God for creating the world and for choosing Israel as his special people. It depicts the Jewish people as engaging in a debate with other nations of the world that seek to persuade Israel to abandon her faith. Despite their suffering, however, the Jews remain steadfast and resolute, confident in the just rewards that await them in the next world. The Torah portion, including the Ten Commandments (Exod. 19–20), is then read as those assembled rise and symbolically accept the Torah for themselves.

It is customary to read the Scroll of Ruth before the Torah reading on the second day of the festival. The book describes

Ruth, a Gentile Moabite woman, as having married a Jewish man who later died, leaving her childless. Despite the insistence of her mother-in-law, Naomi, that she remain in Moab, Ruth accompanied Naomi to Israel where she accepted the Jewish faith. In one of the most beautiful passages in all of Scripture, Ruth declared, "For where you go I will go, and where you lodge I will lodge; your people shall be my people, and your God my God . . ." (Ruth 1:16). Ruth chanced upon Boaz in his field where she was gathering wheat and later married him. The Book ends with a genealogy indicating that King David was from Ruth's offspring.

The tradition of reading the Book of Ruth on Shavuot developed, in all likelihood, because the story took place at harvest time and coincided with the holiday. Moreover, it describes how Ruth the Moabitess embraced Judaism and joined the ranks of the Jewish people, just as we on this day renew our commitment to God and his Torah and accept them anew. Perhaps more significantly, Ruth, a convert, was the great-grandmother of King David, from whose lineage the Messiah will come to usher in a day when "the earth shall be full of the knowledge of the LORD" (Isa. 11:9). The message of Shavuot is that we are never too estranged or distant from God that we cannot accept him. We can even help bring the Messiah, the son of David, and hasten the redemption of the world.

The prophetic reading on the first day of the holiday is from the first chapter of Ezekiel, describing his vision of God's glory. On the second day a selection from Habakkuk (2:20-3:19) is read in which Israel is urged to persist in her faith despite the suffering that may ensue. Shavuot inspires us never to lose faith in God and never to detach ourselves from his Torah. It encourages us to risk the suffering that can befall those who link their lives and destinies with God, Torah, and Jewish peoplehood.

Sukkot (Tabernacles)

"And the LORD said to Moses, 'Say to the people of Israel, On the fifteenth day of this seventh month and for seven days [there shall be] the feast of booths *[chag ha-Sukkot]* to the LORD'" (Lev. 23:33-34).

The Festival of Sukkot, also known as the Festival of Booths or Tabernacles, comes in the fall, four days after Yom Kippur (see below). It is celebrated for eight days. Following on the heels of the somber, introspective High Holy Days, and in stark contrast with them, Sukkot engenders a spirit of joy, gladness, and celebration of life. "You shall rejoice in your feast" (Deut. 16:14), states the Torah of the pilgrim festivals, although Sukkot alone is called "the festival for rejoicing."

Like most other Jewish holidays, Sukkot commemorates a number of religious and historical motifs. Originally it marked the ingathering of the fall harvest when the Israelites gathered their fruit harvest and thanked God for their bounty and for the land of Israel. The holiday, which was also known as *chag ha-asif,* or "festival of ingathering," was so popular among the people that it became known simply as *"The* Festival," with no further identification necessary.

The American pilgrim fathers were, in all likelihood, inspired by the biblical account of Sukkot to pattern the holiday of Thanksgiving after it. Sukkot also commemorates the Jews' wandering through the desert for forty years during which time they lived in temporary "booths," or *sukkot.* "You shall dwell in booths for seven days . . . that your generations may know that I made the people of Israel dwell in booths when I brought them out of the land of Egypt: I am the LORD your God" (Lev. 23:42–43).

The Sukkah. The *sukkah* we build today is a hut consisting of improvised walls and an open roof covered by branches or leaves. It serves as a temporary shelter during the period of the festival. Meals are eaten inside it. Some pious Jews, particularly those living in warm climates, even sleep in the sukkah to fulfill the Torah precept that we are to "dwell in sukkot seven days." Most synagogues build a communal sukkah, although observant families generally erect their own.

On Sukkot we give thanks for our redemption from Egypt and for God's providence during the many years of wandering through the desert. By dwelling in an exposed, insecure hut, we are reminded that true security comes from being sheltered under God's protective wings. In the words of the psalmist, "For he will hide me in his shelter in the day of trouble; he will conceal me under the cover of his tent, he will set me high upon a rock" (Ps. 27:5).

Paradoxically, at the very same time that we offer thanks to God for our material blessings, we take refuge in the sukkah and recall the frailty, vulnerability, and transitory nature of human existence. For lest we become arrogant from our success in amassing material acquisitions, the holiday bids us to leave the permanence and security of our homes and to become humbled by the awareness of our creatureliness and finitude. We are to rejoice over our material blessings but also to recognize that they are insufficient for bringing about our complete spiritual fulfillment. We must also sanctify those blessings by ascribing them to God. Already the Torah warns us of those who "did not serve the LORD your God with joyfulness and gladness of heart, by reason of the abundance of things" (Deut. 28:47). Sukkot bids us to "serve the Lord with gladness," for, in the words of the Talmud, "the *Shekhinah* [divine presence] dwells among us not out of sadness . . . but out of the joy of mitzvah." Sukkot also reminds us that true joy is rooted in the sanctification of materialism and in the acknowledgment of our finitude and dependence on a loving, providential God. For this reason, the *Scroll of Kohelet*, Ecclesiastes, is read on Sukkot. We are to recall the impermanence and vanity of life at the very same time that we celebrate our material blessings.

The sukkah, however, not only symbolizes God's love and concern for his people, it also reflects the singularity of the Jew's willingness to give up the comforts and securities of the home and to risk the elements to follow God wherever he might lead him. For this act of faith, declared Jeremiah, the Jewish people will merit divine loving kindness: "I remember the devotion of your youth . . . how you followed me in the wilderness, in a land not sown" (Jer. 2:2).

The Talmud described this Jewish attribute in the following story: "In times to come, the Holy One, Blessed be He, will embrace a Scroll of the Law and proclaim: 'Let him who has occupied himself with this, come and take his reward.' Thereupon all the nations will crowd together and plead, 'Offer us the Torah anew and we shall obey it.' The Holy One, Blessed be He, will say to them . . . 'I have an easy commandment which is called sukkah; go and observe it' . . . Immediately, every one of them will betake himself and go and make a booth on the top of his roof; but the Holy One, Blessed be He, will cause the summer sun to blaze forth over them [to test their convictions], and every one of them will trample down his booth and flee . . ." (B.T., A.Z. 3a). Sukkot tests the Jew's willingness to sacrifice comfort and convenience for the sake of obedience to God and his word.

After the destruction of the first Jerusalem temple and Babylonian exile in 586 B.C.E., the sukkah assumed the additional symbolic significance of the frailty and impermanence of Jewish life, which is detached from its natural center, the land of Israel. The sukkah came to represent the Jewish quest for sovereignty over their ancient homeland and longing for the coming of the Messiah and redemption of the world. "In that day I will raise up the booth [sukkah] of David that is fallen and repair its breaches, and raise up its ruins, and rebuild it as in the days of old" (Amos 9:11).

Since the sukkah has assumed a universal messianic symbolism in addition to its particularistic Jewish meaning, the Festival of Sukkot has become the only one that Gentiles will also be expected to observe in the messianic era. As we read on the first day of Sukkot, "Then every one that survives of all the nations that have come against Jerusalem shall go up year after year to worship the King, the LORD of hosts, and to keep the feast of booths" (Zech. 14:16).

For this same reason, Jews pray on Sukkot, not only for their own welfare, but for that of the entire world. In addition, Sukkot was the only festival when, in the days of the temple, seventy animal sacrifices corresponding to "the seventy nations of the world" were offered. The universal and messianic character of the holiday was reaffirmed by Zechariah in the prophetic portion of Scripture read on Sukkot: "And the Lord will become king over all the earth; on that day the LORD will be one and his name one" (Zech. 14:9). Indeed, every Shabbat the Jew associates the sukkah with his prayers for messianic peace. In the words of the Sabbath liturgy, "Spread over us your tabernacle [sukkah] of peace. Blessed art thou, O LORD, who spreads the tabernacle of peace over us and over all his people, Israel, and over Jerusalem."

The four species. "You shall take on the first day the fruit of goodly trees *[hadar]*, branches of palm trees *[temarim]*, and boughs of leafy trees *[avot]*, and willows of the brook *[arvei-nahal]*; and . . . you shall keep it as a feast . . . throughout your generations . . ." (Lev. 23:40–41).

In addition to the mitzvah of dwelling in a sukkah, we also take "the four species" and rejoice before God. The oral tradition teaches that the "fruit of the *hadar* tree" refers to the *etrog* or citron, "branches of *temarim*" refers to the palm branch or *lulav*, "boughs of leafy trees" are the myrtle twigs or *hadassim*, and the *arvei-nahal* are the "willows." Together, they form the *arbaah minim*, or "four species."

The myrtle twigs and willows are tied to the palm branch, which is held alongside the etrog. On each day of sukkot we take the four species of harvest produce and wave them in all directions—north, south, east, west, upward, and downward—to symbolize that all our worldly possessions and material blessings come from God. The rabbis offer a variety of explanations as to why these particular types of harvest produce are used. For example, they suggest that the tall palm branch symbolizes man's spine; the drooping willow branches, the mouth; the beautiful and fragrant citron, the heart; and the myrtle leaves, the eyes. Not only our agricultural produce, but our very organs, too—that which we *are* as well as that which we *have*—must be brought together as we worship God. We are to love God with all our being. In the words of the Shabbat liturgy, "All my limbs will proclaim, 'Lord who is like thee.'"

The seventh day of Sukkot, a semi-holiday in its own right, is called Hoshana Rabbah, or "Great Hosanna." In the course of the morning prayer service everyone in the congregation takes the lulav and etrog and joins in a seven-circuit procession around the synagogue while reciting prayers of hosanna calling for God's salvation. These processions commemorate similar ones that were made around the Jerusalem temple in ancient days on Sukkot.

Shemini Atzeret and Simchat Torah. *Shemini Atzeret,* or the "Eighth Day of Assembly," is technically a holiday in its own right, though it is also connected to the festival of Sukkot: "On the eighth day you shall hold a holy convocation . . . it is a solemn assembly . . ." (Lev. 23:36). Despite the fact that the holiday marks the conclusion of the Sukkot pilgrim festival, the rituals of the four species and the sukkah are not observed. The Torah itself provides no explanation for the holiday other than to regard it as essentially the final day of Sukkot. A rabbinic parable, however, compared God to a human king whose children come to visit him in the capital only three times a year. The king, enjoying their company so much and being so saddened by their departure, bids them to stay on an extra day. Similarly, God so loves his children, the people of Israel, and is so pleased that they have come to the temple in Jerusalem to celebrate the festival, that he has difficulty "parting" with them. He, therefore, bids them to stay an additional day.

In the Diaspora, the following day is celebrated as the holiday of *Simchat Torah,* or "rejoicing over the Torah." (In Israel it takes place on the same day as Shemini Atzeret.) The festival, originating in the Middle Ages, marks the completion of the annual cycle of reading from the Torah. As previously mentioned, the Torah is divided into fifty-four portions, one of which is read in synagogue each week so that by the end of the year the entire Pentateuch, or the five books of Moses, will have been completed. Except for Purim, Simchat Torah is the most joyous festival in the Jewish calendar.

On the eve of the holiday all the Torah scrolls are taken out of the ark and carried around the sanctuary seven times amidst singing and dancing. Children customarily lead the procession, waving flags inscribed with scriptural verses or carrying miniature Torah scrolls. Needless to say, traditional synagogue rules of decorum are waived on this holiday. Following the joyous festivities we read the concluding portion of Deuteronomy and then immediately begin reading from the first portion of Genesis. In this way we demonstrate our love for the Torah as well as the fact that we can never come to fully know the word of God. The study of Torah is a never-ending process; there always remains more to learn. Indeed, the Hebrew term for a great Torah scholar is *talmid chakham,* or "wise student." We never stop being students of the Torah. For this reason also, each tractate of the Talmud begins with page number two (there is no page one) to show that there is always more for us to learn. All of the men and children are honored by being called up to the Torah on Simchat Torah so that they might each feel a sense of personal joy and attachment to the Torah. Women are excluded from this practice in Orthodox synagogues.

In recent decades the festival of Simchat Torah has acquired a profound additional meaning. It was then that Jews in the former Soviet Union, prohibited from studying and practicing their ancestral faith freely, gathered in front of synagogues in cities like Moscow and Kiev to sing, dance, and celebrate the holiday in defiance of the authorities. Many Jews living behind the Iron Curtain rediscovered their links with Judaism through the joy engendered by the festival. The spark of Judaism still flickers despite the many years of Communist religious intolerance and repression. The courageous spirit of the Russian Jews is a reminder that no possible form of tyranny will forever endure.

THE HIGH HOLY DAYS

The High Holy Days, commencing in the fall with Rosh Hashanah, the Jewish New Year, and climaxing ten days later with Yom Kippur, the Day of Atonement, are the most widely observed of all Jewish holy days. Even those Jews who normally do not attend synagogue services are inclined to observe them.

The preceding Hebrew month of Elul is set aside as a time for reflection and soul-searching in order that we might enter the "Days of Awe," as the High Holy Days are sometimes called, in the proper spirit. The dominant theme during this forty-day period from the beginning of Elul through Yom Kippur is *teshuvah,* or "repentance," literally, "returning to one's self."

The rabbis suggest that this forty-day period of repentance corresponds to the biblical one in which Moses pleaded with God to forgive the people of Israel for their sin of worshiping the Golden Calf (see Exod. 32–34). The spirit of teshuvah grows and intensifies in the course of those forty days. The *shofar,* or "ram's horn," is blown at morning prayer services, and special prayers of *selikhot,* or "penitence," as well as Psalm 27, are added to the liturgy. By the time New Year's Day arrives, we are already deeply immersed in reflection and in the meticulous observance of mitzvot. We are anxious to "wash our slates clean" and begin life anew.

Rosh Hashanah: New Year's Day

Rosh Hashanah, literally meaning "head of the year," is celebrated for two days. It marks the beginning of what is alternately called "the ten days of repentance," "the Days of Awe," or "the High Holy Days." According to tradition, it is during this period that God determines "who shall live and who shall die" in the coming year. Axiomatic to all of Judaism is the notion that man possesses the freedom and capability to atone for his sins and to transform his life. He has the power to gain reconciliation with both God and his fellow man. Just as God sought out Adam, Cain, and Jonah when they tried to flee from him, so God seeks out all humankind, confronting them with the inner contradictions of their lives and hoping that they will repent. Through an act of "grace," God responds a thousand-fold to humankind's even slightest turning toward him. God, in the words of the midrash, declares, "My children, give me an opening of repentance no bigger than the eye of a needle, and I will widen it into openings through which even wagons and carriages will pass through" (Song of Songs Rab. 5:2; see also chapter 1).

The Jewish New Year is not a time of hilarity or frivolous rejoicing, but of solemnity and intense moral and spiritual introspection, as befits a plaintiff coming before the Supreme Judge and Ruler of the world, appealing for his life. The mood pervading the day is one not only of "fear and trembling" before judgment, but also of trust in a merciful and beneficent father who desires our repentance and is eager to grant forgiveness. In the words of the prophet, "But if a wicked man turns away from all his sins which he has committed and keeps all my statutes and does what is lawful and right, he shall surely live; he shall not die. . . . Have I any pleasure in the death of the wicked, says the Lord God, and not rather that he should turn from his way and live? . . . Cast away from you all the transgressions which you have committed against me, and get yourselves a new heart and a new spirit! Why will you die, O house of Israel? For I have no pleasure in the death of any one, says the Lord God; so turn, and live" (Ezek. 18:21, 23, 31–32).

Rosh Hashanah brings together a variety of different motifs, all rooted in the conviction that God is the Creator of the world and Ruler over all life. It is known by a number of names, each underscoring a different dimension of the holiday. According to tradition, it is *hayom harat olam,* the anniversary of the creation of the world, as well as *yom ha-zikaron,* or "day of remembrance," when both we and God reflect upon our deeds over the past year.

The shofar. The Torah itself refers to it only as "the day of the blowing of the shofar." "On the first day of the seventh month, you shall have a holy convocation. . . . It is a day for you to blow the trumpets . . ." (Num. 29:1). "In the seventh month, on the first day of the month, you shall observe a day of solemn rest, a memorial proclaimed with the blasts of trumpets, a holy convocation. You shall do no laborious work . . ." (Lev. 23:24-25. See also Neh. 8:2-12 which vividly describes how Ezra read the Torah to the people of Israel who then rededicated themselves to serving God).

By the time of the second commonwealth, i.e., in the fifth century B.C.E. Rosh Hashanah also became associated with the idea of atonement for sin. The blowing of the shofar retained its biblical significance as the main ritual of the holiday. According to Jewish tradition, three distinct types of blasts are sounded—a long, drawn-out sound *(tekiah),* a broken plaintive sound *(shevarim),* and a series of sharp, wailing, staccato sounds *(teruah).* One hundred blasts are sounded on each of the two days of Rosh Hashanah, followed by the congregational recitation of biblical verses reminding them of their covenant with God.

There are a variety of explanations proffered for the sounding of the shofar.

Symbol of revelation: The shofar figured prominently in the drama of the giving of the Torah on Sinai. "On the morning of the third day there were thunders and lightnings, and a thick cloud upon the mountain, and a very loud trumpet blast, so that all the people . . . in the camp trembled" (Exod. 19:16). "And as the sound of the trumpet grew louder and louder, Moses spoke, and God answered him . . ." (Exod. 19:19). By sounding the shofar on Rosh Hashanah, we recall the awesome theophany at Sinai and commit ourselves anew to living according to God's Torah.

Symbol of God's coronation: We sound the shofar on Rosh Hashanah as a reaffirmation of God's sovereignty and kingship over us, just as it was blasted in ancient Israel at the coronation ceremony for kings. In the words of the psalmist, "With trumpets and the sound of the horn make a joyful noise before the King, the LORD!" (Ps. 98:6).

Symbol of the akedah (binding of Isaac): The story of the *akedah* (Gen. 22) which is read in the synagogue on Rosh Hashanah permeates a great deal of the holiday liturgy as well. We recall how Abraham, the knight of faith, was willing to sacrifice his one and only son, Isaac, and how, having passed God's test, he then offered a ram in his son's place. The ram's horn, which was caught in the brushes, became an eternal symbol of Abraham's and Isaac's trust in God, even in the face of death. The akedah motif has served as a paradigm of Jewish martyrdom and self-sacrifice for centuries (see, for example, my comments on Hannah and her seven sons in the section on Hanukkah).

Symbol of humankind's need for repentance: In biblical times the shofar was sounded as a call for the people to assemble or for the camp to move and as a warning of impending disaster. Similarly, it is sounded on Rosh Hashanah to arouse us from our moral reverie, to call us to spiritual regeneration, and to alert us to the need to engage in teshuvah (repentance). The shofar is the clarion call to perform teshuvah—to search our deeds and mend our ways before the awesome day of judgment. It is a reminder of our need to confront our inner selves just as God confronted Adam with the existential question, "Where are you?" (Gen. 3:9).

Maimonides, the great medieval Jewish philosopher and codifier, explained the symbolism of the shofar in the following manner: "Awake, O you sleepers, awake from your sleep! Search your deeds and turn in repentance. O you who forget the truth in the vanities of time and go astray all the year after vanity and folly that neither profit nor save remember your Creator! Look at your souls, and better your ways and actions. Let every one of you abandon his evil ways and his wicked thoughts and return to God so that He may have mercy upon you" *(Mishneh Torah,* Laws of Teshuvah 3:4).

Symbol of the messianic era: The shofar is sounded as a reminder of God's promise to bring the Messiah who will usher into the world an era of physical and spiritual peace, and who will herald Israel's redemption and ingathering to Zion. "And in that day a great trumpet will be blown, and those who were lost in the land of Assyria and those who were driven out to the land of Egypt will come and worship the LORD on the holy mountain at Jerusalem" (Isa. 27:13). The Messiah will bring liberty and freedom to all people. And just as the shofar was sounded in biblical days to proclaim the Jubilee year and to herald the freedom of slaves and property, so it will be blown when the Messiah comes, and freedom will come to the entire world. "Then you shall send abroad the loud trumpet . . . and proclaim liberty throughout the land to all its inhabitants" (Lev. 25:9-10).

Rosh Hashanah observance. Rosh Hashanah is associated with a number of beautiful customs. People greet each other with the words, *"le-shanah tovah tikatevu v'taychataymu,"* meaning, "May you be inscribed and sealed for a good year." This practice stems from the traditional imagery in which God sits in judgment on the Days of Awe, deciding the fate of every living thing. On Rosh Hashanah he opens up three books—one for those who were righteous during the year, one for those who were wicked, and one for those whose good and bad deeds balance. Everyone's fate is inscribed in one of those three books. During the ten days between Rosh Hashanah and Yom Kippur, however, we can alter the course of our destiny by repenting, praying, and doing acts of charity. On Yom Kippur, the final day of judgment, God closes all three books and seals humankind's verdict for the coming year. According to Maimonides, we are to constantly regard both our own fate as well as the destiny of the entire world as balanced between acquittal and guilt. By committing even one additional sin, we effectively tilt the scales of our lives and of the world toward guilt and destruction. Conversely, if we perform even one meritorious deed, we swing the scales toward good and help bring about our own salvation as well as that of the whole world.

It is also customary to dip a piece of *challah* (bread) or apple into honey at mealtime and recite the prayer, "May it be thy will that we be blessed with a good, sweet year."

On the first day of Rosh Hashanah, we perform the *Tashlikh* ceremony in which we throw bread crumbs or stones into a running body of water such as a river or spring, and symbolically cast off our sins into the water and begin life anew. This custom originated in the fifteenth century and, in all likelihood, was derived from the biblical account of the scapegoat. A number of rabbis at the time prohibited the practice, regarding it as based in popular superstition. Today, however, Tashlikh is completely accepted and widely viewed as symbolic of the freedom from sin we can enjoy when we repent and trust in God's miracle of forgiveness. In the words of the prophet recited in the Tashlikh liturgy, "Thou wilt cast all our sins into the depths of the sea" (Mic. 7:19).

White is the predominant color scheme during the Days of Awe. The skullcaps, ark curtain, and Torah mantles are all white, signifying purity, holiness, and atonement for sin— "Though your sins are like scarlet, they shall be as white as snow" (Isa. 1:18). White is also the color of the shrouds in which Jews are buried. It reminds us of the gravity of judgment time and of the frailty of life.

As with most other Jewish festivals excluding, of course, fast days, it is a mitzvah to celebrate by partaking of a festive meal on the two days of Rosh Hashanah. We are to feel joyful and confident even on these Days of Awe that God, our Father and King, will pass merciful judgment on our lives and forgive us of our iniquities.

The liturgy of the Rosh Hashanah morning service is among the most beautiful and moving of the entire year. The following brief prayer expresses some of the different motifs underlying the holiday: "Today the world is born, today in judgment there stand before you all the creatures of the world, as children or as slaves. If we may call ourselves [your] children, show us mercy as a father shows mercy to his children; if we are

[but] slaves, our eyes are focused on you that you might have compassion and decide our case in judgment as brightness in light, awesome and holy God" (Rosh Hashanah Musaf service).

Another example of the kind of powerful soul-stirring poems included in the liturgy is the *Unetane Tokef*, written by a rabbi from Mayence (Mainz), circa the eleventh century, who underwent martyrdom together with his family during the first Crusade.

> Let us acclaim the majestic sanctity of this day, for it is awesome and mighty. Your kingdom is triumphantly proclaimed. Your throne is established in mercy, and you occupy it in truth. In truth, you are judge and prosecutor, knowing motives, giving evidence, writing, sealing, counting, measuring, remembering all, even things we have forgotten. You open the book of remembrances and it speaks for itself, for every person's signature is affixed to his deeds.
>
> The great Shofar is sounded. A muted small voice is heard. The angels too are frightened, fear and trembling seize them, and they declare: "This is the day of judgment, of mustering the host on high!" In your sight not even they are exempt from judgment. And all that have come into the world pass before you as a flock of sheep. As a shepherd gathers his flock, making his sheep pass beneath his staff, even so do you make pass, count, and muster the souls of all the living. You determine the latter end of every creature and record their ultimate verdict. On Rosh Hashanah it is written down for them, on Yom Kippur it is sealed. How many shall leave [life] and how many shall be born, who shall live and who shall die, who shall attain his full span of life and who shall not, who shall perish by fire, and who by water, who by the sword and who by wild beasts, who by hunger and who by thirst, who by storm and who by plague, who shall have rest and who shall be restless, who shall find repose and who shall be wandering, who

shall be free from sorrow and who shall be tormented, who shall be exalted and who shall be humbled, who shall be poor and who shall be rich. But Repentance, Prayer, and Good Deeds can avert the severity of the decree.

For your renown is as your name; slow to anger, ready to be soothed. You do not desire the guilty one's death, but that he turn from his way and live. You wait for him up to the very day of his death; if he returns you accept him at once. Verily you are their Creator and you know their inner drives; they are but flesh and blood.

As to man, his origin is dust and his end is dust, at the risk of his life he earns his bread, he is like a broken vessel of clay, like withering grass, a fading flower, a passing shadow, a drifting cloud, a fleeting breath, scattering dust, a transient dream.

But you are King, God, living and enduring!
(High Holy Days Musaf service)

The Sabbath falling in the intervening ten days between Rosh Hashanah and Yom Kippur is called *Shabbat Shuvah,* or "Sabbath of returning," in light of the predominant theme of the season and of the prophetic portion read on that day which begins with the words, "Return, O Israel, to the LORD your God" (Hos. 14).

Yom Kippur: Day of Atonement

"And it shall be a statute to you for ever that in the seventh month, on the tenth day of the month, you shall afflict yourselves, and shall do no work, either the native or the stranger who sojourns among you; for on this day shall atonement be made for you, to cleanse you; from all your sins you shall be clean before the LORD. It is a sabbath of solemn rest to you, and you shall afflict yourselves; it is a statute for ever" (Lev. 16:29–31). The month of Nissan, when the Jewish people left Egypt and became a free nation, is the first month of the year in the biblical calendar; both Yom Kippur and Rosh Hashanah the "New Year" therefore fall in the Hebrew month of Tishrei which in the Biblical calendar is the seventh month.

Yom Kippur, the Day of Atonement, is the culmination of the entire High Holy Day drama—our final opportunity to repent from our sins. It is also the holiest day in the Jewish year or, in the Torah's words, the "Sabbath of Sabbaths." During the twenty-four hours of Yom Kippur, Jews fulfill their obligation to "afflict" their souls by fasting (both food and water are prohibited), soul-searching, and praying. From the eve of the holiday until sundown the following day (except for the few hours when they go home to sleep), Jews are in the synagogue beseeching God for forgiveness and reflecting upon the course of their lives. An entirely new liturgy is used only on this one day of Yom Kippur. It is a day of purification and reconciliation with one's God and fellow human beings. However, the rabbis repeatedly pointed out that repenting through acts of fasting and prayer atones only for those sins that are committed between man and God. For those between man and his fellow man, we must seek forgiveness from the other party himself. Fasting on Yom Kippur is not to be seen as an end in itself but rather as an act that should prod us to focus on spiritual matters. It is a reminder of the frailty of human existence and of our duty to act charitably and compassionately toward the less fortunate. It is also a means of self-discipline and a sign of penance. In order that we remember the true meaning of the fast, the rabbis selected the inspiring words of Isaiah as among those to be read in synagogue on Yom Kippur:

> Is not this the fast that I choose:
>   to loose the bonds of wickedness,
>   to undo the thongs of the yoke,
> to let the oppressed go free . . . ?
> Is it not to share your bread with the hungry,
>   and bring the homeless poor into your house;

when you see the naked, to cover him,
and not to hide yourself from your own flesh?
(Isaiah 58:6–7)

It is customary to go to a *mikvah*, or "ritual bath," before Yom Kippur in order to fulfill the biblical mitzvah: "You shall immerse yourselves in water and be purified." This practice, from which Christian baptism originated, symbolizes man's act of purification and regeneration, as well as his "new birth" through *teshuvah* (repentance). We greet each other with the words, *"gemar chatimah tovah,"* or "May you be sealed [i.e., in God's Book of Life] for good." Parents bless their children before the holiday, wishing them a happy and healthy New Year. (It is still regarded as the New Year season since God yet sits in judgment.) The following is an example of such a parental blessing:

May it be the will of our Father in Heaven to put into your heart love for him and reverence for him. May the reverence for God accompany you all the days of your life that you may not come to sin. May your longing be for Torah and mitzvot. May your eyes be directed straight, your mouth speak wisdom, your heart strive for reverence. May your hands be occupied with mitzvot, your feet hasten to do the will of your Father in Heaven. May he give you pious sons and daughters who will occupy themselves with Torah and mitzvot all the days of their lives; may your womb be blessed. May he vouchsafe your sustenance through legitimate means, without stress and with profit, out of his hand that is wide open and not through the handouts of other human beings, a sustenance that will direct you toward the service of God. May you be inscribed and sealed unto a good, long life, you and all the righteous of Israel. Amen.

(Code of Jewish Law [abridged] 131:16)

We give charity before the holiday and also light memorial candles in memory of departed family members. As with all Jewish festivals, it is the woman who formally ushers in the holiday with the lighting of the candles at sundown. We attend synagogue where the mood is one of solemnity and awe, but also of hope. A spirit of holiness and love pervades the assembly as everyone stands before God during this final twenty-four-hour period, appealing to the eternal Judge for a merciful judgment. Evening services commence with the recitation of the *Kol Nidrei* (meaning "all vows"), one of the most powerful and emotionally evocative prayers in all of Jewish liturgy. The Kol Nidrei prayer is a plea for absolution from vows that were made but not fulfilled during the course of the year. As stated earlier, the vows referred to are only those between man and God, since those between man and his fellow man must be reconciled by the parties involved.

While it is true that we are to treat our words with the utmost seriousness and to keep all our promises (see Deut. 23–24), it is puzzling that the central prayer on this, the holiest day of the Jewish year, would focus on the relatively trivial matter of asking absolution for vows. Moreover, it is difficult to account for the fact that, despite the relative triviality of its theme, the Kol Nidrei service is one of the most emotionally intense and evocative experiences for observant and nonobservant Jews alike. The fact that this is the first service of the Yom Kippur holy day and our final opportunity to come before God to plead for merciful judgment, no doubt, plays a major role. And yet, this explanation is insufficient to explain the powerful emotional charge of the prayer.

In truth, the moving, heightened emotions associated with the service are due more to the history and melody of the Kol Nidrei prayer than to the meaning of the words themselves. The prayer originated some time between the sixth and tenth centuries when Jews were faced with the choice of either converting to Christianity or suffering martyrdom. Many of those forced to convert, however, secretly recited this Kol Nidrei prayer on Yom Kippur, declaring before God that the vows they had made denying their Jewish faith and accepting Christianity were done under duress and were, therefore, null and void.

By the sixteenth century the prayer achieved even greater significance as it was invoked by the Spanish *Marranos*. (Marranos, a Spanish term meaning "pigs," were Jews who outwardly converted to Christianity to escape death, but who secretly continued to practice Judaism.) The haunting melody of Kol Nidrei originated in the 1500s in southern Germany. Jews bring to this Yom Kippur service an abundance of emotions as they listen to the indescribably sorrowful strains of the Kol Nidrei melody and recall their history of suffering. However, both the words of the prayer as well as its melody end in a triumphant note of optimism, leading us from despair to hope.

The services on the following morning and afternoon contain a number of features unique to Yom Kippur. We recite a series of confessionals for sins we committed during the course of the year, as well as a special *Avodah* service in which we recall how the high priest in ancient days entered the Holy of Holies to purge it of uncleanliness and to pray for forgiveness for the House of Israel (see Lev. 16). In another portion of the service we recall how ten great rabbis during the time of the Roman Hadrianic persecution suffered martyrdom rather than abandon their Jewish faith. Prayers of *Yizkor*, or "remembrance," for the deceased members of one's family are also recited. Today most synagogues add two additional Yizkor memorial prayers, one for those who died in the Holocaust and one for those killed defending the State of Israel. The prophetic portion from Isaiah 58 describing the true nature of fast days is read in the morning service (see above). In the afternoon we read the Book of Jonah as a reminder that no one can flee from the Lord and his judgment, but that God is a loving, merciful, and forgiving God who cares for man and, indeed, for all his creation.

Emotions reach their acme at the *Neilah*, or "closing" service, as nightfall approaches and Yom Kippur is about to come to an end. The pervasive imagery depicted in the liturgy is of heavenly gates closing, leaving man, the petitioner, with his final opportunity to plead his case before final judgment. "Open unto us the gate at the gate's closing time, for the day is almost over. The day is passing fast, the sun is going home and setting, do let us enter your gates. Forgive us, pardon us, have mercy . . ." (Neilah liturgy).

In a final dramatic burst of spirit and faith, the prayer service reaches its crescendo as the congregation declares, "Hear, O Israel, the Lord our God the Lord is One. Blessed be his glorious kingdom for ever and ever. God is the Lord." The service concludes with one blast of the shofar as the congregation, trusting in God and confident in his favorable judgment, proclaims, "Next year in Jerusalem!" The drama of the Day of Atonement has reached its finale; the High Holy Days of awe and repentance have come to a close.

Repentance. The central theme of the High Holy Days is repentance, or *teshuvah,* literally meaning "returning to one's self." According to Maimonides and Jewish tradition, there are four conditions necessary for teshuvah—regret for the past, desisting from sinful behavior, confession before God, and resolving not to sin in the future. Complete repentance occurs when we are thrust into the same circumstances in which we had previously sinned, but which we now overcome. (See Maimonides' *Mishneh Torah,* Laws of Repentance, for his excellent treatment of the overall subject.) True repentance, therefore, involves not only a "change of heart," but a "change in action" as well—a turning away from bad and a turning toward good. In the words of the psalmist, "Depart from evil, and do good" (Ps. 34:14).

The notion that man is created with free will and is capable of doing either good or bad underlies the doctrine of teshuvah. And while Judaism recognizes that sin is an integral part of the human condition and that "there is not a righteous man on earth who . . . never sins" (Eccles. 7:20), the Jewish faith also professes that man is not inherently evil but rather that he has a predilection toward sin (see chapter 2). Moreover, man has the capacity to change his ways and to repent from his transgressions.

The rabbis insisted that teshuvah is an act of will that we are all capable of asserting. It involves a "turning" away from evil and "returning" to God and to our true (pure) selves. Man is never too ridden with sin that he cannot turn toward God and initiate his own moral regeneration and renewal. For while God created man with both evil and good inclinations, he also provided him with the antidote to the power of evil—the Torah. Man's power to initiate reconciliation and inner healing is itself a divine miracle and act of grace. Indeed, it is a profound mystery. God extends his love to man even further, however, by responding a thousandfold to his "turning" from sin. This Jewish view of repentance was inspired by the prophets who declared, "Return to me, says the LORD of hosts, and I [then] will return to you" (Zech. 1:3). "Seek the LORD while he may be found, call upon him while he is near; let the wicked forsake his way, and the unrighteous man his thoughts; let him return to the LORD, that he may have mercy on him . . ." (Isa. 55:6-7). Three times daily the Jew prays, "The LORD is near to all who call upon him . . . who call upon him in truth" (Ps. 145:18).

Teshuvah is also predicated on the notion that God does not desire ". . . the death of the wicked . . . but that [he] turn from his way and live" (Ezek. 33:11). God is a merciful and compassionate Father, as well as judge of justice. The rabbis taught that God created and governs the entire world through a combination of his attributes of mercy and justice. The midrash, for example, draws an analogy between God and a mortal king who had in his possession fragile glassware. The king was concerned that if he poured hot water into the glasses, they would burst, but if he poured cold water, they would crack. And so, he decided to pour a mixture of both. So, too, states the midrash, if God were to guide the world only with his attribute of compassion, it would never survive but instead would be overrun by sinners. And if he were to rule it only with strict justice, it would also not last since no human being could withstand his judgment. And so, God rules the world with a mixture of both justice and compassion (Gen. Rab. 12:15).

Furthermore, unlike biblical critics who view the different names for God in the Torah as proof that the Bible was authored by different writers at different times, the rabbis claimed that the term *elo-im* refers to God's attribute of justice and *adon-y* to his quality of mercy. Both of God's names and attributes are necessarily involved in his rule of the world. (Note, for example, when God tells Noah that he would bring a flood, the Torah uses the term *elo-im,* but when Noah is safely in the ark, it is *adon-y* who closes the door and secures him and his family. Similarly, when God tells Abraham to sacrifice his son Isaac, the term *elo-im* is used, but when he stops him from killing Isaac, it is "an angel of *Adon-y.")* We recite God's thirteen attributes of mercy many times during the course of the High Holy Day services. We ask that he judge us accordingly, with compassion, love, and mercy. And we recall that, "As a father pities his children, so the LORD pities those who fear him" (Ps. 103:13).

God waits for man to show the slightest sign of teshuvah, even until the time of his death, so that he may forgive him. Rabbi Eliezer, states the Talmud, taught that if a man were to repent even on the day of his death, all his sins would be forgiven. "But does a man know the day of his death?" asked his disciples. Therefore the rabbi responded, "We must repent daily lest we, in fact, die that day." Such an attitude gives urgency and meaning to life. It compels man to "count his days" and to grasp the moment to the fullest. Man is to live in the present and to reconcile himself through repentance from the inner contradictions of his life.

The reward for doing a mitzvah, states the Talmud, is being inclined to do more mitzvot. By renouncing sin and doing mitzvot, we are rewarded with an even greater desire to pursue good. Teshuvah lifts a tremendous burden from man's heart. It brings him spiritual tranquillity, inner purity, and a cleansing of his soul; it brings him reconciliation with God and man. According to the Talmud, one who engages in repentance is so meritorious that, "where repentant sinners stand, the thoroughly righteous cannot stand" (B.T., Ber. 34b). In fact, "If a man repents he converts into pious deeds even the many sins of which he may be guilty" (Exod. Rab. 31:1).

The redemption of the world is dependent on man's doing teshuvah. "Were Israel to practice repentance even for one day," claims the midrash, "forthwith they would be redeemed, and forthwith the scion of David would come" (Song of Songs Rab. 5:2). According to the Mishnah, "Better is an hour of repentance and good works in this world than the whole life of the world to come; and better is one hour of bliss in the world to come than the whole life of this world" (Avot 4:17). Judaism insists that the possibility and miracle of teshuvah are always present. For while "the gates of prayer are sometimes open and sometimes locked, the gates of repentance are always open" (Deut. Rab. 2:7 or 12). It is up to man to avail himself of that opportunity and to walk through its gates.

THE MINOR HOLIDAYS

Purim

Purim is the most joyous festival in the Jewish year. It is so cherished that the Talmud even equates it with the day of revelation at Sinai. And while all other Jewish holidays will be abolished when the Messiah arrives, Purim alone will continue to be celebrated (T.Y., Meg. 1:5). The importance ascribed to the holiday by Jewish tradition is, however, rather surprising. For Purim is one of only two festivals commemorating an event taking place in the post-biblical period, i.e., after the death of Moses and the compilation of the Torah (Pentateuch or Five Books of Moses), and the only one that occurred in the Diaspora. There are even those who claim that the entire series of events of Purim never transpired but that they are adaptations of ancient spring folk festivals. Nevertheless, the holiday is widely and enthusiastically celebrated by Jews. It commemorates the averting of a terrible calamity, the triumph of good over evil, and the victory of the Jewish people over their enemies.

The familiar story of Purim dates back to the fifth century before the Common Era in Persia. King Ahasuerus made a great feast and commanded his Queen, Vashti, to come before him and his guests to parade her beauty. (Ahasuerus, the King of Persia described in the Scroll of Esther, is believed to be either King Xerxes, who ruled from 485–464 B.C.E., or King Artaxerxes II, who reigned from 404–361 B.C.E.) Vashti refused and was summarily deposed. A search for a new queen was conducted throughout the empire, and from among all the maidens in the land, a Jewish girl, Hadassah, also known as Esther, was selected to be the new queen. Meanwhile, Haman, the king's prime minister, was outraged at Mordecai the Jew, Esther's uncle, for refusing to bow down to him. Haman plotted to destroy not only Mordecai, but the entire Jewish people. King Ahasuerus, who relied entirely on Haman's counsel, ordered that the Jews be eradicated and that their property and possessions be confiscated. "Lots," or *purim*, were cast to ascertain the date for the Jews' destruction. The date of doom was fixed on the thirteenth day of the twelfth Hebrew month, Adar. When Mordecai learned of the impending disaster, he immediately went to Esther, urging that she intercede on behalf of her people. Esther decreed that all the Jews in Persia observe a three-day fast after which she would go before the king at great personal risk. The king received Esther who proceeded to invite him and Haman to two successive banquets.

On the night before the second banquet, the king could not sleep. He asked that the national chronicles be read to him. Coincidentally, the section that was read told of Mordecai's having saved the king's life by reporting an assassination plot against him. The account also revealed the fact that Mordecai had never been rewarded for that act. Precisely at that moment

Haman, who was in the hallway, came before King Ahasuerus to ask permission to hang Mordecai.

Ahasuerus, who was preoccupied with Mordecai's unrewarded deed, asked, "What shall be done to the man whom the king delighteth to honor?" Haman, convinced that the king was referring to him, suggested that such a person be escorted in a royal procession so that the people would give honor to him and realize that he was the king's most trusted and closest advisor. Instead of hanging Mordecai, Haman became his chief attendant in a magnificent pageant.

That night at the banquet Esther made an impassioned plea to the king on behalf of her people, and Ahasuerus and Haman learned for the first time that she was a Jewess. The king ordered Haman to be hanged in Mordecai's place.

Since it was not possible for the king to rescind his edict that all Jews should be killed, Esther and Mordecai implored him to issue an edict granting Jews the right to protect themselves from their enemies. Their wish was granted, and the Jewish community of Persia was saved from destruction. To commemorate this miraculous turn of events, Esther and Mordecai inaugurated the festival of Purim, which is celebrated annually on the fourteenth day of the twelfth month, Adar.

The festival of Purim is celebrated in the spring, one month (in a leap year, two months) before Passover. It is a day of great rejoicing, gladness, and levity, with even a degree of frivolity, much like a Mardi Gras. The Shabbat before Purim is known as *Shabbat Zakhor*, or "Sabbath of Remembrance." The special portion of the Torah that is read (Deut. 25:17–19) describes the commandment to remember the treacherous deeds of the Amalekites who attacked the Israelites from behind as they left Egypt. We are never to forget that treacherous act, and we are to obliterate the name of Amalek from the face of the earth. A portion from the prophets describing Saul's encounter with Agag, King of Amalek, 1 Samuel 15, is also read.

The reason we recall the Amalek motif before Purim is because Haman is described in the Scroll of Esther as an

"Agagite" (Esther 3:1), a descendant of King Agag the Amalekite. Moreover, Amalek and Haman became seen as the Jewish prototypes of pure, unadulterated evil, paradigms of the incarnation of radical and absolute evil in the world. In every generation, say the rabbis, there are Amalekites like Haman seeking to destroy the Jewish people. They are those who declare, "Come, let us wipe them [the Jews] out as a nation; let the name of Israel be remembered no more!" (Ps. 83:4). God's dominion over the world is incomplete so long as Amalek, symbolizing evil, exists. It is, therefore, humankind's duty as copartner with God to eradicate evil and to replace it with good (Deut. 25:19). The obligation to blot out the names of Haman and Amalek is probably the origin for the custom of making noise (stomping, jeering, turning the *gregers* or "noisemakers") still practiced on Purim today when Haman's name is mentioned during the reading of the Scroll of Esther.

The major ritual of the holiday is the public reading of the *Megillah,* or "Scroll of Esther," in the synagogue during the evening and morning services. The day before Purim is a fast day called *Taanit Esther,* commemorating Esther's decree that the Jews fast and repent before she went before the king.

On Purim day we partake of a festive meal and share our joy with others by giving articles of food to friends and gifts of money (or food) to the poor. For it is only when others, especially those less fortunate than ourselves, share in the joy of the holiday that our own joy truly becomes complete. The origin of these customs is the Scroll of Esther itself, which states, "They should make them days of feasting and gladness, days for sending choice portions to one another and gifts to the poor" (9:22).

Jewish thinkers elaborated on this mitzvah. Maimonides, for example, writes, "When giving gifts of money one must not count one's pennies but must give to whoever asks. It is more praiseworthy for a man to be extravagant in giving gifts to the needy than to be extravagant in preparing his own *seudah* (festive meal) or in giving gifts to his own friends. There is no greater joy than to give happiness to the poor, to the orphan, to

widows, and to strangers. Whosoever gives happiness to those
less fortunate than himself can be compared to the Divine
Presence, for it is said (Isa. 57:15), 'I dwell in the high and holy
place, and also with him who is of a contrite and humble spirit,
to revive the spirit of the humble, and to revive the heart of the
contrite.'"

The Purim holiday, while joyous and spirited, has a serious
and instructive dimension, as well. It reminds Jews that in each
generation they may have to confront a Haman, but that God
and the forces of good will ultimately triumph over those of
evil. The holiday inspires us to have courage in the face of danger and adversity. It urges us never to despair, even when our
survival is threatened. It also reminds us not to be silent in the
presence of evil, nor to place our reliance either upon God or
man alone. Instead, we are commanded to confront evil and to
eliminate it by combining our human initiative with our trust in
God's *yeshuah,* or "salvation." God has an ongoing battle with
the demonic Amalek and we, his human emissaries, are obligated to fight with him against those forces. Man is God's instrument for salvation: "For if you keep silence at such a time as
this," Mordecai warns Esther, "relief and deliverance will rise
for the Jews from another quarter, but you and your father's
house will perish" (Esther 4:14).

Purim also reminds us of the frailty and vulnerability of
human life which can be wiped out overnight at the whim of a
foolish or capricious leader. Jews are particularly reminded of
the precariousness of their condition and of the common destiny they all face. Yet, Purim also affirms that while oppressors
may come and go, God's promise and covenant with his people
is everlasting. The calamity was averted; the Jews of Persia were
saved. God will not desert his people.

Purim provides great insight into the mysterious way in
which God acts in the world. The rabbis suggest that the biblical source for the holiday of Purim is found in the verse
"Anochi Haster asteer panai bayom hahu"—"I will surely *hide*
my face in that day" (Deut. 31:18, emphasis added). They also

point out that the name "Esther" stems from the same Hebrew root, *seter,* or "hiddenness" (her real name was Hadassah).

The incidents described in the Scroll of Esther, in fact, appear to have taken place entirely at random without any divine providential guidance at all. The name of God does not appear even once. Even the very name of the holiday, Purim or "lots," reflects the capriciousness of the events and the element of chance involved. In reality, however, the coincidence of events forms an inescapable pattern of redemption. God was present in every action and in every event. He worked through persons like Esther, as her name itself (hiddenness) indicates. She and Mordecai were the human instruments of God's power of salvation.

Nachmanides, along with other Jewish thinkers, suggests that there are two basic categories of miracles—those which are supernatural and which transcend and defy the laws of nature, such as the parting of the Red Sea, and those which are hidden, such as Purim, in which God's redemptive actions take place *through* nature and in the course of normal events.

While almost everyone would acclaim the first category as a miracle, the second tends to be one of perspective. For example, two people witnessing the same military victory of a nation such as Israel over her enemies, be it in the time of the prophets or today, might differ in what they "saw." One might attribute the victory to factors such as superior military training, morale, technology, and so on—all of which may very well be true— while the other might claim that the victory is, on a deeper level, to be ascribed to God who acted *through* man and natural phenomena. To this second type of person, life itself is an amazing miracle, though our sense of awe and wonder may be blunted by its everyday occurrence. To others, life is "natural," something taken for granted and not pointing beyond itself.

While Passover and Shavuot commemorate the miracle of God's supernatural intervention in human history, Purim celebrates his miraculous hidden way of working through the natural process. Purim teaches us that the natural order is infused with God's presence, that hiddenness is penetrated by divine salvation, and that those who genuinely seek to find God's hand in history can surely do so.

"The Jews ordained and took it upon themselves and their descendants and all who joined them, that without fail they would keep these two days . . . and . . . that these days [of Purim] should be remembered and kept throughout every generation, in every family, province, and city, and that these days . . . should never fall into disuse among the Jews, nor should the commemoration of these days cease among their descendants" (Esther 9:27–28). Renewing our belief in a God who acts in history and who continues to perform miracles is one of the most fundamental affirmations a Jew can make. It is, indeed, cause for great joy and jubilation.

Hanukkah

Hanukkah, historically a minor Jewish festival, is the only one without a biblical basis (although it is cited in the Christian Bible, see John 10:22). Nevertheless, it has evolved into one of the most festive and widely celebrated of all Jewish holidays, perhaps because it falls so close to Christmas. Children especially get caught up with the overall excitement of the season. Hanukkah is observed for eight days, beginning on the twenty-fifth day of the Hebrew month Kislev, which usually falls in December. All forms of work are permitted during this time.

Hanukkah, meaning "Feast of Dedication," commemorates the victory of the Maccabees over King Antiochus Epiphanes and his Syrian-Greek forces in 165 B.C.E. The Antiochus regime tried to impose the dominant Hellenism and paganism of its time upon the Jews, many of whom, such as the High Priest Joshua who changed his name to Jason, were already fully assimilated and eager to cooperate in imposing Hellenistic "enlightenment" upon their "backward" brethren. Some Jews even reversed their circumcisions through a painful operation as a demonstration of their acceptance of Hellenistic universalism and rejection of Jewish distinctiveness and separateness.

Antiochus imposed a number of restrictions on the Jews' religious freedom. He placed a pagan altar in the Jerusalem temple for the adoration of Zeus and offered swine flesh upon it, an especially abominable desecration; he forbade the act of circumcision, which Hellenistic culture viewed as especially irreverent since it marred the beauty of the human form; he prohibited Jews from studying Torah and even burned Torah scrolls; and he erected gymnasiums and forced Jewish youth to participate naked as was the Greek custom. The punishment for not abiding by these decrees was death. The very survival of Judaism was at stake.

Finally, a small band of Jews led by Mattathias of the priestly Hasmonean family and his five sons, including Judah Maccabee who organized them into a guerrilla fighting army, arose in defiance of the Hellenist authorities and revolted. Their struggle endured for three years and culminated in 165 B.C.E. on the twenty-fifth day of Kislev with the reestablishment of Jewish political sovereignty over Jerusalem and their control over the temple. The Jews cleansed and purified the defiled temple of pagan idolatry and restored Jewish worship in its place. They celebrated the rededication of the temple by kindling the *menorah,* or "candelabrum," for eight days as Solomon had done in the first temple. Hence, the festival is called Hanukkah, meaning "dedication," and is celebrated for eight days. Another view is that the eight-day celebration was modeled after the consecration ceremony of the desert tabernacle, not after the dedication of Solomon's temple (see Lev. 8:8–10). The second book of Maccabees offers a third explanation that because the Maccabees were in hiding on Sukkot and could not observe it properly, they celebrated the holiday belatedly upon their victory. This rationale would be very much in line with the fact that Hanukkah was originally called "the Sukkot of the month of Kislev" (see 2 Macc. 1:9; 10:6–8).

The primary sources for our knowledge of the events of Hanukkah are the first and second books of the Maccabees which, although not canonized as part of the Jewish Bible itself, do constitute part of Jewish apocryphal literature. They describe the events of Hanukkah in the following way:

> Then said Judah and his brothers, "Behold, our enemies are crushed; let us go up to cleanse the sanctuary and dedicate it." So all the army assembled and they went up to Mount Zion. And they saw the sanctuary desolate, the altar profaned, and the gates burned. In the courts they saw bushes sprung up as in a thicket, or as on one of the mountains. They saw also the chambers of the priests in ruins. Then they rent their clothes, and mourned with great lamentation, and sprinkled themselves with ashes. They fell face down on the ground, and sounded the signal on the trumpets, and cried out to Heaven. Then Judas . . . chose blameless priests devoted to the law, and they cleansed the sanctuary (1 Macc. 4:36–43).

> Early in the morning on the twenty-fifth day of the ninth month, which is the month of Kislev, in the one hundred and forty-eighth year, they rose and offered sacrifice, as the law directs, on the new altar of burnt offering which they had built. . . . All the people fell on their faces and worshiped and blessed Heaven, who had prospered them. So they celebrated the dedication of the altar for eight days. . . . There was very great gladness among the people and the reproach of the Gentiles was removed.
> Then Judas and his brothers and all the assembly of Israel determined that every year at that season the days of the dedication of the altar should be observed with gladness and joy for eight days, beginning with the twenty-fifth day of the month of Kislev (1 Macc. 4:52–53, 55–56, 58–59).

The Talmud, on the other hand, offers a somewhat different reason for the holiday. "What is Hanukkah? Our rabbis stated:

'Commencing with the twenty-fifth day of Kislev, there are eight days during which mourning and fasting are forbidden. When the Greeks entered the Temple, they defiled all the oils therein, and when the Hasmonean dynasty prevailed against them and defeated them, they made search and found only one cruse of oil, sufficient for but one day's lighting, which lay with the seal of the High Priest. Yet a miracle was wrought therein and with it they lit the lamp therewith for eight days. The following year these days were appointed a Festival with the recital of Hallel and thanksgiving'" (B.T., Shab. 21b).

Like the book of Maccabees, both Maimonides and the special liturgical prayer recited on this holiday suggest that the principal miracle celebrated on Hanukkah is that of the military victory that enabled the Jews to rededicate the temple and to worship God freely. Hanukkah marks the victory of the few over the many, of the weak over the mighty, and of those with faith in God and commitment to religious freedom over the pagan tyrants of the world. The Talmud and later tradition maintain that in addition to the miracle of the military victory, another miracle took place. They suggest that as the Jews purified the temple, they were able to find only one remaining flask of pure olive oil, capable of keeping the eternal light burning for only one day. Miraculously, the oil lasted for eight days and eight nights, after which time they were able to find new oil.

Hanukkah was a controversial holiday for a number of centuries and did not achieve total acceptance until well into talmudic times. The rabbis' reluctance to sanction the holiday can, perhaps, be attributed to the fact that they felt uneasy about commemorating a military victory. That may also be why they insisted that the primary reasons for celebration were that the temple was rededicated and that the menorah oil miraculously burned for eight days. Not surprisingly then, the prophetic portion selected by the rabbis to be read on Hanukkah comes from the Book of Zechariah and includes the verse, "Not by might, nor by power, but by my Spirit [shall you prevail], says the LORD of hosts" (4:6). And yet, the motif of the military victory did remain important if not central to the commemoration of the holiday. For were it not for the successful Maccabean revolt, paganism and Hellenism would likely have been imposed upon the Jews. Had that happened, the very foundations of Judaism might have been destroyed and Christianity might never have come to be. In other words, if not for the miracle of the Jewish military defeat over the Syrian-Greek tyrants, there might be no Judaism and no Christianity in existence today.

Josephus, a Jewish historian who lived in the first century, was also ambiguous about the meaning of the holiday. He claimed that the festival was called the feast of lights "because the free practice of our religion was to us like a rising day of light."

Nowhere does he even mention the miracle of the oil that the Talmud later affirmed to be the holiday's central event. Despite all of these factors, by the fifth century C.E., Hanukkah was fully entrenched in the Jewish calendar.

Hanukkah celebrations center around the home. The lighting of the nine-branched menorah (as distinguished from the one with eight branches that was used in the temple) serves as the predominant holiday ritual. On the first night we light one candle, and on each successive night we light an additional one so that on the eighth and final day of the holiday, all nine candles are lighted (the ninth candle, or *shamash*, is used to light the others). The menorah is placed near a window facing the outside so that passersby will see it and be reminded of the miracle.

It is customary for children to play with a *dreidel,* a small, four-sided, spinning top inscribed with the four Hebrew letters, *N. G. H. SH.,* one on each of its sides. The letters are an acronym for the Hebrew words *Nes Gadol Hayah Sham,* meaning "a great miracle happened there." The origin of this custom is uncertain. However, it is believed to have evolved from the fact that, in spite of Antiochus's tyrannical decrees, many Jews defied the authorities and gathered secretly to study and practice the Torah. To protect themselves, they posted children outside playing dreidel and keeping a lookout for the soldiers. That way they would be alerted in case of a raid. There is also an old custom, independent of the Christmas one, of giving *gelt,* or "money," to the children (although today people usually give presents) so that they will rejoice in the holiday, too.

The festival of Hanukkah bids us to rededicate our lives to the Jewish values and ideals that were preserved by the Maccabean victory, just as the Jews then rededicated the temple. The theme of martyrdom, dying *al kiddush hashem,* "in sanctification of God's name," became central to the Jewish understanding of the Hanukkah story and profoundly influenced later Jewish and Christian life and thought, as well. Jews were tenacious in their convictions. They sacrificed their lives for the right to practice their faith freely.

The book of Maccabees describes one such incident in which the king tried to force Hannah, a Jewish woman, and her seven sons to eat swine. Rather than transgress the laws of God, each of the sons submitted to gruesome torture and death, encouraged and strengthened by their mother who assured them that they would meet in the next world where they would be resurrected together. In the end Hannah also was killed. Unlike Abraham who was willing to sacrifice his one and only son but in the end was prevented from doing so, Hannah gave up all seven of her sons, as well as her own life, in "sanctification of God's name" (see 2 Macc. 7:1–41). Martyrdom, as well as the rewards of resurrection, immortality, and the world to come, became powerful motifs later on in Jewish history. Jews came to realize that the survival of their faith, at times, required the supreme sacrifice of individual lives.

The book of Maccabees describes another episode in which a group of entrapped Jews refused to fight on Shabbat, believing that it would constitute a violation of the law and a defilement of the sanctity of the day. As a result, they were slaughtered without offering any resistance. When the rest of the Jews realized that both they and their faith could be totally destroyed if they did not defend themselves, they made the determination that, in this case, saving human lives superseded the laws of the Torah; the community had to be protected to ensure the preservation of the faith. Later on, this concept was further developed by the rabbis who declared that, with the exception of three circumstances, the laws of the Torah were to be suspended when human life was at stake (see chapter 3). The Jewish struggle for religious liberty and willingness to endure martyrdom on behalf of their faith became powerful paradigms for centuries to come for Jews and Christians alike.

Hanukkah reminds us of the importance of *bitachon,* or "trust in God." It was the Jews' trust in a loving and caring God that prompted them, the few and the weak, to rise up against the many and the mighty. It was their faith in God that prompted them to light the temple menorah, despite the fact that they knew there was only enough pure oil to keep the fire burning for one day and that it would take eight days to bring back new oil. In both cases the Jews acted against the odds, trusting in God's *yeshua* (salvation). Moreover, in both instances, they relied on God's saving grace only after exhausting their own human powers. For the Jews recognized that God performs miracles through the human agent and by way of the natural order. And while man is to trust in God, he must also initiate action himself. Only then will God also act. Like Purim, Hanukkah celebrates God's *nes nistar,* or "hidden miracles." In addition, it stresses man's duty to help bring about such redemptive miracles through his own efforts and initiative. Even in the classic example of a supernatural miracle, the parting of the Red Sea, the waters did not split until the Israelites acted and entered into the sea.

While Hanukkah bids the Jew to remain staunch in his Jewish convictions, it does not urge that he categorically reject all outside values and cultures. It is possible for the Jew to embrace both Hellenism and Judaism, both Athens and Jerusalem, both aesthetics and morality, and both universalism and particularism. Greek and Jewish values are not necessarily diametrical opposites but are in need of being selectively synthesized. As the late Rabbi Abba Hillel Silver, orator and Zionist leader, once wrote, "There is no unbridgeable gulf between the culture of the Greeks and the culture of the Jews. They are not in polar opposition. . . . the peoples of the Western World at the close of the Classical Age turned for their scientific and artistic needs to Greece, and for their spiritual and ethical inspiration to Judea."[3]

While the Jew may participate in outside culture and society, he should also be sufficiently removed from it so that he is able to judge and, if necessary, confront it. And while he should maintain a universal outlook, he should also reconcile such views with his particularistic Jewish heritage. The Jew's point of departure, however, must always be his Jewish faith, through which all other values ought to be refracted.

Hellenistic culture was, undoubtedly, a very powerful, seductive force at the time. Many Jews, blinded by its attractiveness, were seduced from their ancestral faith. There were probably also those who were able to synthesize its positive values and incorporate them into their lives. However, it was the simple, unenlightened, small-town folk, in all likelihood, not too well versed in the sophisticated avant-garde mores of Hellenistic culture—the Jewish fundamentalists—who were the ones who recognized that limits had been breached and that integration into society had given way to assimilation. It was they who rose up in defiance and saved Judaism. Like Elijah in his confrontation with the worshipers of Baal on Mount Carmel (1 Kings 18), these fundamentalists declared that the time had come for Israel to choose between God and Zeus.

American Jews are a minority group, living within two great cultures—Western and Jewish civilizations. The challenge they face today is whether or not they can live in both without in the process surrendering their unique Jewish faith and heritage. Only when Jews remain true to their covenant can they hope to fulfill their divine mission of serving as a holy people and a blessing to all the nations of the world.

The holiday of Hanukkah reminds us of our duty to uphold the principles of religious freedom, liberty, and justice for all people. It strengthens the Jew's resolve to worship God even under oppressive conditions. The Jewish struggle on behalf of these values continues even today. As Theodor Herzl, the "father" of modern political Zionism once wrote, "The Maccabeans will rise again. The Jews who wish for a State will have it. We shall live at last as free men on our own soil."[4]

As Jews light the Hanukkah candles, they recall that the rise and continued survival of the embattled State of Israel lends testimony, no less than that of the Maccabean victory, to God's miracles and acts of salvation. The spirit of God still hovers in the world; faith, in fact, ultimately triumphs over the brute forces of evil.

Fast Days

The most solemn time in the Jewish year falls in the summertime when we mark the destruction of the two Jerusalem temples and the exile of the Jewish people from their homeland. A period of three weeks is devoted to commemorating these tragic events, beginning with the fast of *Shivah Asar b'Tammuz,* meaning "the seventeenth day of (the Hebrew month) Tammuz," and culminating with *Tisha b'Av,* or "the ninth day of Av," the saddest day on the Jewish calendar.

The fast of Shivah Asar b'Tammuz was instituted to commemorate the first breach of the Jerusalem walls during the Babylonian siege in 586 B.C.E. According to tradition, it also marks a number of other tragedies that befell the Jewish people after that day, including the halting of the daily temple sacrifices at the time of the Babylonian invasion, the burning of Torah scrolls, and the erection of idols in the temple during the Roman incursion. It is also the day on which Moses broke the first set of tablets.

The fast begins at dawn and ends at nightfall. No food or water may be consumed. Shivah Asar b'Tammuz initiates a three-week period of mourning, during which time we gradually increase the intensity of our feelings of sadness. Throughout the entire three weeks, we do not conduct celebrations such as weddings, nor do we wear new clothes or have our hair cut. During the last nine days, we also desist from eating meat, drinking wine, and bathing for pleasure. (Bathing for hygienic purposes is, of course, permitted.) As usual, on Shabbat all laws of mourning are suspended. The rabbis introduced these and other such customs in order to set us in a proper mournful mood and to prepare us for the day of Tisha b'Av.

The fast of Tisha b'Av culminates the three-week period of mourning. It is the blackest, most sorrowful day in the Jewish year. Although it, too, marks a number of tragedies that have befallen the Jewish people throughout history, it was instituted mainly to commemorate the fatal coincidence of the destruction of the two Jerusalem temples, one in 586 B.C.E. and the other in 70 C.E. For it was on the ninth day of the month of Av that each was razed. Unlike the fast of Yom Kippur, which is one of repentance, that of Tisha b'Av is one of mourning and sadness.

Among the other Jewish tragedies that have taken place on that day are these: God decided not to allow the generation of the Exodus to enter the Promised Land; Bar Kochba's revolt was brought to an end and the city of Betar was captured (135 C.E.); sacred Jewish books were burned in Paris (1242); and, more recently, Jews were deported from the Warsaw ghetto to the Treblinka concentration camps (1942).

The various laws and customs of the fast day, such as the prohibitions against working, shaving, wearing leather shoes, and sitting on regular chairs are similar to those of a bereaved mourner (see chapter 5). They attempt to create within us the same kind of solemn mood experienced by someone mourning the death of a close family member. We are to vicariously feel the depth of grief and sadness that has marked this day throughout history. For we, too, are mourners on Tisha b'Av; we, too, "let tears stream down like a torrent day and night" over the fall of Jerusalem, the "daughter of Zion" (Lam. 2:18).

Because of its importance, the fast of Tisha b'Av, like that of Yom Kippur, begins at sundown and concludes twenty-five hours later at nightfall on the following day. The synagogue is dimly lit and the congregation is plunged into mourning. The curtains covering the ark are removed, symbolizing that the Torah, too, is in mourning. The congregation sits on the floor or on low stools like mourners, and the *Megillat Aichah,* or "Scroll of Lamentations," bemoaning the sacking of Jerusalem and the fall of the first temple, is chanted. *Kinot,* or "dirges," lamenting the various episodes of Jewish suffering that occurred on this day are recited. Included in the kinot are poems recalling the destruction of the Jerusalem temples, the martyrdom of Jews throughout the centuries, and the slaughter of entire Jewish communities during the time of the Crusades. Today it is also customary to add special dirges in remembrance of those Jews killed in the Holocaust.

Yet even this, the saddest day of the Jewish year, is injected with a note of hope and optimism. In the afternoon we rise from our lowly mourning stools and recall the tradition that the Messiah will be born on Tisha b'Av and that in messianic times this mournful fast day will be transformed into one of great joy and celebration. We attest that redemption will sprout forth from the very depths of suffering and despair. For the same reason, we refer to the Sabbath following Tisha b'Av as *Shabbat Nachamu,* or "Sabbath of Consolation," since the prophetic portion beginning with the words "Comfort, comfort my people, says your God" (Isa. 40:1-26) is read in synagogue. For the next seven consecutive Sabbaths until Rosh Hashanah, other prophetic selections of consolation are read as a reminder that despite the adversities and affliction marking Jewish history, God's covenant with his people, Israel, remains in effect; his promise of redemption will yet be fulfilled: "The LORD your God will restore your fortunes and have compassion upon you, and he will gather you again from all the peoples where the LORD your God has scattered you" (Deut. 30:3). We are inspired by such prophetic readings and encouraged never to despair from salvation, for "there is hope for your future, says the LORD, and your children shall come back to their own country" (Jer. 31:17).

In our own day, we have witnessed the fulfillment of some of these divine promises. Israel has been restored! Jews from all corners of the earth have begun to return to their ancestral homeland, *Eretz Yisrael!* Indeed, God will not desert his people!

Chapter 5

THE JEWISH LIFE CYCLE

RITES OF PASSAGE

Birth

Historically, it has been the family, even more than the synagogue, that has served as the primary vehicle for the transmission of Jewish values from generation to generation. Celibacy was rarely, if ever, accepted as a Jewish ideal. Indeed, the more saintly and scholarly the Jew, the more obligated he is to fulfill the first mitzvah in the Torah, to "be fruitful and multiply" (Gen. 1:28). For this reason Jews have tended to have large families, and this continues to be the case among most Orthodox Jews even now.

Today, however, the integrity of the Jewish family is threatened by many of the same forces that affect all of Western society—greater frequency of divorce, later marriages, fewer children, greater acceptability of single life, and so on. These and other such factors seriously undermining the traditional family unit pose a major challenge to Jewish life.

In Judaism the birth of a boy is marked with a *berit milah,* or "covenant of circumcision" ceremony, on the eighth day after birth. (If the infant is ill or not strong enough, the ceremony is delayed.) "He that is eight days old among you shall be circumcised; every male throughout your generations. . . . So shall my covenant be in your flesh an everlasting covenant" (Gen.17:12–13). Circumcision involves the removal of the foreskin covering the glans of the penis by a *mohel,* one who is trained in the surgical procedure as well as the accompanying religious ceremony. The circumcision ritual marks the male child's formal initiation into the covenantal Jewish community: "This is my covenant, which you shall keep, between me and you and your descendants after you: Every male among you shall be circumcised. You shall be circumcised in the flesh of your foreskins, and it shall be a sign of the covenant between me and you" (Gen. 17:10–11). The act of circumcision symbolizes the Jewish covenant and partnership with God in all areas of life, including in that of his own creation and completion.

"Circumcision," writes Herschel Matt, "does not 'make' a person Jewish, for he is Jewish already by birth. The circumcision, rather, testifies that he who bears this sign sealed in his flesh is under the covenant which is what gives meaning to life. Through the covenant he is bound to all of the children of Israel, and through them to God; through the covenant he is made aware of how he sinfully falls short; through the covenant he is promised the coming of the Messiah . . . and life eternal . . . yes, circumcision is for us a sign that the Lord who called to Abraham our father, calls yet to us of Abraham's seed, summoning us . . . to renew the covenant."[1]

Throughout Jewish history, circumcision has been viewed as the sign of the covenant linking God with the Jewish people (see chapter 1). Abraham, the first Jew, circumcised himself at the age of ninety-nine and later circumcised his entire household, including his son Ishmael (see Gen. 17:22–27). Isaac was circumcised on the eighth day after his birth, and this has been the custom ever since. Joshua and the people of Israel carried out the rite before entering Canaan, although it was apparently not performed during their wandering in the desert, perhaps because of the hazards of journeying (see Josh. 5:2).

By the time of the prophets the term *arel* or "uncircumcised," was commonly used metaphorically, as well, as an allusion to the covering and hardening of the heart obstructing people from obeying God's word (see, for example, Ezek. 44:1-9 and Jer.

6:10). Later, Paul and the Christian church spiritualized the concept entirely by claiming that the physical act of circumcision was no longer necessary, only the removal of the spiritual foreskin covering the heart. Judaism (as well as some of the more extreme Judaizers in the early church), however, insisted on preserving the physical connotation of the circumcision rite, too. It maintained that those born of a Jewish mother, as well as Gentiles seeking to enter the Abrahamic covenant and community, must be physically circumcised. Jews have been unswerving in their performance of this important mitzvah—at times under the most trying of circumstances. The Bar Kochba revolt in 135 C.E., for example, erupted when Hadrian the Roman emperor forbade circumcision.

In addition to the berit milah, traditional Jews also conduct a *pidyon ha-ben,* or "redemption of the first-born," ceremony on the thirty-first day after a woman's first birth in the event that she bore a male. This practice serves symbolically to redeem the child from consecrated service to God, which became incumbent upon him after God spared the Israelite first-born in the tenth plague in Egypt: "For all the first-born among the people of Israel are mine . . . I consecrated them for myself . . ." (Num. 8:17). After the sin of the Golden Calf, however, the Levites assumed that consecrated role. "I have taken the Levites instead of all the first-born among the people of Israel" (Num. 8:18; see also Num. 18:15-16). The first-born, nevertheless, remained consecrated to God and in need of "redemption" from temple service, hence the ceremony. Despite the destruction of the temple and the absence of any distinctive Levite role in religious life thereafter, the ceremony continues to be practiced by traditional Jews today.

Historically, there was no religious celebration marking the birth of a girl and her entrance into the covenant as there was for boys. In recent years, however, many parents have marked the occasion with some sort of religious ceremony in which the female child, too, is formally welcomed into the Jewish covenantal community. This practice is becoming ever more popular and is likely, in time, to become an integral part of Jewish tradition.

Bar/Bat Mitzvah

The *Bar/Bat Mitzvah* ceremony is one of the most widely celebrated events in Jewish life today. A boy becomes *bar mitzvah,* meaning "son of the commandments," at the age of thirteen; a girl becomes *bat mitzvah,* or "daughter of the commandments," at twelve (since girls reach physical maturity earlier) (see B.T., Kidd. 16b). At that time the child is formally initiated into the Jewish community and becomes obligated to observe all the mitzvot. And while heretofore the parents were "responsible" for the child's moral and religious behavior, at Bar/Bat Mitzvah the child assumes that responsibility as well as the other rights, privileges, and obligations of being a Jew.

The Bar Mitzvah celebration is conducted in the synagogue on the Sabbath following a boy's thirteenth birthday when he is called up to the Torah for the first time. He recites a blessing in which he thanks God for giving the Torah to the Jewish people. He then reads the appropriate weekly portion from the Torah and Prophets.

The girl's Bat Mitzvah ceremony usually takes place in the synagogue, too, although the degree of ritual participation permitted to women differs among the denominations. Orthodoxy prohibits women from being called up to the Torah (when men are present); however, Reform and most Conservative congregations permit it.

Despite its importance and widespread observance, the Bar Mitzvah celebration has no real precedent in either biblical or talmudic literature, and it can be traced back only as far as the fifteenth century, to customs originating in Germany and Poland. The Bat Mitzvah celebration, which originated in France and Italy in the nineteenth century, still often lacks the import of the Bar Mitzvah even among many of those who, in fact, celebrate it. Nevertheless, the fact that boys become obligated to observe the commandments at thirteen and girls become responsible at twelve is alluded to in the Talmud. The Talmud states, for example, that vows made by thirteen-year-old boys and twelve-year-old girls take effect upon *them,* not their parents. Moreover, it states that at those ages children become obligated to observe the Jewish fast days. Thus, while the formal Bar/Bat Mitzvah ceremony is of relatively recent vintage, the underlying principle that the child then becomes fully responsible for observing the Torah is, in fact, at least fifteen hundred years old.

The other major ritual associated with the Bar Mitzvah is the donning of *tefillin,* or "phylacteries." From the time of Bar Mitzvah, boys are obligated to wear tefillin every day during morning prayers (except on Shabbat and festivals) for the rest of their lives. Also, they may then be included in the quorum of ten adults required for public prayer. They may even lead the services and read from the Torah on behalf of the congregation. They are Jewish adults in the fullest sense of the term.

The occasion of the Bar/Bat Mitzvah marks the time when a Jewish child personally and voluntarily reaffirms his commitment to the covenant and his responsibility to observe the mitzvot. He is then granted the equal right to participate in every facet of synagogue life and, indeed, in all the religious expressions of the community.

Marriage

Marriage is one of the most important and sanctified institutions in all of Judaism. It represents the biblically sanctioned way in which we are to fulfill our religious obligation to procreate and fill the earth. Marriage is also the biblical existential ideal for man and woman in that it provides couples with the religious framework within which they can find love, comfort, security, and companionship. "Then the LORD God said, 'It is not good that the man should be alone; I will make him a helper fit for him.' . . . Therefore a man leaves his father and his mother and cleaves to his wife, and they become one flesh" (Gen. 2:18, 24).

The prophetic and rabbinic traditions often portrayed a variety of other relationships in terms of lovers or married partners, such as those between God and Israel, Israel and the Shabbat, and Israel and the Torah. While polygamy was practiced in biblical times, it came into disuse among Jews long before the Common Era and was formally prohibited by the edict of Rabbi Gershom in the beginning of the eleventh century C.E.

Celibacy was utterly rejected by biblical and rabbinic teaching. Those who refused to bear children were regarded not only as having violated the first mitzvah of procreation, but also as if they had shed blood and diminished the image of God from the world, since man is created in his image. And, according to the rabbis, they even caused the divine presence to depart from the Jewish people. The rabbis further state, "No man without a wife, neither a woman without a husband, nor both of them without God" (Gen. Rab. 8:9). Moreover, "He who marries a good woman is as if he fulfilled the whole Torah from beginning to end" (Y.S., Ruth 60b). They also claim that an unmarried man is an incomplete person, bereft of joy, blessing, and goodness (B.T., Yev. 62b, 63a). An unmarried high priest was not even allowed to officiate in the temple on the Day of Atonement. Sexuality was seen as a potentially positive drive in rabbinic thought, for without those desires, "no man would build a house, marry a wife, or have children" (Gen. Rab. 9:7). Such energies, however, are obviously capable of abuse and in need of being regulated and channeled through the institution of marriage.

Judaism recognizes that successful marriages are not easily achieved. The Talmud states, for example, that God himself must enter into the process of selecting mates since loving marriages are as much a miracle as was the parting of the Red Sea (B.T., Sotah 2a). God also dwells amidst married couples, say the rabbis. This is alluded to in a fascinating rabbinic hermeneutical play on words. The Hebrew word for "man" is *ish* and for "woman," *ishah*. The Hebrew letters are the same except for an additional *yud* in the word for "man" and a *heh* in the word for "woman." Together these additional letters form the name of God. Thus, when a couple shares a common devotion to God, his presence dwells in their midst.

The Hebrew term for marriage is *kiddushin,* meaning "sanctification," from the root *kadosh,* or "holy," which in biblical thought implies separateness. Man and woman consecrate each other through marriage and set each other apart from all others. The husband is biblically obligated to provide food, clothing, and conjugal rights for his wife (see Exod. 21:10). The rabbis extended these obligations and, in addition, demanded that he respect his wife and not make her cry (B.T., B. Metzia 59a), that he deny himself to provide her with her needs (B.T., Hul. 84b), and that he give her the kind of material lifestyle to which she was accustomed before marriage. "Let a man be scrupulous about honoring his wife," states the Talmud, "because whatever blessing prevails in a man's home is there because of his wife" (B.T., B. Metzia 59a).

Long before most other religions and civilizations, Judaism also obligated the husband to provide for the financial security of his wife when he dies or in the event they are divorced. Already in the first century B.C.E., the *ketubbah,* or "marriage contract," was instituted. It sets forth the various responsibilities incumbent upon the spouses toward each other. The ketubbah remains part of the Jewish marriage ceremony even today. The laws of marriage are both numerous and complex (see Lev. 18–21 upon which they are mainly based). Since the slightest deviation from the law can invalidate a marriage, rabbinic guidance and involvement is essential.

It is a special mitzvah to rejoice at a wedding feast. Even the study of Torah must be interrupted to bring joy to newlyweds (B.T., Ket. 17b). Traditionally, the groom wears a white *kittel,* a robe similar to the Jewish burial shrouds, and the bride wears a white gown. This symbolizes that at marriage, as on the Day of Atonement, all of the couple's sins are forgiven and they now can begin life anew with their slate wiped clean. For this same reason, the bride and groom fast on the day of their wedding and beseech God for forgiveness from their past sins. It is also customary for the bride to wear a white veil as a sign of modesty, as Rebekah did when she first saw Isaac.

The marriage ceremony is conducted under a *chuppah,* or "canopy," symbolizing the bridal chamber, to demonstrate that the couple now enters their own "home" and, in addition, that God's love and abiding presence always hovers over them. The groom gives the bride a wedding ring (actually, anything of value), and in the presence of two witnesses recites the traditional marriage vow, "Behold thou art consecrated unto me with this ring in accordance with the law of Moses and Israel." Blessings over wine are recited, the ketubbah is read, and a brief message is delivered by the rabbi. The ceremony concludes with the groom breaking a glass to symbolize that even at this moment of the couple's greatest personal joy, they have not forgotten Jerusalem, nor have they ceased to hope and pray for the world's redemption. They reaffirm the conviction that "if I forget you, O Jerusalem, let my right hand wither! . . . if I do not set Jerusalem above my highest joy" (Ps. 137:5-6). They recall that their joy is incomplete so long as the Messiah has not come and world peace and spiritual fulfillment have not been achieved.

Divorce

Although Judaism treats marriage with the utmost sanctity, it also acknowledges situations in which it would be far better to dissolve the marriage with a divorce: "When a man takes a wife and marries her, if then she finds no favor in his eyes because he has found some indecency in her, and he writes her a bill of divorce and puts it in her hand and sends her out of his house, and she departs out of his house, and if she goes and becomes another man's wife . . ." (Deut. 24:1-2). Divorce is, nevertheless, viewed as a tragedy and a course of action that should be taken only out of calamitous necessity, after exhausting all other possibilities of maintaining harmony and tranquillity in the marriage. It should not be treated lightly or resorted to casually. Indeed, the rabbis taught that "over one who divorces the wife of his youth even the altar of God sheds tears" (B.T., Git. 90b; see Mal. 2:13-16 upon which this view is based).

Still, the possibility of divorce exists and is even to be regarded as meritorious in certain instances. "The law of divorce is given for the sake of peace. . . . And those who divorce when they must, bring good upon themselves, not evil" (Eliyahu Kitov). It was because of Judaism's fundamental concern that relationships be imbued with love and harmony and that marriage truly be a sanctified institution, that divorce was made possible, tragic as it may be. To minimize its occurrence, however, the rabbis prohibited a man from marrying a woman without first seeing her, since he may come to dislike her and contravene the law, "Thou shalt love thy neighbor as thyself." Moreover, they required the couple to first seek mediation and to have a "cooling off" period before they could become divorced. And the rabbi conducting the divorce proceedings was also to protract the ceremony in the hope that reconciliation might come about.

A Jewish *get,* or "bill of divorcement," is required before remarriage can take place; a civil divorce is insufficient. Divorce proceedings are conducted by a special "court" of three rabbis who are intricately familiar with the complex laws involved. An entire talmudic tractate, *Gittin,* meaning "documents of divorce," is devoted to the subject. Among the questions discussed therein are: May a husband appoint a scribe to write the divorce document or must he write it himself as the Torah seems to suggest? May one use a standard form or printed document and simply fill in the names of the parties or must each document be written expressly for the couple involved? Can a man appoint a messenger to bring the divorce papers to his wife? What if she refuses to accept the document? Are witnesses necessary? Is a rabbinic court essential? May a woman divorce her husband, and if so, how and under what circumstances? What are proper grounds for which a man can divorce his wife? May a man issue a conditional get such as on the condition that she not go back to her father's home? May a man going to war issue a get on the condition that it become effective in the event that he is missing in action so that his wife would not be left an *agunah* (i.e., a woman who is still legally married because her husband never gave her a get or was never proven dead, and who, therefore, may not remarry)? Does the obligation of the levirate marriage exist today—when a man dies without children, must his brother marry his wife? These and many other complex questions are treated by the Talmud and later *responsa* literature in light of the principles set forth in the biblical verses allowing for divorce and of the varying conditions and circumstances of the times. They continue to be studied and applied by rabbis today.

Of special concern to the Talmud was the question of what constitutes legitimate grounds for divorce. The Torah states that a man may divorce his wife if he finds in her *ervat davar,* often translated as "an unseemly thing" (see Deut. 24:1). Talmudic authorities, however, differed in their interpretation of these two Hebrew words. The school of Shammai claimed that *ervat davar* possessed a sexual connotation and implied "a thing of [sexual] indecency." They, therefore, permitted divorce only for the wife's unchastity. The school of Hillel, on the other hand, interpreted the phrase liberally as "anything unseemly" and permitted divorce when anything at all disrupted domestic tranquillity (see B.T., Git. 90a and Yev. 112b). The law was decided in favor of Hillel's lenient view. Jesus and the early church, however, favored the more conservative interpretation of the school of Shammai (see chapter 1).

Death and Mourning

Judaism acknowledges the inevitability of death: "Those who are born of necessity will die . . . for perforce were you created . . . and perforce you will die" (Mishnah, Avot 4:22). But why must man die? According to one strain in rabbinic thought, death comes as a punishment for sin. Since "there is not a righteous man on earth who . . . never sins" (Eccles. 7:20), death is an inevitable part of the human condition. "There is no death," states the Talmud succinctly, "without sin" (B.T., Shab. 55a). A second strain, however, regarded death as part of the very fabric of the world's creation, as an integral part of affirming life and creation. Despite the differences between these two schools of thought, both regarded death as an atonement for sin; both subscribed to the talmudic adage that the wicked are considered as if dead while yet alive and the righteous are as if living even in death (B.T., Ber. 18a, b). Both also agreed with Rabbi Yochanan that "the end of man is death" (B.T., Ber. 17a).

At the same time, the rabbis professed that man's soul lives on after death in an afterlife when (or where) the wicked are punished and the righteous receive their due rewards. Immortality, in Judaism, entails the notion "that man contains something independent of the flesh and surviving it—his consciousness and moral capacity, his essential personality—a soul."[2] Life in this world, according to the rabbis, is merely transitory, a preliminary to the next—"this world is like a corridor leading to the world to come" (Mishnah, Avot 4:16)—while our bodies are palaces for our souls, which depart from us upon death and return to God. (Certain kabbalistic traditions affirmed, in addition, the concept of *gilgul*, or "reincarnation," although this never became part of mainstream Jewish beliefs.)

Judaism was far less precise and elaborate, however, in its treatment of such eschatological matters than it was, for example, in elucidating the mitzvot, which are incumbent upon man in the here and now. Moreover, the little that was said on such themes was usually intended to be understood allegorically, rather than literally, for the issue of primary concern to the rabbis was how the Jew ought to lead and sanctify his life in *this* world. They insisted that those engaging in the study and practice of Torah, something that is well within man's grasp, would be amply rewarded in the world to come. Such people had nothing to fear from death because it is written that "a good name is better than precious ointment; and the day of death, than the day of birth" (Eccles. 7:1; see also B.T., Ber. 17a). For this reason, explained Rabbi Meir, when God said of the sixth day of creation that "it was very good" (Gen. 1:31), he was referring to the day of man's death, not to the creation of man. For man's true rewards come in the afterlife.

When God breathed a divine soul of life into man's body, it was transformed from mere matter into a holy vessel bearing the image of God. Since man is, therefore, not only an earthly but also a divine being, his body must be treated with the utmost reverence and respect. This doctrine underlies virtually all of the Jewish laws relating to burial. It forms the basis of the Jewish concept of *kibbud hamet,* or "honoring the deceased."

Before dying the Jew is to confess his sins and then is to recite the Shema, "Hear, O Israel, the Lord our God the Lord is one." As a sign of respect, we are not to leave the body of the deceased unattended from the time of death until the funeral. It is also customary to recite psalms when in its presence.

Most communities have a group of men and women called the *Chevrah Kaddisha,* or "Sacred Society," which assumes the responsibility for the preparation of the body (washing and dressing it) and for the burial arrangements. (In some communities these acts are done by the funeral home.) Members of the Chevrah Kaddisha do not receive any remuneration for their services. Their deeds of loving kindness are, however, regarded by Jewish tradition as among the holiest and most meritorious possible. God himself, note the rabbis, participated in burying Moses (Deut. 34:6).

The body is thoroughly washed (this is referred to as the *taharah,* or "act of purification") and clothed in a plain white linen garb called *takhrikhim,* or "shrouds." Men are buried with their tallit over their shrouds. This custom of dressing the dead in takhrikhim originated in talmudic times when the affluent went to extreme lengths to bury their dead in ornate, expensive clothing, bringing shame and embarrassment to the poor. This often prompted them to spend beyond their means in order to compete with the lavish arrangements made by the rich. To show the equality of rich and poor alike in death, and the transitory, ephemeral nature of material possessions, the rabbis decreed that all Jews be buried in the same unadorned white shrouds. Similarly, since the rich buried their dead in expensive, ornate beds while the poor could afford only plain, wooden boxes, the rabbis decreed that all Jews be buried in plain, unadorned wooden caskets. Through such laws the rabbis sought to teach the true nature of the mitzvah of honoring and burying the dead.

These and many other Jewish mourning laws and customs that evolved over the centuries and are practiced today serve to honor the deceased, to console the living, and to help mourners accept the reality of death. They provide great cathartic value by giving vent to the mourner's feelings of grief. They help alleviate his anguish and renew his commitment to God and everyday living. Jews are prohibited, in fact, from mourning excessively and from wallowing relentlessly in grief. (The Talmud derives this law from the verse, "Weep not [in excess] for him who is dead, nor bemoan him [too much]" (Jer. 22:10). Jewish mourning laws and customs also generate a feeling of solidarity among family members and friends by providing them with an opportunity to reflect upon the course of their lives, relationships, and commitments.

Only burial in the earth is permitted by traditional Judaism. This is derived from biblical passages such as, "You are dust, and to dust you shall return" (Gen. 3:19), and "You shall bury him" (Deut. 21:23). Cremation or burial either above ground or in the sea is strictly forbidden. All parts of the body must be buried; nothing may be discarded. (The question of the permissibility of transplants revolves, inpart, around this law.) The blood also must be buried, and for this reason embalming is forbidden. Since autopsies are regarded as a desecration to the body of the deceased, they are strictly prohibited unless they contribute in some way to the saving of another human life.

It is customary for the funeral to take place within twenty-four hours after death, in keeping with the biblical edict not to leave a corpse lying unburied (Deut. 21:23). The period may be extended for an additional day, however, to enable family members from out of town to attend. Burials are not held on the Shabbat or on most other festivals. Upon learning of a death (or at the funeral), the mourner recites the blessing, "Blessed art thou, O Lord our God, Master of the universe, the true Judge." The immediate relatives of the deceased perform the act of *keriah* in which they tear their garments, with children tearing the portion covering their hearts, symbolizing the emotional tear in their hearts. It also recalls the ancient Jewish custom of rending one's clothing and wearing sackcloths as a sign of grief and mourning.

Interment is followed by three successive stages of mourning that decrease in intensity, and gradually bring the family members from the solitude of their anguish back into the community. The first period, known as the *shivah,* meaning "seven," refers to the seven days of deepest mourning commencing after interment. Members of the immediate family of the deceased remain at home and do not attend work or even synagogue (except on Shabbat and festivals when most mourning laws are suspended). Instead, friends and relatives visit the mourners' home and conduct daily prayer services there. As a sign of their grief, the mourners sit either on the floor or on low stools rather than on regular chairs. It has, therefore, become customary to characterize a person in this first period of mourning as "sitting shivah." Mourners in this first stage may not wear leather shoes or cosmetics, shave, cut their hair, or engage in sexual relations. They are to remove themselves briefly from the pleasures of life and to experience grief and sorrow. Mirrors are covered in the mourners' home to symbolize that life and beauty are but vanity and transitory and also to show that God's image, which is evident in man, has been diminished from the world with the death of that person. We greet the mourner with the phrase, "May the Lord comfort you among the mourners of Zion and Jerusalem," and thereby demonstrate that personal grief, like personal joy, is linked with the collective Jewish condition (see earlier section on marriage).

The second stage of mourning, less intense than the first, is known as the *sheloshim,* meaning "thirty," and refers to the period from the end of shivah through the thirtieth day after burial (totaling twenty-three days, since the first seven days of the shivah are included). During this time, the mourner is permitted to work, wear leather shoes, and sit on regular chairs, although he is still to refrain from shaving, having his hair cut, listening to music, and attending parties or celebrations. In the third period, extending from the end of sheloshim until twelve months after the death, most earlier restrictions such as shaving and having haircuts are lifted and only a few restrictions such as listening to live music remain in effect.

Immediate family members attend daily prayer services and recite the mourner's *kaddish,* or "prayer for the dead," throughout all three stages of mourning. Few prayers in the Jewish liturgy can equal the kaddish in terms of the depth of emotion it hypnotically elicits, in spite of the fact that it includes no reference whatsoever to death and that it is recited in its original Aramaic language, which most mourners, in all likelihood, do not even understand. The kaddish glorifies God and expresses the hope that he might soon establish his kingdom of peace in the world. It is a declaration of faith in both God and redemption, in the face of personal loss and grief. Indeed, at the very moment of such anguish and despair, we are bidden to testify faithfully, "The LORD gave, and the LORD has taken away; blessed be the name of the LORD" (Job 1:21).

Through the kaddish, the mourner, like Job, renews his commitment to sanctified Jewish living. He professes that, "though he slay me, yet I will trust in him" (Job 13:15, KJV). The kaddish inspires him to reflect upon his life and faith, and also provides him with the daily opportunity to remember his loved one.

Novelist Herman Wouk described the almost magical power of the Kaddish in the following way:

This narrative of the facts hardly explains the hypnotic power of Kaddish as a custom. For one thing, there is the prayer itself. It is a beautiful dithyramb with strong rhythms and stirring sounds. For sheer word-music it is admirable, and though perhaps one mourner out of five knows what the words mean, the utterance itself is moving. There is the emotional impact of speaking it together with others who have recently suffered death in the family. There is the powerful aura of respect for the dead with which long custom has impregnated the kaddish. The mourner who speaks it feels an instinctive solace and release in the act, as though for the moment he is stretching his hand to the far shore and touching the hand of his departed. I am not saying that this is a rational feeling, but it is a strong one.[3]

A *matzevah,* or "tombstone," is erected at the gravesite after either the thirty-day or one-year period of mourning. Annually, the mourner observes the anniversary of the death with the *yahrzeit,* named after the German term meaning "time of year." This custom, originating in the early 1400s, provides the mourner with a day on which to remember his departed loved one. It is one of the most widely observed Jewish practices today. Year after year on the day of the yahrzeit, family members recite the kaddish, recall the life of the deceased, and reflect upon their own lives. Most Jews have as their deepest and most fervent prayer, the hope that their children will, in turn, recite the kaddish after them. A memorial lamp lasting for the twenty-four-hour duration of the yahrzeit is lit in the home to symbolize that the memory of the deceased has not been forgotten and that while man's body dies, his soul lives on eternally.

THE SERVICE OF THE HEART

Prayer

The reason why we pray, said William James, is simply that we cannot help praying. Prayer is the most natural and universal human urge, man's spiritual ladder linking him with ultimacy itself. It springs almost instinctively from the human condition in which man, a finite being, encounters a personal, infinite, and loving God, one who hears man's cries and is deeply concerned for his welfare. Prayer represents the language and music of our souls. Its enrapturing power penetrates to the very core of our being. Prayer gives expression to man's longing for *devekut* ("union with the divine") and to his feelings of awe and wonder over God's creation. It stems from man's quest to encounter the living God and from his thirst to communicate with him. It flows from our abiding faith in God's immanence and from our unswerving trust that "the LORD is near to all who call upon him . . . in truth" (Ps. 145:18). The mystical tradition describes the purifying, regenerative magic of prayer in the following manner: "As the flame clothes the black, sooty clod in a garment of fire and releases the heat imprisoned therein, even so does prayer clothe a man in a garment of holiness, evoke the light and fire implanted within him by his Maker, illumine his whole being, and unite the Lower and the Higher Worlds."[4] Indeed, "would that man would pray all day" (B.T., Ber. 21a).

The Jewish obligation to pray was derived by the rabbis from the verse ". . . to serve him with all your heart . . ." (Deut. 11:13). "What," they ask, "is the service of the heart? It is prayer" (B.T., Taan. 2a). For whatever form prayer may take—petition, penitence, thanksgiving, or praise—it must always involve introspection, meditation, and self-scrutiny. The very term for "to pray" in Hebrew is the reflexive *lehitpallel,* meaning "to judge oneself." For whatever else prayer may be, it must be sincere and be a "service of the heart." In the pithy words of the rabbis, "The All Merciful One desires the heart."

Prayer lies at the very foundation of the Jewish faith, at the heart of Jewish convictions. From the Torah we learn that Abraham prayed to God to save the righteous people of Sodom (Gen. 18:23-33); Jacob prayed for deliverance from his brother, Esau; Eliezer prayed for a fitting wife for his master; Moses and Aaron prayed for the people of Israel, as did the kings and prophets later on. Indeed, an entire book of the Bible, the Psalms, can effectively be called a book of prayer.

While prayer in biblical times was often offered in conjunction with sacrifices, it also came independently of them, as a spontaneous emotional outburst of thanks or petition to God. Indeed, the biblical accounts of Hagar's plea for Ishmael (see Genesis 21:14–19) and Hannah's prayer for a son (see I Samuel 1:10–11), neither of which involved sacrifices, became viewed as the Jewish paradigms of genuine prayer. In the aftermath of the destruction of the temple and therefore the end of sacrificial worship, prayers substituted entirely for the offerings and also corresponded to them. Thus, the three daily services— *Shacharit* (morning service), *Minhah* (afternoon service), and *Maariv* (evening service)—as well as the additional *Musaf* service on Shabbat and festivals, were instituted to supplant and correspond with the daily sacrifices offered in the time of the temple. Other traditions link the three daily prayer services to each of the patriarchs. Thus, Abraham is said to have instituted the morning Shacharit prayers, Isaac the afternoon Minhah ones, and Jacob the evening Maariv prayers.

Judaism insisted, however, that prayer not be restricted to the synagogue or to the three formal daily worship services. We ought to experience prayerful moments many times during the course of the day. For this reason, the observant Jew recites at least one hundred *berakhot,* or "blessings" (singular, *berakhah*), throughout the course of each day. In the morning, for example, he recites a series of blessings, including ones thanking God for giving man his eyesight, intelligence, and strength. He offers blessings before and after partaking of material pleasures such as wine, bread, fruit, vegetables, and water, and even upon hearing thunder, or seeing lightning, comets, mountains, or rivers.

A blessing is recited upon hearing good news and bad news, when we wear new clothes, and even after purchasing a new home. Every mitzvah is preceded with a blessing, too, in which we thank God for sanctifying Israel and giving her the opportunity to follow God's commandments. The berakhot enable the Jew to transform virtually every moment of life into a prayerful experience wherein mundane time and events become sanctified with profound spiritual import. The berakhah does not transfer holiness to the object itself, but rather entitles us to partake of the world's pleasure. In blessing food, for example, we give thanks to the Lord and testify thereby that the earth is his and we are but its caretakers.

Blessings are recited in Hebrew (or in the vernacular for those who do not understand Hebrew). They all begin with the same standard core formula—"Blessed are you, Lord our God, Ruler of the universe . . ."—followed by mention of the specific object, such as ". . . Creator of the fruit of the vine" (for wine), or ". . . who brings forth bread from the earth" (for bread), or ". . . Creator of the fruit of the tree" (for fruit). The *birkat ha-mazon,* or "grace after meals," is recited when bread has been eaten, while other shorter forms of grace are recited when it has not.

The specific content and structure of the three daily prayer services originated in the fifth century B.C.E., following the return of the Babylonian exiles to Palestine under Ezra and Nehemiah. By the beginning of the second century C.E., the service was well established and essentially identical to ours today. Additional poems and liturgies were introduced, however, over the course of the next few centuries. The prayer book, or *Siddur* (meaning "order of service"), was completed by the ninth century. The traditional Siddur, written almost entirely in Hebrew, organized prayer along set liturgical lines. The introduction of a formal, structured set of prayers to be offered at specific times during the day, however, created a new problem—whether or not emotional spontaneity and freedom in worship could be reconciled with the more static factors of prayer rules and set liturgies.

In the view of Dr. Joseph Hertz:

> . . . fixed prayer alone prevented chaos at the individual centers of worship and rendered possible uniformity . . . something of vital importance in Jewry, with its children scattered to the four winds of heaven. At the same time, private prayer and the free effusion of the heart were duly esteemed. . . .
>
> The regulations concerning the minutiae of prayer are many; the opening treatise of the Talmud, Berachoth [sic], is entirely devoted to that subject. Schürer and other Christian theologians contend that these regulations must have stifled the whole spirit of prayer. But this is a controversial fiction; as if discipline in an army, or laws in a country, necessarily suppressed patriotism. In fact, rule and discipline in worship *increase* devotion. . . . He who prays must remember before Whom he stands, they [the rabbis] said; and it was neither the length, nor the brevity, nor the language of the prayer that mattered, but the sincerity.[5]

Although we recite the same set of prayers daily, the rabbis advised that we guard against allowing them to become routine or lacking in *kavvanah,* or "intention," specifically, in spiritual concentration and devotion. We are to bring to our standardized prayers the new experiences we encounter daily, and we are to feel as if we are reciting them for the very first time. "And when you pray," states the Talmud, "make not your prayer routine, but [a plea for] mercy and supplication before God" (Mishnah, Avot 2:13). It is habit, said the great Hasidic Rabbi of Kotsk, which is the defeat of the spirit, the destroyer of the soul, and the downfall of man. One who prays today only because he prayed yesterday, he once noted, does not properly fulfill his prayer obligation. In ancient days, pious Jews would arrive at synagogue an hour before services in order to meditate, study Torah, and prepare themselves for their prayerful encounter with God (B.T., Meg. 28a).

Prayer is a force for reconciliation not only in the Jew's devotion and attachment to God, but in his bonds with other Jews, as well. It is fascinating to note that today we offer the very same prayers that, with but slight variations, have been recited by Jews from different countries and diverse cultures for centuries. Jews can visit foreign lands and still feel comfortable and familiar with the prayer service, although most of the melodies in use would reflect the particular culture. Thus, despite the rigid structure and uniformity of the prayer service—perhaps, even because of those very factors—participating in a Jewish prayer service can be a profound spiritually uplifting experience.

While the Jewish ideal is to pray in a synagogue with a *minyan*, or "quorum," of at least ten people, one may recite the daily prayers alone and outside a synagogue, as well. There are certain prayers, however, that may not be recited without the presence of a minyan, for the Jewish concept of prayer and personal supplication is inextricably linked with Jewish peoplehood as a whole. Indeed, the Siddur contains very little in the way of personal, first-person supplication but rather invokes the collective plural form such as in the following phrases: our God, give us, save us, heal us, redeem us, and so on.

The two pillars of the prayer service are the *Shema* and the *Amidah*. The Shema consists of the verses, "Hear, O Israel, the Lord our God the Lord is One. Thou shalt love the Lord thy God with all thy heart, with all thy soul, and with all thy might . . ." (i.e., Deut. 6:4-9, followed by Deut. 11:13-21 and Num. 15:37-41). The Shema, which proclaims the unity of God, constitutes the central affirmation of the Jewish faith. It is recited twice daily, in the morning and in the evening. It is one of the first things a Jewish child learns to recite and one of the last things the Jew utters before death. Through the centuries Jews have died with the holy watchwords of the Shema on their lips. Saintly Jews faithfully recited the Shema even before entering the gas chambers during the Nazi Holocaust. They affirmed the oneness of God, their love for him, and their acceptance of his mitzvot in the very face of death and in the midst of despair. Somehow, they were able to find the spiritual resources to declare that the world was infused with divine purpose and unity.

The Shema is followed by the recitation of the *Amidah,* meaning "standing" (since it is recited while standing up), which is also known as the *shemoneh esreh,* or "eighteen," because it originally consisted of eighteen benedictions. (Today the Amidah contains an additional nineteenth benediction condemning *minim,* or "apostates." This benediction was added after the original redaction. Some scholars suggest that it was directed against the early Jewish-Christians, though this remains uncertain.) The Amidah, the highpoint of the prayer service, is a prayer of silent devotion. It forms the liturgical core of all three daily services and includes prayers of praise, thanksgiving, petition, and confession to God.

In addition to these two cardinal prayers, there are other blessings, liturgies, and psalms that together constitute the three daily prayer services. Jews face in the direction of *Eretz Yisrael* (Israel) during prayer, which in America is toward the east. In Israel, Jews face Jerusalem. In Jerusalem, they face the Western Wall which once surrounded the holy Temple Mount, the most sacred spot in Judaism (see Dan. 6:11 and B.T., Ber. 30a). On Shabbat and on Monday and Thursday mornings, a selection from the Torah is read in synagogue since Torah study is an integral part of the Jewish worship experience. According to some rabbinic sources and traditions, the study of Torah is an even greater mitzvah than prayer. (See, for example, B.T., Shab. 11a and R.H. 55a. See also chapter 8 on the Hasidic response to this view.)

The Synagogue

The introduction of the synagogue was one of Judaism's foremost contributions to Western civilization. Few other institutions in Jewish life can rival it in importance. The synagogue has served as one of the most effective keys to Jewish survival, particularly since the time of the destruction of the second temple when exile and dispersion marked the Jewish condition. It was the synagogue that, in large measure, sustained the Jewish faith and ensured its vitality. Historically, the Jew's entire life tended to revolve around the synagogue, or *shul* as it is sometimes affectionately called.

The term "synagogue," stemming from the Greek word meaning "assembly" or "congregation," is a translation of the original Hebrew term *bet knesset,* or "house of assembly." The Jewish synagogue was more than just a "house for God," as the temple was often described, since "the earth is my [God's] footstool; what is the house which you would build for me, and what is the place of my rest?" (Isa. 66:1). The rabbis also point out that the Torah deliberately uses the expression, "And let them make me a sanctuary, that I may dwell in *their* midst" (Exod. 25:8, emphasis added), rather than, ". . . in *its* midst," to teach us that the physical edifice of the synagogue (i.e., "its midst") merely facilitates the people's assembly, but that it is man's prayers and heartfelt devotion that bring God into their hearts (i.e., into *"their* midst").

The synagogue was a "house of assembly" for prayer as well as a *bet ha-midrash,* or "house of learning." It was the communal study hall where both children and adults came to study Torah and Talmud. Its function as a "study hall" was, in fact, regarded by the rabbis as of greater importance than its role as a house of worship. For this reason, a synagogue may be converted into a house of learning, although the reverse is not permitted, for transforming a house of learning into one of prayer constitutes a decrease in holiness and to do so would violate the rabbinic principle of "elevating items in holiness, not lowering them."

The synagogue also served as a "house of assembly" or community center for Jews' social and humanitarian needs. Historically, the elderly, the needy—even the traveler just passing through—would come to the synagogue to find food, shelter, and fellowship. In its various functions as an assembly place for prayer, study, and fulfillment of social needs, the synagogue came to represent the microcosm of the mosaic of Jewish life. It served at the very heart of the Jew's devotion to God and commitment to his fellow man.

The synagogue was, in all likelihood, created during the Babylonian exile in the sixth century B.C.E., although it did not achieve its prominence in Jewish life until after the destruction of the second temple and exile in the first century C.E. Jews took the synagogue with them wherever they went. By the time the New Testament was written, it had already become a central gathering place for Jews to pray, preach, and study the word of God, and also to fulfill their charitable social obligations.

A Jewish house of worship need not be architecturally any different from other buildings, although symbols such as the Star of David or a menorah are commonly used as designs. Sculptures or paintings depicting the human form, however, are strictly forbidden in Judaism, due to the biblical admonition against making a graven image. They would not be found adorning any synagogue. The sanctuary is to face in the direction of Israel and should have windows so that the worshipers can gaze outside and be inspired by God's creation. It is the presence of the Torah that transforms a mere building into a holy "synagogue."

In the front of the sanctuary is the *bimah,* or raised "platform," where the ark containing the Torah scrolls rests and from where the rabbi and cantor officiate. The Torah is generally adorned with a silver crown, breastplate, and small silver bells—all reminiscent of the adornments used during the time of the tabernacle (see Exod. 28:15-34). The Torah is made of strips of parchment from the skins of kosher animals sewn together and tied on two wooden rollers in the form of a scroll. It is covered with a cloth mantle that is often embroidered with a design such as a tree since the Torah is described as "a tree of life to those who lay hold of her" (Prov. 3:18).

Ezra instituted the custom of reading a portion of the Torah weekly. Despite centuries of exile and dispersion, and despite their diverse cultural, liturgical, and musical heritages, Jews the world over still read the same Torah portion each week, with essentially the same special tune.

Torah scrolls may not be printed or mass-produced but are hand-written in the traditional manner by pious Jews called *soferim,* or "scribes." The average Torah scroll takes about one year to complete at a cost of ten to thirty thousand dollars. Scrolls are treated with the utmost reverence since they contain the name of God. As the ark containing the Torah is opened, the congregation rises respectfully; and as the scroll is carried around the synagogue, we kiss it. If a scroll falls, the entire congregation must fast. When a scroll (or even printed Bible) becomes too old or worn out to be used, it must be buried in the ground *(geniza)* just like a human being. It may not be thrown away since it contains the name of God. For this reason, many ancient scrolls and religious books that otherwise would never have survived are extant. The perpetually lit *ner tamid,* or "eternal light," hangs in front of the ark, symbolic of the one that was aglow in the ancient sanctuary (see Exod. 27:20-21).

The rise of the Enlightenment and Jewish denominationalism in Western Europe brought major changes to the structure of the synagogue and to the form of the prayer service. Reform Judaism made the most drastic revisions by introducing such things as the organ, mixed seating, mixed choirs in which women and non-Jews participated, as well as prayers in the vernacular (see chapter 8). In addition, the introduction of decorum by all three Jewish denominations changed the character of the synagogue service from its earlier, more informal style. Today Reform and Conservative congregations (Reform generally use the term "temple" rather than "synagogue") have mixed pews, unlike Orthodox congregations in which the men and women sit separately. Reform Jews often do not wear a tallit, tefillin, or kippah (see below); Conservative and Orthodox Jews do.

The role of the cantor is to conduct the prayer service and to serve as the *shaliach tzibbur,* or "messenger of the congregation." He plays no special grace or sacramental role. Anyone knowledgeable in liturgy (preferably someone with a pleasant voice) can be appointed cantor and lead the congregation in prayer. The rabbi is also not a sacramental figure and is ordained by virtue of his religious piety and knowledge of the Torah and Talmud. (The requirements for *semikhah,* or "ordination," differ among the denominations.) In previous centuries rabbis received no remuneration for serving as teachers, scholars, and spiritual leaders to their communities; it was an avocation that they performed in conjunction with their regular professions. Today, however, the rabbinate is a full-time occupation. In addition to serving as teacher and spiritual leader of a community, the rabbi is expected to perform various pastoral duties such as visiting the sick and burying the dead, functions that actually are equally incumbent upon all Jews.

The synagogue continues to serve as the central institution in Jewish life, although admittedly, many of its earlier functions such as serving the social and educational needs of the community are now performed by other, more specialized bodies such as the day school and federation movements.

Tefillin, Tzitzit, Mezuzah

He who wears tefillin on his head and arm, tzitzit on his garment, and has placed a mezuzah on his doorpost is well protected. He will not fall into sin, as we are told (Eccles. 4:12) a threefold cord will not easily break (B.T., Men. 43b).

"Bind them [God's words] as a sign upon your hand, and they shall be as frontlets between your eyes" (Deut. 6:8).

Tefillin, or "phylacteries" as they are known in English, are two black boxes to which are attached black straps. The boxes contain small pieces of parchment on which are written portions of the Torah including the verse, "Hear, O Israel, the Lord our God the Lord is one." One box and strap is wrapped around the left arm (opposite the heart), the other is wrapped around the head (so that the box lies on top of the brain). Tefillin are worn by men over the age of bar mitzvah (thirteen) during the daily morning prayer service (except on festivals) as a sign of the covenant (see Deut 6:8). According to the midrash, God himself wears tefillin since he, too, is bound by the covenant. And while the Jew's tefillin contain verses praising God, in God's tefillin it is written, "Who is like unto thee, O Israel, a unique nation in the world?" By enwrapping his arm and head with the tefillin, the Jew demonstrates that his love for God and devotion to his word involve his hands (actions), heart (emotions), and mind (thoughts)—all united in service to him.

"The LORD said to Moses, 'Speak to the people of Israel, and bid them to make tassels *[tzitzit]* on the corners of their garments throughout their generations, and to put upon the tassel of each corner a cord of blue; and it shall be to you a tassel to look upon and remember all the commandments of the LORD, to do them . . .'" (Num. 15:37-39).

The *tallit,* or "prayer shawl," on which are attached the tzitzit, is worn daily (including on Shabbat) at morning prayer services. There are 613 knots in the four tzitzit corresponding to the 613 mitzvot in the Torah. We enwrap ourselves in the tallit to symbolize that our entire being should be devoted to fulfilling God's mitzvot.

"Write them on the doorposts of your house and on your gates" (Deut. 6:9; 11:20).

The *mezuzah,* a small, often ornately designed box unlike the plain black ones of the tefillin, contains a piece of parchment on which is written the prayer of the Shema ("Hear, O Israel . . ."). It is placed on the outside doorpost of the home and on the doorposts of all the rooms inside, except in the washroom, since we are prohibited from uttering God's name or carrying in a book containing his name there. The outside of the box is usually inscribed with the Hebrew letters *shin* (sh), *daled* (d), and *yod (y),* which together form one of the names of

God and which also form an acronym for *shomer daltot Yisrael,* meaning "guardian of the doors (i.e., houses) of Israel." The midrash points out that unlike an earthly king who dwells inside his home and surrounds it with guards to protect him, God, the true King, surrounds the homes of his children, Israel, and protects them. It is, therefore, customary to kiss the mezuzah as a sign of affection and reverence upon entering and leaving the home.

Kippah

The *kippah,* or "headcovering," (sometimes referred to as a *yarmulka)* does not have any biblical precedent and, in fact, was not even a requirement in talmudic times. Its origins and rationale remain unclear, although it was likely instituted as a sign of reverence for God's sovereignty and as a reminder that there is always a power transcending man. Orthodox Jews wear it at most, if not all, times; Conservative Jews wear it especially when praying or reciting a *berakhah;* and some Reform Jews wear it at prayer services, although it is generally optional even then.

KOSHER DIETARY RULES

Foods which may be eaten by observant Jews are called *kosher;* those which may not are *treif.* The term kosher is used by the Bible on only three occasions (Esther 8:5; Eccles. 10:10; 11:6), all with the meaning of "fit" and "proper"—none of these refer to food. Today the word is generally used in reference to foods that are permissible according to Jewish law. Foods that are ritually pure and that may be eaten are described by the Torah as *tahor* rather than kosher, while those that are ritually impure and prohibited are called *tameh.* These terms are often mistakenly translated as "clean" and "unclean," conveying the notion of physical uncleanliness rather than ritual impurity.

The Jewish dietary laws *(kashrut)* are both numerous and complex. They are derived primarily from passages in Leviticus

11 and Deuteronomy 14, although they were developed and amplified by the rabbis over the centuries.

Reform Judaism does not insist on the observance of kashrut. The overwhelming number of Reform Jews today, in fact, disregard those rules, although many would be inclined not to eat pork. Conservative and Orthodox Jews continue to uphold the observance of these laws, albeit to different degrees and with different levels of meticulousness.

Fruits and Vegetables: All produce from the ground, such as fruits and vegetables, are permitted and may be eaten with either dairy products or meat. "And God said, 'Behold, I have given you every plant yielding seed which is upon the face of all the earth, and every tree with seed in its fruit; you shall have them for food'" (Gen. 1:29).

Fish: Only fish with fins and scales, such as tuna, salmon, bass, trout, sole, and so on, may be eaten. All seafoods such as lobster, oyster, and shrimp are prohibited (see Lev. 11:9-12).

Birds: The Torah lists those birds that may not be eaten rather than categorizing their features as it does in the case of fish and animals (see Lev. 11:13-19; Deut. 14:11-18). Most of the prohibited birds, however, share the characteristic of being wild birds of prey, such as the eagle, stork, owl, and vulture. Permitted fowl include chicken, turkey, ducks, geese (not wild), and doves.

Animals: Animals that walk on four legs, chew their cud, and have split hooves, such as cattle, sheep, goats, and deer, are permitted. Others such as horses, donkeys, camels, and pigs are prohibited (see Deut. 14:4-8).

Other: Products such as eggs, milk, or oil that are derived from kosher animals are permissible; those that came from non-kosher animals may not be eaten with the exception of honey, which comes from bees (all insects and swarming things are forbidden) but is, nevertheless, kosher. Eating blood, even from kosher animals, is strictly prohibited (see Lev. 7:26-27, 17:10-14).

Whether or not various animals and birds are inherently

kosher, however, is only one aspect of whether or not they may be eaten. For unless they are slaughtered and prepared properly, according to Jewish law, they remain treif and may not be eaten. For example, cows and chickens, which are inherently kosher animals but which were not slaughtered properly by a *shochet* (a trained, observant, and licensed Jewish slaughterer), may not be eaten. If the animal died through any other means or was diseased, it is rendered non-kosher. Proper slaughter involves cutting the animal's windpipe (trachea) and foodpipe (esophagus) in one motion with a razor-sharp knife, bringing about its instant, painless death. (These laws do not apply to fish, which may be killed in any manner.) According to Maimonides, "The commandment concerning the killing of animals is necessary because the natural food of man consists of vegetables and the flesh of animals. . . . Since, therefore, the desire of procuring good food necessitates the slaying of animals, the law enjoins that the death of the animal should be the easiest. We are not permitted to torment the animal by cutting the throat in a clumsy manner, by poleaxing, or by cutting off a limb whilst the animal is alive."[6]

Observant Jews buy their meat from kosher butcher shops that are under special rabbinic supervision so they may be assured that the various dietary rules have been followed. They would not eat chicken or meat even from a kosher animal such as a cow at a non-kosher home or restaurant, since these were not slaughtered correctly and lack rabbinic supervision.

Because eating blood is strictly forbidden (Lev. 17:10–14), meat must be soaked and salted so as to remove all excess blood. Failure to do so renders the animal non-kosher. For the same reason, we are prohibited from eating an egg with a blood spot in it. In addition, certain fats (Lev. 7:23-24), as well as the "sciatic nerve," or *gid ha-nasheh,* in the hind quarter or rump (filet mignon), even from kosher animals that were slaughtered and prepared correctly, always remain prohibited as decreed in the Torah's account of Jacob's struggle with the angel: "Therefore . . . the Israelites do not eat the sinew of the hip which is upon the hollow of the thigh" (Gen. 32:32). Non-kosher foods that are mixed with kosher ones render the entire mixture prohibited.

Meat and Milk

Kosher meat or chicken, even if it was prepared properly, may not be eaten if it is mixed with milk or milk products. Separate utensils, such as silverware, dishes, pots, pans, and even towels, are used for dairy and for meat to ensure that the two do not come into contact with each other. It is also customary to wait a period of time (anywhere from one to six hours, depending on one's family tradition) after eating meat or chicken before eating dairy products to ensure the two have no contact even after ingestion. The reverse (i.e., eating meat after dairy), however, is permitted since dairy products are much more easily digested.

The prohibition against combining meat and milk, which is part of the oral tradition, is derived from the threefold mention of the verse, "You shall not boil a kid in its mother's milk" (Exod. 23:19; 34:26; Deut. 14:21; see B.T., Hul. 115b). The rabbis deduced from this thrice-repeated verse that a mixture of meat and milk is prohibited in three ways—one should not cook the two together, eat them together, or profit from the mixture. Chicken is treated as "meat" in this regard, although fish, which may be combined with milk, is not.

Fruit, vegetables, bread, and other products not containing either dairy products or meat are referred to as *parveh,* or "neutral," and may be eaten with either dairy or meat meals. Once they are cooked with either one, however, they assume its character and are treated accordingly. Many food companies stamp their product with a symbol such as "Ⓤ" (for Orthodox Union) or "K" (for kosher) to certify that it is kosher and to assure the observant Jewish consumer that it is under rabbinic supervision. They may also add the letter "P" for parveh to show that it contains no milk products and can be eaten after or together with meat.

Meaning of Dietary Laws

The Torah itself does not provide a rationale for what on the surface appears to be a meaningless set of dietary regulations. As with other mitzvot, however, we are free to proffer explanations for the kashrut laws, provided we do not make their observance contingent on the meaning we ascribe to them. For mitzvot are the divine call beckoning for a human response. As such, they have a binding force independent of the particular rationale we may give them. Man can never hope to fully penetrate the divine intent of the commandments, "For my thoughts are not your thoughts, neither are your ways my ways, says the LORD" (Isa. 55:8). Those who trust in God and his eternal word, however, believe that the mitzvot are not arbitrary, whimsical, or capricious on his part, but are motivated by his ever-abiding love and concern for his people, Israel.

Certain biblical commandments called *chukim* were viewed by the rabbis as deliberately lacking any real rationale other than to teach us unconditional obedience to God's will. They test our love and devotion to him and our willingness to yield our will before his. Ultimately, the Jew is to observe the mitzvot dutifully *because God commanded them in his eternal Torah,* not because of any benefits that might be gained or relevance we perceive them to have, although these are certainly useful factors adding to their meaningfulness. In fact, Rabbi Samson Raphael Hirsch, nineteenth-century leader of neo-Orthodoxy, went so far as to say, "There is no other reason for all the dietary laws other than that God gave them." Kosher regulations, therefore, cannot be invalidated by scientific or hygienic discoveries, making one of the rationales obsolete.

Providing explanations for the mitzvot, however, does significantly add to the meaningfulness of our observance and sheds insight into the divine will and intent. In the case of the kashrut laws, the Torah is notably silent in providing a rationale other than linking those rules with the Jewish obligation to be a holy people: " 'For I am the LORD who brought you up out of . . . Egypt, to be your God; you shall therefore be holy, for I am holy.' This is the law . . . to make a distinction between the unclean and the clean and between the living creature that may be eaten and . . . that may not be eaten" (Lev. 11:45-47).

The Hebrew term *kadosh,* or "holy," implies separateness and apartness. That which is holy is set apart from all else. One rationale for the kosher laws, therefore, is that they set the Jews apart from all others and help shape them into a distinctive and holy people. Even today the dietary regulations serve as a major bulwark against the rising tide of Jewish assimilation. In addition, the kosher laws enable the Jew to sanctify his mundane act of eating by transforming it into a spiritual exercise wherein the table becomes his altar, the food his sacrifice, and his body a holy vessel for his soul.

One of the most common explanations provided for the dietary laws is that they are of hygienic benefit. Modern science and medicine have demonstrated rather conclusively that there exists a strong interdependence between our physical well-being and our diet—between that which we are and that which we eat. The medieval Jewish scholar Nachmanides claimed that fish with fins and scales were kosher since they tended to swim in fresh water areas and were, therefore, healthier. Maimonides, the most renowned medieval rabbinic scholar who also served as the private physician to the sultan, claimed that, "All the foods which the Torah has forbidden us to eat have some bad and damaging effects on the body. . . . The principal reason why the law forbids swine's flesh is to be found in the circumstances that its habits and its food are very dirty and loathsome."[7] (It is very possible that historically Jews were seldom afflicted by diseases such as trichinosis because they observed kosher laws and did not eat pork.) Maimonides also insisted that "the general purpose of the Torah is twofold, the well-being of the soul and the well-being of the body. The well-being of the soul is ranked first, but . . . the well-being of the body comes first."[8]

Other rabbinic commentators, however, expressly opposed this medical rationale. "God forbid that I should believe that the reason for forbidden foods is medicinal," wrote Isaac Abarbanel. "For were it so, the Book of God's law would be in the same class as any of the minor brief medical books. . . . Furthermore, our own eyes see that people who eat pork and insects and such . . . are well and alive and healthy at this very day. . . . all of which points to the conclusion that the Laws of God did not come to heal bodies and seek their material welfare but to seek the health of the soul and cure its illness."[9]

The fact that there are ways to avoid contracting diseases associated with eating non-kosher animals does not invalidate the dietary laws or make them antiquated, as noted earlier. For while kosher regulations may indeed be beneficial to our hygiene and health, their observance should not be contingent on such factors.

Another rationale provided for the kosher laws is that they help man build a disciplined moral character able to subordinate desires to God's will. "Who," asks the Mishnah, "is a courageous person? One who conquers his inclination to sin." Interestingly, the rabbis teach that we ought to be tempted by non-kosher foods but that we must overcome our desires and declare, "I want them, but what can I do since our Father in heaven decreed that I not have them?" For the one who is tempted by sin but overcomes it, they claim, is more saintly than the one who is not tempted by it at all.

It is also suggested that some of the dietary rules, such as the prohibition against cooking a kid in its mother's milk, have their origins in ancient heathen idolatrous practices that Israel was commanded to renounce.[10]

Yet a further interpretation of the dietary laws is that they sensitize the Jew to the value of life and to the need to act kindly toward animals. For this reason, we are prohibited from slaughtering a cow and its calf on the same day (see Lev. 22:28) and from eating meat and dairy products together, since "it is a matter of cruelty to cook a kid in its mother's milk."[11] We are also commanded to send away a mother bird before taking her eggs lest we become callous and insensitive to her feelings. Even the laws regulating the slaughter of birds and animals reflect this humanitarian concern for bringing about their instant, painless death. The Torah wished to sensitize the Jew to the pain and suffering of others. "What does it matter to God," asks the midrash, "whether an animal is slaughtered by the throat or not, whether man eats kosher or not; it neither benefits nor injures him? Rather, the divine laws are not obeyed for God's benefit, but so as to purify man and sanctify his acts" (see Gen. Rab. 44:1).

It is also suggested that the dietary laws help bridge the gap between the Jewish ideal of vegetarianism and the present fractured human condition. In the Garden of Eden, representing the Jewish ideal (see chapter 2), man was permitted to eat only fruits and vegetables, not meat: "And God said, 'Behold, I have given you every plant yielding seed which is upon the face of all the earth, and every tree with seed in its fruit; you shall have them for food'" (Gen. 1:29). After the flood, however, God said to Noah, "Every moving thing that lives shall be food for you; and as I gave you the green plants, I give you everything" (Gen. 9:3). As a concession to man's frail, imperfect condition, God permitted him to eat meat. But in order that man preserve the ideal of vegetarianism and be constantly reminded of it and drawn closer to it, Jews were commanded to observe the dietary restrictions and to limit the kinds of animals they may or may not eat.

By regulating their daily eating habits Jews are constantly reminded to bridge the gap between the present human condition and that of the biblical ideal. Rabbi Sam Dresner writes, "Human consumption of meat, which means the taking of animal life, has constantly posed a religious problem to Judaism, even when it has accepted the necessity of it. The Rabbis of the Talmud were aware of the distinction between man's ideal and his real condition, regarding food. . . . We are permitted to eat meat, but we must learn to have reverence for the life we take. It is part of the process of hallowing which kashrut proclaims. Reverence for life, teaching an awareness of what we are about when we engage in the simple act of eating flesh, is the constant lesson of the laws of kashrut."[12]

While the New Testament cites Jesus as saying that it is not what goes into the mouth that is important so much as what goes out of it (Mark 7:15), this need not be interpreted as his absolute rejection of kosher laws. Indeed, it is likely that Jesus (and the Jerusalem church) observed them his entire life and that it was Paul who regarded them as obsolete. (Moreover, while Paul was opposed to the Gentiles' observing kosher laws, it is unclear whether he also rejected the continued observance of them by Jews.) Rather, Jesus in that New Testament passage seems to have been underscoring the seriousness of the sin of slander by contrasting it with the dietary laws. The rabbis also saw *lashon ha-ra*, or spreading either true or untrue gossip, as one of the most serious offenses in all of Judaism. They repeatedly preached, "Keep your tongue from evil, and your lips from speaking deceit. Depart from evil, and do good; seek peace, and pursue it" (Ps. 34:13-14).

A Hasidic story tells of a gossipy woman who came to a rabbi seeking a way to atone for her grave sin. Upon the rabbi's instructions, she tore open a pillow in the village square. The rabbi then told her to return to the square and to retrieve all the feathers. The woman exclaimed that it would be impossible to do so since the wind had blown them all away. So too, said the wise rabbi, it is terribly difficult to atone for gossip, which also travels in all directions and is equally impossible to completely "retrieve" once said.

Despite the seriousness with which the rabbis treated this sin, they at no time claimed that the divinely ordained kosher laws, i.e., that which comes into the mouth, were no longer valid. The ancient prophets often excoriated Israel for inflicting pain and anguish upon others, although that never prompted them to disavow the dietary rules (see, for example, Isa. 66:17; Ezek. 4:14; Dan. 1:8).

Jews have an abiding love and commitment to God's law. At various times in their history, they have chosen martyrdom rather than transgress the kosher regulations. Their refusal to eat non-kosher foods even touched off the entire series of events marked by the Hanukkah festival. For while kosher laws, like all others—except for the three cardinal sins—are suspended under life-threatening conditions (see chapter 3), in the event that a government engages in a coordinated effort to wean Jews away from their faith, the Jew is dutifully commanded to give up his life even for the smallest item. This was the case with the events of Hanukkah in which the Greek Hellenists publicly and systematically tried to force the Jews to abandon their faith by eating pork. Their actions prompted the Jews to rebel (see chapter 4). Even today there are Jews living in very tenuous situations and remote areas who go to great length, even risking their lives, to procure kosher food.

Whatever their origin, their divine intent, and their rationale, the laws of kashrut constitute a most significant link in the chain of Jewish tradition and survival. They strengthen the moral character of the Jewish people and shape them into a holy nation.

Chapter 6

FACING THE CHALLENGES OF THE HOLOCAUST

Never shall I forget that night, the first night in camp, which has turned my life into one long night, seven times sealed. Never shall I forget that smoke. Never shall I forget the little faces of the children, whose bodies I saw turned to wreaths of smoke beneath a silent blue sky.

Never shall I forget those flames which consumed my faith forever.

Never shall I forget the nocturnal silence which deprived me, for all eternity, of the desire to live. Never shall I forget those moments which murdered my God and my soul and turned my dreams to dust. Never shall I forget these things, even if I am condemned to live as long as God Himself. Never.[1]

The *Holocaust,* a term taken from the burnt sacrifice that was offered in the temple and that was totally consumed, refers to the systematic slaughter of six million Jews by Adolf Hitler and the Nazis during the period of World War II. Jews at times refer to it as the *shoah,* meaning "terrible catastrophe."

Until recently, there was widespread ignorance and misunderstanding among Americans about the Holocaust. Studies reveal that even those schoolchildren who were familiar with the term often were unaware of what it referred to. Some even believed it to be a Jewish holiday! Today this is no longer the case. There is now greater awareness than ever before of the events surrounding the Holocaust. This, however, has created a new set of problems. For perhaps too much is now being said that is either inaccurate or that trivializes the subject and takes away from the horror of that event. Indeed, there are those who invoke the Holocaust too frequently and those who do not talk of it enough; those who speak of it appropriately and those who do so insensitively; those who wish to forget about the past and those who seek to learn from it; those who use the Holocaust to their own advantage and those who are humbled by its magnitude and awesomeness.

According to the Torah, when Moses approached the burning bush, God said to him, "Do not come near; put off your shoes from your feet, for the place on which you are standing is holy ground" (Exod. 3:5). To speak of the Holocaust is to tread on *terra sancta*, holy ground. Indeed, the blood of its victims has barely congealed; its voice still "is crying to me [God] from the ground" (Gen. 4:10). Survivors with concentration camp numbers tattooed on their forearms bear witness to the power of the demonic, as well as to the resilience of the human spirit. There is a difference, of course, between the biblical story of Moses at the bush and that of the Holocaust. In the former, the bush burned but was not consumed. In the latter, six million Jewish men, women, and children burned; and their bodies *were* consumed—although not entirely so. The Jewish people continue to live! By their very survival they bear testimony to the world that good ultimately triumphs over evil; by their very tortured death they give witness that the Messiah has not yet come; and by their continued faithfulness to God's covenant, they still declare, like Job long ago, "Though he slay me, yet will I trust in him" (13:15, KJV).

All Jews alive today regard themselves as Holocaust survivors since Hitler's plan was genocidal—to eradicate the entire Jewish nation. All bear the awesome responsibility of telling the story of those excruciating years. Nevertheless, the morally sensitive person trembles in awe and trepidation before uttering anything at all about the Nazi conflagration. Just as Aaron, the high priest, was so stunned by the death of his two sons that he could not speak (see Lev. 10:1–3), so our initial response to the Holocaust must be one of silence. We ought to feel dumbstruck by the magnitude of suffering and enormity of manifest evil. Even the survivors themselves were incapable of speaking of their experiences for many years.

We are faced, therefore, with an incredible dilemma. To speak of the Holocaust is to risk the inevitability that our words will be inadequate to the task and responsibility at hand. To remain silent, on the other hand, is to assume the even greater risk that the Holocaust might be forgotten and that such monumental evil and human anguish might occur again. As Santayana has warned, those who do not learn from the errors of history are doomed to repeat them. The only solution is to commemorate the Holocaust through both silence and words. Only after mourning our terrible loss may we dare speak of it; only after initially remaining silent do we have the moral right to talk of it.

In learning about the Holocaust one immediately finds that, unlike most other subjects, it can never be fully mastered, grasped, or understood. The more it is studied, the more it eludes our grasp, and the more beguiling and incomprehensible it becomes. It forever remains a profound mystery to theologians, social scientists, and survivors alike. The thoughtful student feels humbled by the Holocaust. And yet, he refuses to view it detached from its core as a historical event involving human misery and suffering of incredible magnitude. In speaking of the theological lessons or social implications to be drawn from it, he is mindful that what is being spoken of, first and foremost, is an actual historical event in which real, live children and adults suffered excruciating pain, unmitigated suffering, and horrible deaths.

The question of whether the Holocaust actually constitutes a qualitatively different form of evil from anything ever experienced before by humanity, or whether it only differs in its staggering proportions, has been debated for some time. There are those who believe that the Holocaust was a unique episode in the annals of history, one in which evil reached a qualitatively new level never before attained. "The uniqueness of the position of the Jews in the Nazi world," writes Holocaust historian Yehuda Bauer, "was that they had been singled out for the total destruction . . . simply because they had been born of three Jewish grandparents. In other words, for the first time in history a sentence of death had been pronounced on anyone guilty of having been born, and born of certain parents."[2] Others maintain that while it was quantitatively more tragic than other instances of evil or Jewish suffering, it was not qualitatively different. As theologian David Hartman wrote, "It is childish and often vulgar to attempt to demonstrate how the Jewish people's suffering is unique in history."[3] The Holocaust, this position would claim, is no more theologically perplexing or incomprehensible, and no less compelling, than the tragic, premature death of even a single child.

In whichever manner the student of the Holocaust approaches the subject, however, he ought to remember that just as the Torah prohibits us from uttering God's name in vain lest we trivialize it, so we dare not invoke the Holocaust gratuitously, callously, glibly, or inappropriately.

Although the Holocaust has a strong universal component, it should not be universalized to the point where its particularity is lost. Certainly, millions of Gentiles whose lives were equal in value to those of Jewish victims died at the hands of the Nazis. No attempt should be made to rob their deaths of meaning or to minimize the significance of their witness. And yet, the slaughter of the Jews was, somehow, radically different. Whether they were young or old, religious or irreligious; whether they were actively opposed to Nazism or silent in the face of it; even if they were converted Christians with but three Jewish grandparents—what mattered was the fact that they had "Jewish blood" in them. That alone made them subject to extermination. The Nazi aim was to purify and cleanse society of Jews, to bring about a "final solution" to what was perceived to be the Jewish problem. Jews were regarded as vermin contaminating the Aryan race and poisoning German society. Every single one of them had to be hunted down and annihilated.

The Holocaust raises many questions among people of faith and countless challenges to both Christians and Jews. We will explore a few of those issues.

Challenges to Christian and Jewish Faiths

I die peacefully, but not complacently; persecuted but not enslaved; embittered but not cynical; a believer but not a supplicant; a lover of God but no blind amensayer of His.

I have followed Him even when He rejected me. I have followed His commandments even when He has castigated me for it; I have loved Him and I love Him even when He hurls me to the earth, tortures me to death, makes me the object of shame and ridicule. . . . God of Israel . . . You have done everything to make me stop believing in You. Now lest it seem to You that You will succeed by these tribulations to drive me from the right path, I notify You, my God and God of my fathers that it will not avail You in the least! You may insult me. You may castigate me. You may take from me all that I cherish and hold dear in the world. You may torture me to death—I shall believe in You, I shall love You no matter what You do to test me!

And these are my last words to You, my wrathful God: nothing will avail You in the least. You have done everything to make me renounce You, to make me lose faith in You, but I die exactly as I have lived, a believer!

Hear, O Israel, the Lord our God, the Lord is One. Into your hands, O Lord, I consign my soul.[4]

The Holocaust poses a number of serious challenges to traditional Christian and Jewish theologies. Some of the most sacrosanct affirmations of both faiths are brought into radical questioning by those who have genuinely confronted the Holocaust. Is it possible, for example, for Christians and Jews to speak of God in the post-Auschwitz era in the same way that they did before? Can they ever again have perfect faith in a loving and caring God, or rather, as theologian Irving Greenberg has suggested, are only "moments of faith" now possible? Can they speak as they did earlier of God's love and concern for man and the world, and his guidance of the course of history while bearing witness to events reflecting the utter absence of such love, guidance, and concern? Can they continue to profess doctrines such as the covenant, chosenness, and divine providence? Can Judaism any longer affirm the doctrine of the inherent purity and goodness of man in the face of his manifest depravity? Is it still possible for Christians and Jews to believe in a God who is omniscient and omnipotent in light of his deafening silence? Can they speak of God's miraculous presence in 1948 when the State of Israel was born at the same time that they speak of his absence in Europe between 1938 and 1945? Does God indiscriminantly play peekaboo with man, sometimes here, sometimes not? Does he close his eyes to the world? Does he guide events? Can God stand up to the burdens of history? Can man?

No matter how we may work out these and other such vexing theological problems, one thing is clear—neither Christians nor Jews can ever be quite the same after Auschwitz as they were before. And neither can their faiths. Confronting the Holocaust admittedly involves great risk in that it forces the morally sensitive individual to reevaluate, and perhaps even alter, aspects of his or her most treasured values and sacrosanct religious convictions.

To confront the Holocaust is to begin a process of reflection and reappraisal without knowing where it will lead ultimately.

And yet, the devout person of faith feels compelled to embark on such a path, for he deeply believes in God and trusts that his divine goodness and grace can withstand such questioning. Such a person is not afraid to confront the burdens of history, even those of the Holocaust, for he is confident that his God can withstand the challenge and that his faith can be sustained despite his encountering such events. Like Abraham, whose deep, abiding trust in God prompted him to leave the security of his home and to go to an unknown land to which God promised to lead him, so those who confront the Holocaust today must be prepared to abandon the security and smugness of their lives of faith and to struggle trustingly toward a new stage of belief.

To confront the Holocaust genuinely is to open ourselves up to the inescapable, painful questions and anguishing challenges it poses. We cannot but face history, however, and we cannot but attempt to reconcile both God and man with its burdens. For only those who are willing to risk such insecurities can ever hope to become disciples of father Abraham and a source of blessing to "all the families of the earth." Only those who struggle with God and with man can merit the title "Israel," for they have "striven with God and with men, and have prevailed" (Gen. 32:28).

Intelligibility of Suffering

> Women carrying children were [always] sent with them to the crematorium. Children were of no labor value so they were killed. . . . When the extermination of the Jews in the gas chambers was at its height, orders were issued that children were to be thrown straight into the crematorium furnaces, or into a pit near the crematorium, without being gassed first.[5]

Jewish tradition is replete with sources indicating that suffering comes as a consequence of sin. The Torah, for example, posits this correlation on a number of occasions (see Deut.

8:19–20; 28:15–68), as do the prophets who often admonish Israel, warning her either to repent or to suffer a punishment (see Jer. 16:10–13; 22:8–9).

The rabbis in the talmudic period also accepted the cause-and-effect nexus between sin and suffering. They offered a variety of sins as explanations for the Jewish condition of exile and for the destruction of Jerusalem. One rabbinic view attributed the destruction of the first Jerusalem temple (586 B.C.E.) to the sins of murder, sexual licentiousness, robbery, and idol worship, and the destruction of the second temple (70 C.E.) to the sin of fratricide.

Another view maintained that the second temple was destroyed because the Jews did not bless the Torah before studying it. In other words, although they studied Torah, they did so more for its historical and ethical content than because they acknowledged it as the Word of God.

There is even a view that "Jerusalem was destroyed because the children did not attend school and instead loitered in the streets" (B.T., Shab. 119b). It is clear that for centuries Jews have believed that their suffering was neither haphazard nor coincidental, but was deliberately inflicted upon them by God as a consequence of their sins.

The rabbis offered a variety of other explanations for Jewish suffering in general. In one instance they suggested that it comes, paradoxically, as a result of their belovedness in the eyes of God, as reflected in Amos's statement, "You only have I known of all the families of the earth; therefore, I will punish you for all your iniquities" (Amos 3:2). According to this view, God is more demanding of Israel and exacting in his relationship with her than he is with the other nations of the world, who could not withstand a relationship guided by justice and who, unlike Israel, are in need of divine mercy.

Another rabbinic rationale for Israel's suffering is that God's love and mercy for the Jewish people is so great that he chooses to punish them immediately for their sins instead of letting the sins accumulate over generations. That way, God is not forced into punishing them all at once, in a measure they could not bear. The sins of other nations, however, are not punished immediately but are allowed to accumulate until they become so numerous that the nations cannot withstand the overwhelming severity of the punishment.

A further explanation is that just as righteous individuals are punished for their sins in this world but receive their just rewards in the next, so Israel as a whole will be amply rewarded in the next world, even though she may suffer in this earthly one. In whatever manner the rabbis rationalized Jewish suffering, there was widespread agreement that it was deserved and that it came as a punishment for sin. Nowhere is this correlation more clearly expressed than in the traditional holiday liturgy, which states, "Because of our sins we have been exiled from our land . . ." (This prayer was eliminated from the Reform prayer book.)

There is an additional strain of thought, however, that rejects the connection between sin and suffering, and that suggests instead that man cannot comprehend the reason for his suffering. The theodicy problem of why the righteous suffer and the wicked prosper has been raised repeatedly throughout Jewish history. When Abraham challenged God's intentions to destroy the entire city of Sodom, the righteous along with the wicked, and asked, "Shall not the Judge of all the earth do right?" (Gen. 18:25), in reality, say the rabbis, he was raising the theodicy problem. And when Moses asked to see the fullness of God's glory (Exod. 33:18), he was really asking, the rabbis claim, to learn the answer to that same profound mystery. God responded, however, by telling Moses that he would show him only his back, symbolizing that mortal man will never fully comprehend God's immutable ways. It was this idea that, in fact, prompted one talmudic rabbi to suggest that Moses was the author of the biblical Book of Job.

The entire Scroll of Job is devoted to the theme of suffering, and more particularly, to the classical theodicy problem. The story is a familiar one. Satan challenges God to take away all of

Job's possessions to prove that under such conditions Job would curse, not praise, God. God accepts the challenge, believing that whatever the circumstances, Job's faith and devotion would remain inviolable. He proceeds to take away Job's family, wealth, and good name. In spite of Job's anguish and terrible losses, however, he refuses to revile God and, instead, continues to serve him righteously. Friends come to console Job throughout his ordeal, urging him to examine his deeds and to repent from his sins, which were surely the root cause of his suffering. But Job refuses to accept either the rebuke of his friends or their assertion that his sins, which were few and relatively minor, warranted such severe retribution or that they were even the cause of his suffering in the first place. Finally, God himself appears, speaking from out of a whirlwind, and asks Job a series of rhetorical questions that demonstrate man's inability to probe the mysteries of God's ways and Creation. Ultimately, Job is vindicated from the accusation of his friends that it was his sins that brought on his suffering. (I have often felt that it was not so much the specific content of God's non-answer that finally brought Job solace but the fact that he heard God speaking to him and that he felt God touching his soul.)

The message of the Book of Job seems clear—the theodicy problem, and suffering in general, are humanly incomprehensible. Man cannot penetrate the divine mystery of why humans suffer. God and humankind will always be separated by an unbridgeable gulf. As Isaiah declared, "For my [God's] thoughts are not your thoughts, neither are your ways my ways, says the LORD" (55:8).

There appear to be two major strains of Jewish thought on the matter of suffering—one claiming that it comes as a punishment for sin and the other, disputing any cause-and-effect connection, insisting that mortal man simply cannot ever hope to comprehend suffering, since God's ways transcend human reason and understanding.

After the slaughter of almost two million innocent Jewish children in the Holocaust, the notion that there exists an intrinsic link between the sins of the people of Israel and their suffering, or that suffering is somehow deserved or meaningful in light of Jewish faith, has come into widespread disrepute. Jews today find it difficult, if not obscene, to profess that the suffering and death of those children was in any way a consequence of their sins. And while prayers linking suffering with sin are kept intact in the traditional Jewish prayer book, many Jews recite such prayers with great moral anguish and theological ambivalence. It has also become difficult after the Holocaust to believe in the kind of this-worldly *quid pro quo* scheme of reward and punishment that is described so categorically in the Bible (Deut. 11:13–21) and in the holiday Musaf service ("Because of our sins we have been exiled from our land"). The notion that suffering is in some way meaningful in light of our Jewish faith has become one of the foremost theological casualties of the Holocaust.

Just as the Indian caste system can lead to a fatalistic acceptance of one's lot and as the Buddhist ethos that all of life is *dukkha,* or "suffering," can lead to a negative view of man and the world, so the danger exists that if Jewish suffering were to be regarded as theologically intelligible, it might become fatalistically accepted as the natural lot of Jews. Instead, the Holocaust should jar us to the recognition that suffering is *not, necessarily,* the mark of the Jewish condition. Neither should suffering, in fact, necessarily be the mark of the human condition as a whole. It is man who can stop it from ever occurring.

Man can even play a crucial role in mitigating natural disasters such as storms, earthquakes, floods, and famine, as well. For if man were to direct his monies and energies toward researching cures and causes instead of toward destructive or less worthy purposes, he might find a way to eliminate such ailments and disasters, too. The Talmud states that there is no ailment for which there is no cure already built into the structure of Creation, awaiting man's discovery.

After the Holocaust we must confront ourselves not only with the question of "Where was God?" but even, more important, with the question of "Where was man?" For it was man who administered the suffering, and it was man who had the power to prevent it. The slaughter of Jews was not inevitable; their suffering was not a given; their wretched plight could have been alleviated, and indeed averted, since it was evil men who imposed it in the first place. We dare not forget that there were righteous Gentiles who risked their lives to save Jews, and who demonstrated by such acts that the Jewish agony could have been mitigated, if not altogether avoided. In fact, it is those who accept suffering as the divinely predestined Jewish condition who also would be inclined to be passive and acquiescent in the face of such suffering rather than to intercede and oppose it. *Acceptance* of the inevitability of Jewish suffering invariably leads to the *expectation* of such suffering, so that if and when it actually occurs, it is regarded as comprehensible and, indeed, a confirmation of the need for Jews to suffer. *To accept Jewish suffering either as inevitable or as meaningful in light of one's faith is to make oneself and one's God a party to the infliction of that suffering.*

Christians today should be especially wary of linking the suffering of others, particularly that of the Jews, with sinfulness, since such views have historically contributed to the infliction of such suffering. It should never be forgotten that the real sinners are those who inflict suffering upon others, not the innocent victims of it. Moreover, it is important to note the talmudic insistence that while we may attribute our own personal suffering to our sins, we may not say this about other people's suffering (B.T., B. Metzia 58b).

Certain Christian writers and best-selling novels speak of the creation of the State of Israel as the fulfillment of biblical prophecies signaling the imminent attack by Russia and Arab nations on Israel, which will result in a Holocaust of Jews, one even more devastating than that of World War II.

What is disturbing about such thinking is that it was a similar type of theological reasoning that entered into European consciousness centuries ago and that, many scholars would agree, ultimately contributed to the outbreak of the Holocaust. The very founders of the church implanted many of these ideas into Western civilization with devastating results.

Early Christian literature and theology often found complete religious justification for, and even the *necessity of,* Jewish suffering by rooting such views in their interpretation of the Bible, "God's word." Yet, while Scripture may very well be divine and intrinsically infallible, it is man who interprets it and who can read into it all sorts of *a priori* viewpoints. History has demonstrated that man can justify virtually any action by abusing and manipulating the word of God. Even religion can be transformed into an instrument for idolatry. Jews have experienced inquisitions, expulsions, forced conversions, pogroms, blood libels, and *autos-da-fé* at the hands of Christians who defended their actions by pointing to Scripture. Jewish suffering was comprehensible in light of the Christian faith; it was a sign of Jews' divine accursedness for having crucified the Christians' Lord, Jesus Christ. After all, did not the (Christian) Bible say that at the time of the Crucifixion *the Jews* declared, "His blood be on us and on our children" (Matt. 27:25)? Jews were expected to suffer. Indeed, it was Jewish suffering that shaped the theological framework within which many Christians viewed the mystery of the continued existence of the Jewish people. After all, they reasoned, if Jews were to remain alive in this world while maintaining their ongoing testimony of their rejection of Christ, it was to be in a state of degradation so that all people would recognize the supremacy of Christianity and the triumph of the church. For centuries, the suffering, debased Jew was the only kind of Jew much Christian theology had room for.

Such theological reasoning, and particularly the deicide accusation that Jews killed Christ and were therefore to suffer eternally, contributed to a vicious cycle of violence against Jews. As the Jews increasingly suffered, the theological arguments citing their need to suffer became more meaningful and convincing. And the more suffering, humiliation, and degradation Jews were forced to endure, the more convinced their tormentors became of the righteousness of their cause and of their obligation to administer even further suffering. It should be recalled that while popular images such as the "wandering" and "suffering" Jew may have been historically accurate and even theologically grounded in the Bible (see Isa. 53), such views presuppose the existence of those who forced these conditions upon the Jews.

For a Christian to affirm today a theological paradigm that justifies Jewish suffering as a sign either of their accursedness or special chosenness in the eyes of God is to set up a system that leads to the very administering of such suffering or, at best, to passivity and nonintercession in the face of it. To espouse a "theology of expectation" of further, more catastrophic Jewish suffering is to set up the dynamics that could, God forbid, serve as a catalyst to bring about such an event. In light of the Holocaust, to claim that Jewish suffering is intelligible and meaningful within the Christian faith or that it somehow fulfills biblical prophecies calling for such suffering is to justify murder, blaspheme God, and pervert his sacred word. To espouse a theology that even indirectly leads either to the administering of suffering or to passivity and acquiescence in the face of it is to implicate God himself in the crucifixion of man millions of times over.

Maimonides has written that just as a piece of metal shaped in the form of a horseshoe must be bent to the opposite extreme before it can be made straight, so man must go to the opposite extreme in rooting out sin from his personality before he can arrive at the ideal middle road. Humankind's paramount response to the absolute evil of the Holocaust must, therefore, be to bend to its opposite—extreme compassion and activism on behalf of good. As Rabbi Kook, the late chief rabbi of Israel, once wrote, since the temple was destroyed because of fratricide and senseless hate, it will only be restored when we demonstrate their opposites—senseless love and compassion. Today, therefore, it should be the Christian and Jewish obligation to categorically reject the theological strain of thought present in both traditions that suggests that it is the Jews' sins that bring upon them suffering or that the Jews are predestined to be the world's eternal suffering servants. Nothing less than such a radical response is sufficient to ensure that such a Holocaust will never happen again.

Untermensch vs. "In the Image of God"

In Treblinka there was a man named Yankel Wiernik, a carpenter. During the uprising, together with those who participated in it, he managed to escape and he wrote his story. "Dear reader," he says, ". . . I who saw the doom of three generations must keep on living for the sake of the future. The world must be told of what happened.

"Between 450 and 500 persons were crowded into a chamber measuring 125 square feet in Treblinka. Parents carried their children in the vain hope of saving them from death. On the way to their doom they were pushed and beaten with rifle butts and gas pipes. Dogs were set on them, barking, biting and tearing them. It lasted a short while. Then the doors were shut tightly with a bang. Twenty-five minutes later everybody was dead and they stood lifeless; there being no free space, they just leaned against each other. They no longer shouted because the thread of their lives had been broken. They no longer had any needs or desires. Mothers held their children tightly in their arms. There were no more friends, no more enemies. There was no jealousy. All were equal. There was no longer any beauty or ugliness, for all looked yellow from the gas. There were no longer any rich or poor. All were equal. And why all this? That is the question I keep asking myself. My life is hard, very hard. I must live to tell the world about all this."[6]

Holocaust scholars note that in the early stages of the geno-cide, when Jews were rounded up and shot, Nazi morale became seriously impaired. How was it possible for the most cultured of Western societies to be transformed into one that systematically murdered millions of human beings for no rea-son other than that they were Jews? The Nazis, after all, were a civilized and cultured people. For them to wantonly slaughter innocent and defenseless men, women, and children in cold blood must have taken a great mental toll. The killing task became so gruesome and repugnant that soldiers began to defy orders from authorities. The extent of the revulsion toward the mass killing on the part of those soldiers actually engaged in it soon reached crisis proportion, threatening the integrity of the entire genocidal program. To resolve this crisis of disobedience, the Nazi leaders created physical and psychological distance between the killers and their victims. They were able to accom-plish this by first sending the Jews away to concentration camps where a select group of hard-core "experts" would methodically conduct the slayings. That way the vast majority would be spared the gruesome task and responsibility for conducting the slaughter.

Second, this psychological distance was accomplished by propagating the idea that Jews were *untermenschen,* or "sub-humans," and were the single most corrupting feature of European society. While it may be difficult for civilized people to murder human beings, killing animals or subhumans would be far more palatable. The Jews were not only portrayed as untermenschen, they were transformed into the essence of satanic evil and painted as devils with supernatural powers capable of corrupting the purity of the Aryan race; Jews were like vermin infecting the entire European civilization. To reinforce this stereo-type, Jews were placed into the most degrading conditions to make them feel like animals, or at least appear as such.

Thus, the Holocaust occurred because the Nazis became convinced that Jews were untermenschen, not human beings, whose lives were of no value. It stands to reason that a similar

Holocaust of Jews or any other group could be avoided if we came to perceive all people not as detached objects of utilitarian value, but as human beings, created "in the image of God," of absolute worth by their very existence. To destroy man is, in a very real sense, to destroy a part of God that is manifest in the world. To take responsibility for the welfare of man is to bring the day of salvation that much closer. In the nuclear age in which we live today, the Holocaust must serve as a warning to humankind, alerting him to his power to bring the entire world and history of civilization to an irreversible end.

Questioning Authority

> The basic factor in the Ghetto's lack of preparation for armed resistance was psychological. . . . We fell victim to our faith in mankind, our belief that humanity had set limits to the degradation and persecution of one's fellow man.[7]

When the prosecution at the Nuremberg trials conducted after World War II asked the Nazi prisoners why they committed such horrible atrocities, their response invariably was that they were just following orders. Some twenty-five years later, American soldiers, defending their role in the incidents at My Lai, offered a similar rationale. The fact is that soldiers are inculcated with the idea of obeying orders from their superiors. Indeed, we are all taught to respect authority and to abide by the law. What is so disturbing is that people tend to blindly follow orders from authority figures, particularly ones wearing official uniforms, such as policemen, doctors, or priests. This was demonstrated rather dramatically and conclusively by the Milgram scientific experiments on obedience conducted at Yale University.[8] In the study, a man posing as a doctor told an unwitting subject to administer electric shocks to a man sitting behind a glass wall each time he answered a question incorrectly. The subject could see the man and hear his feigned cries;

in reality, the man was not being shocked but was part of the experimental team. The study found that despite the fact that the subjects genuinely believed that the actors were being hurt, the majority of them were willing to continue administering what they thought were high-voltage shock currents at the urging of the doctor conducting the experiment. Even after the actor pretended to fall into a state of unconsciousness from the shock treatment, there were many who continued to administer shock. The study revealed that even responsible and decent people were willing to inflict pain and even death upon others, against their better judgment, due to their trust of an authority figure who reassured them by his status that what they were doing was all right.

It is revealing to note that the closer in proximity the subject was to the conductor of the experiment, the more inclined he was to abide by the experimenter's orders to administer shocks. Conversely, the closer the proximity between him and the actor being shocked, the more likely he was to refuse to abide by the orders to administer shock. Physical distance from a subject apparently plays a major role in creating psychological detachment from him, as well. Thus, people are inclined to be sympathetic toward those to whom they are closer, and more likely to inflict harm upon those distant from them.

While society must obviously be based on a healthy respect for the law and on obedience to authority, it should be equally obvious that we must learn to question the moral resoluteness of authority figures and the moral integrity of their orders. We ought not to obey authority figures blindly. We ought to obey them, not because of their titles, degrees, or uniforms, but because of their superior knowledge and experience, and the ethical correctness of their views. We ought also to be morally discerning and resolute enough to disobey laws and orders that go against our conscience. This is a radical, albeit necessary, solution. None other will suffice after the Holocaust.

That people in Western society tend to feel alienated, estranged, and detached from each other is well-known. So is the fact that as a result of those feelings, people often are not inclined to come to the aid of someone in distress. This pervasive "bystander apathy" was at work in the tragic case of Kitty Genovese who was raped and murdered on a New York street in 1964 while dozens of people hearing her cries for help did nothing to intervene. No one even bothered to call the police. The fact that the bystanders could easily have alerted the authorities anonymously but chose not to suggests that more was at work than a fear of becoming involved.

In fact, it was the pervasiveness of these very same forces that enabled German society to be swept away by Nazism. Hard-core Nazi anti-Semites were able to rely not only on the widespread, deeply ingrained antipathy toward Jews, but also on basically good people's passive acceptance of and indifference to the drastic measures the Nazis were taking. The Nazi seizure of power proved Edmund Burke's statement that the only thing necessary for the triumph of evil is for good men to do nothing. The Holocaust demonstrated that silence and lack of involvement in realpolitik can inevitably lead to the triumph of evil and injustice.

The Torah presents a fundamentally different model of how humans should interact in society. When Cain killed Abel, God asked, "Where is Abel your brother?" (Gen. 4:9). The rabbis point out that God, of course, knew what had happened to Abel but that he posed the question so that Cain would confront himself and take responsibility for his actions.

Underlying God's question was the notion that man is responsible for the welfare of his fellow man. He is his brother's keeper! The Torah bids us to come to the aid even of an animal suffering under a heavy burden. The prophets stressed this same theme repeatedly, although none perhaps as eloquently as Isaiah, who posited that man's primary duty is "to loose the bonds of wickedness, to undo the thongs of the yoke, to let the oppressed go free, and to break every yoke . . . to share your bread with the hungry, and bring the homeless poor into your house; when you see the naked, to cover him, and not to hide yourself from your own flesh" (58:67).

One of the few anecdotes emanating from the Holocaust tells of two Jews who were lined up against a wall, about to be shot. One Jew began kicking, screaming, and cursing at the Nazis. The other, turning to him, said, "Quiet, you might get them angry and who knows what they'll do to us then!" In fact, silence and passivity can be blasphemous and obscene, while action and resistance can be a divine obligation. Arthur Morse writes, "If genocide is to be prevented in the future, we must understand how it happened in the past—not in terms of the killers and the killed, but of the bystander."[9] Hitler proceeded slowly and cautiously with his genocidal plans, constantly testing the nations of the free world and evaluating their response at each step of the way. What he found was little, if any, worldwide outrage or criticism. It was that silence that convinced him that Jewish lives were expendable and that no one would act to save the Jews from annihilation. He was even convinced that the world would, in the end, thank him for ridding it of Jews.

When Hitler began killing the infirm and handicapped in his euthanasia program there was an immediate, massive demonstration of public outrage which forced him to stop. Dare we consider the possibility that had there been a similar, spontaneous demonstration of overwhelming revulsion to the murder of Jews, the Holocaust might not have taken place? Dare we not?

Martyrdom and Power

> Thus says the LORD:
> "A voice is heard in Ramah,
>   lamentation and bitter weeping.
> Rachel is weeping for her children;
>   she refuses to be comforted for her children,
>   because they are not."
>   (Jeremiah 31:15)

When the Roman emperor Vespasian destroyed the second temple, he granted the Jewish leader Rabbi Yochanan ben

Zakkai his request that the village of Yavneh be spared from destruction and designated as a site for a *yeshiva,* or "seminary." While ben Zakkai's request may very well have saved Pharisaic Judaism and enabled Judaism as a whole to survive, it also established a pattern of helplessness and powerlessness, which would characterize the Jewish condition for centuries to come. Indeed, from the time of the destruction of the second temple in 70 C.E. until the establishment of the State of Israel in 1948, Jews have been a people devoid of power.

Throughout their long exile, Jews have lived at the good graces and, often, at the capricious whim of other nations. At times they were permitted to participate in the economic, social, and cultural life of society, at times they were not. Like ben Zakkai, they were willing to relinquish their quest for power and to assume a low social profile in the hope of finding a haven in which to live and to practice their ancestral faith. For the most part, however, this was not to be. Jews have suffered inquisitions, *autos-da-fé,* ghettos, pogroms, blood libels, and wholesale slaughter. They were expelled at one time or another from virtually every country in "Christian Europe." Their fate was determined by the fact that they were at the total mercy of the host countries and utterly powerless to alter their situation. Even the theological disputations in which Jews were forced to engage during the Middle Ages did not provide them with a genuine opportunity to wield power or to demonstrate the veracity of their faith. Whether they won or lost the debates, the tragic results remained the same—the persecution of the local Jewish community.

It was Jewish powerlessness that made their persecution possible. It was that condition that made them attractive targets and that may even have invited their oppression, although one must take care not to ascribe blame to the innocent victims. Tragically, often the only element of power Jews wielded over their destinies lay in their freedom to decide whether to give up their faith or to suffer martyrdom. Jewish martyrdom became so common that, in time, the theological doctrine of *kiddush hashem,* or "sanctification of God's name," became associated more with acts of sanctification through death than through life.

It should be abundantly clear that powerlessness, combined with an absolute reliance on the good will of others, including God, has a rather poor track record in Jewish consciousness and experience. For it was precisely those factors that made the Holocaust possible. Jews, along with many Christians, have developed a new understanding of God, history, and the divine-human relationship after that conflagration.

Jews today have overwhelmingly resolved—often unconsciously—to reject the deeply ingrained, centuries-old tradition of sanctifying God's name through death and passive acts of martyrdom. Instead, they have collectively resolved to hallow God's name by surviving and by leading a sanctified life in this, as yet, unredeemed world. No longer will Jews accept martyrdom as a religious ideal. They have vowed to live! Like the psalmist long ago, Jews today collectively declare, "I shall not die, but I shall live, and recount the deeds of the LORD" (Ps. 118:17).

Noted philosopher and Holocaust survivor, Emil Fackenheim, has written that a six-hundred-fourteenth commandment is now incumbent upon Jews (the traditional rabbinic view is that the Torah contains 613 commandments): to survive and not grant Hitler a posthumous victory. Hitler sought to destroy the entire Jewish people. The Jewish response must be to live and rob him of that victory. Jews have solemnly vowed never to allow such a catastrophe to recur. Never, ever, again. Failure to appreciate fully the intensity of this Jewish conviction portends the failure to understand either the contemporary Jew or his faith.

This Jewish commitment to survive, however, also means that Jews must be willing to reenter the arena of power after having been without it for almost two thousand years. Jews have overwhelmingly decided in favor of such a course. Those living in the State of Israel, the embodiment of this collective

Jewish spirit, have exemplified the Jews' struggle to secure power in order to survive. Jews are preeminently aware that the difference between Entebbe in 1976 and Auschwitz in 1943 is that in the case of the former, they were able to exercise power and strength of will. As a result, dozens of Jewish lives were saved.

Jews continue to abhor war. They remain uncomfortable even with their moral and responsible exercise of power. Their pledge to survive, however, has required them to take up arms and, at times, bring bloodshed both upon themselves and upon their enemies seeking to destroy them. Men who never raised a hand in violence against others, of necessity, became fighter pilots. Fathers, who perhaps more than all others appreciated the value of human life, became paratroopers and tank operators.

Israelis are often characterized as having a "Masada complex." (Masada was the fortress where the Jewish Zealots made their last stand against the Romans in 73 C.E. and where they committed mass suicide rather than succumb to the Romans.) In truth, their collective psyche might better be described as "Samsonite." For like the biblical Samson, Israeli Jews today are prepared to sacrifice their lives through acts of resistance, not through passive martyrdom. In the nuclear age in which we live, such a "Samsonite complex" is a very dangerous thing, indeed. It can, in a very real sense, bring down the whole house.

American Jews have also resolved to enter the realm of power, albeit in a different manner than their Israeli coreligionists. They are deeply conscious of the fact that while they were vocal during the Holocaust, they had neither the political resolve nor clout to affect change in United States policy.

American Jews learned of their need for political, economic, and social power. They recognized that it was those forces that bring about greater freedom, autonomy, and control over their destiny. They also realized their vulnerability without power and the ineffectiveness of pleas based solely on good will and not backed by organized muscle.

The new American Jewish political assertiveness on behalf of oppressed world Jewry, even their activism in lobbying for such things as the sale of guns, planes, and bombs to Israel, stems from their determination to survive and, out of necessity, to enter the realm of power. For, while bombs may destroy and war may seem like hell, these necessary evils can also help ensure the preservation of the Jewish people and civilization. Post-Holocaust Jews have learned that while power can corrupt and absolute power can corrupt absolutely, as Irving Greenberg has noted, "Absolute powerlessness corrupts even more."[10]

This new worldview admittedly involves great risk because it can so readily be abused. For while the possession of power has many positive consequences (most notably, the ability to exert control over one's destiny), it also frequently carries with it many negative ones (such as the immoral use of power and the insatiable quest for more).

It is easy for a society to move from one that "supports a military" to one that "is militaristic"; from one that hates war to one that makes war; from one that uses power sparingly, responsibly, and only when absolutely necessary, to one that is intoxicated by power and that wields it constantly. Nevertheless, Jews have chosen to risk these dangers, believing that they have no choice if they are to survive. The real test of their ethical character comes now that they do possess power.

One of the greatest challenges facing the Jewish people today is whether they can avoid the abuses that often accompany power and strength. Golda Meir, the late prime minister of Israel who was preeminently conscious both of the pitfalls and necessities of power, once remarked that while Jews might some day forgive the Arabs for killing their sons and daughters, it would be much harder for them ever to forgive the Arabs for making them into killers. Such is the toll Jews have, of necessity, had to pay. She also stated, however, that if the choice for Israel is between exercising power and being alive and unpopular among the nations of the world, or being destroyed and lauded, Israel will unequivocally choose the former. If the choice for Jews in this, as yet, unredeemed and imperfect world is either not to wield power and to be slaughtered, or to assume the risks and responsibilities of power and to survive, Jews have unanimously resolved to accept the latter. For survival is itself a moral act and for the post-Holocaust Jew it is also his religious obligation.

In one of his sermons, Protestant thinker Reinhold Niebuhr said, "Love without power simply surrenders the world to power without love. How to make power express love, and love humanize power, is the distinctive task of the church of Christ for the next hundred years." It is also one of the most compelling challenges facing Jews today. For the first time in centuries Jews can be judged, not by the way they have suffered under the abuse of power by others, but by the manner in which they themselves wield power. And therein lies the profound test to Jewish life today.

Failure of a Universalist Ethos

> I pinched my face. Was I still alive? Was I awake? I could not believe it. How could it be possible for them to burn people, children, and for the world to keep silent? No, none of this could be true. It was a nightmare. . . . Soon I should wake with a start, my heart pounding, and find myself back in the bedroom of my childhood, among my books.[11]

Nineteenth-century Jewish reactions to the seductive call of modernity and emancipation, and to the newfound Jewish acceptance in Western Gentile society, varied tremendously. Some Jews dropped out of Jewish life entirely and chose to assimilate into secular nationalistic culture instead. Some converted to Christianity, mainly to advance their social and economic stations in life. Still others continued to affirm their Jewishness through the new movements of Reform, Conservative, and neo-Orthodox Judaism. What was common to virtually all the Jewish responses was their rootedness in a strong optimistic belief in the equality of man and universality of the human condition.

The Jews' willingness to embrace such a universalist ethos, however, often came at the expense of their essential Jewish character. Many Jews willingly shed aspects of their traditions and distinctive Jewish traits in order to become fully accepted by mainstream Gentile society. The pressures upon Jews to accommodate the mores of Gentile society became so intense that even committed Jews tended to subscribe to the pithy advice of the time: "Be a person in your outside life but a Jew in your tent."

Nineteenth-century western European Jews more than repaid their debt to society for giving them their freedom by becoming proud, loyal citizens of the countries in which they lived. Jews prided themselves in being first and foremost good nationalists, referring to themselves, for example, as Germans or Frenchmen "of the Mosaic (or Israelite) persuasion," but rarely openly calling themselves Jews. Most of them opposed Zionism, which they felt conflicted with their allegiance to their homeland. Reform Judaism even denied the concept of Jewish nationhood entirely.

These and other such categorically optimistic and universal worldviews based on the goodness of man and the progressiveness of modernity were effectively shattered by the events of the Holocaust. After all, the Holocaust was unleashed by Germany, the most enlightened, civilized, and progressive European nation of its time. The Holocaust demonstrated rather persuasively the dangers of giving ultimacy even to (potentially) fine values such as universalism, nationalism, and the traditional Jewish doctrine of the goodness of man.

It was precisely their endorsement of a universalist view of the world, of the oneness of humanity and of the nobility of the German spirit, that blinded Jews to the unfolding disaster and led them to believe that a Holocaust could never happen, certainly not in Germany. Man's strong inclination to sin was tragically forgotten. Highly decorated German Jews who had fought for the fatherland in World War I, secular, universalist Jews who denied their Jewishness, Jews who had converted to Christianity, even those who had only one Jewish grandparent, Jews with a strong German heritage and nationalist loyalties— none could escape their Jewish identities; none could flee from their common destiny. They all met a radically particularistic death at the hands of the Nazis—as Jews.

It was not until 1967, when the Arab-Israeli Six-Day War again threatened the survival of millions of Jews that even American Jews became fully comfortable asserting their distinctively Jewish causes and identities. Then Jews felt abandoned and deserted by the world—again—despite their finest efforts at a dialogue with their non-Jewish friends and neighbors over the years. The deafening silence they met with at their critical time of need, when their very survival was again at stake, prompted most Jews to utterly reject a universalist ethos which was not rooted in Jewish particularism and balanced by self-reliance and unabashed Jewish pride.

Jewish pride and identity soared in the aftermath of the stunning Israeli military victory in 1967. Many secular and assimilated Jews became caught up with their Jewishness for the first time in their lives, and they became concerned with issues such as the security of Israel and world Jewry. The organized Jewish community reflected this shift in Jewish values and consciousness by likewise turning inward and becoming more deeply and aggressively involved in narrower Jewish agendas.

The challenge facing Jews today remains how to balance their belief in the universality and oneness of the human condition with their commitment to the survival of a distinctive Jewish faith and peoplehood. While Jews have shifted in pendulum fashion between these two poles, they have moved much closer toward the ideal balance in recent years. Evidence of this can be found in their renewed involvement in issues such as world hunger, while at the same time maintaining unflinching support for narrower Jewish concerns such as Israel, Russian

Jewry, the Jewish poor and aged, and so on. The rabbis in the Talmud expressed this ideal best: "If I am not for myself who will be for me? But if I am only for myself what am I? And if not now, when?" (Ethics of the Fathers, 1:14).

Duty to Support Israel

When the LORD restored the fortunes of Zion,
we were like those who dream.
(Ps. 126:1)

Of the many Jewish responses to the Holocaust, the obligation to support the State of Israel is perhaps both the most widely accepted and the most deeply felt. And while American Jews support Israel for biblical, historical, political, moral, geo-strategical, and other reasons, their love for her transcends them all; their commitment to her survival is absolute. Israel is the symbol of the contemporary Jewish resolve to live after having been tormented and persecuted for centuries. She epitomizes the Jewish rebirth as a dynamic living people.

In addition to the staggering loss of life in the Holocaust, the annihilation of six million Jews—one-third of the entire Jewish population—brought centuries of European Jewish civilization to an abrupt and irreversible end. Nazi leader Adolf Eichmann defiantly exclaimed that although the Nazis were unsuccessful in destroying all the world's Jews, he would go to his grave laughing, convinced that the Jews could never recover from the Holocaust's devastating blow to their life center. For among the dead were 80 percent of the world's Torah and Talmud scholars, students, and teachers who were alive in 1937. The magnitude and intensity of suffering threatened the remaining Jewish community with radical despair. Remarkably, the remnants of that cataclysm had the strength and determination to rebuild their lives. A national Jewish homeland became the cornerstone of their dreams; its national anthem, the *Hatikvah,* meaning "the hope," became their lifeblood. They dreamed and pledged, in the words of the Hatikvah, "to be a free nation in our homeland, the land of Zion and Jerusalem."

Although Jews have not yet fully grasped the implications of Israel's rebirth upon their lives, many deeply believe that the events of our day, particularly the ingathering of Holocaust survivors and other Jews from all four corners of the world into a free, democratic Jewish state, signal the beginning of the world's redemption. Indeed, the Israeli chief rabbinate has introduced a prayer characterizing Israel as the "beginning of the sprouting of our redemption" into the weekly Shabbat prayer service. Like Ezekiel, Jews in this generation gazed into the valley of death and saw only dry, lifeless bones (Ezek. 37). They, too, asked, "Will these bones ever live?" And behold, a miracle—the bones were revived, Israel came into being, and her people came into life reborn.

The State of Israel is not merely some political entity or geographical area of casual interest for Jews. Her existence as a free, sovereign, and secure nation is the most central affirmation Jews have salvaged from the rubble of history and from the ashes of Auschwitz. The existence of Israel goes to the very core of Jewish identity today. Not surprisingly, Jews have backed up their convictions with an almost obsessive activism on her behalf. They have collectively declared, "For Zion's sake I will not keep silent, and for Jerusalem's sake I will not rest . . ." (Isa. 62:1). For Jews believe very deeply that if the Holocaust, indeed, imposes a new six-hundred-fourteenth commandment upon them to survive, it is the State of Israel that will ensure that survival.

A delicate but powerful analogy can be drawn between the Jew's commitment to Israel and the Christian's commitment to Christ. Just as Christians affirm that an indissoluble link exists between Jesus' death and resurrection, so Jews today profess that an inexorable tie links them in their death at Auschwitz and their rebirth in Jerusalem. And just as the bond between death and resurrection shapes the very backbone of the Christian identity, so it constitutes the driving force of the contemporary Jewish psyche.

Israel offers the Jew redemptive hope after having been engulfed by death, darkness, and despair. She represents the Jewish Easter Sunday! Just as Christians mark that solemn day by proclaiming, "Behold, Christ has risen," so Jews declare, *"am Yisrael chai"*—the Jewish people has arisen again and continues to live! Just as Christians cannot sever Good Friday from Easter Sunday, so Jews cannot speak only of death without celebrating its concomitant reality, the resurrection of their people through Israel. And just as the theological nexus linking Good Friday with Easter Sunday shapes the character of Christians and constitutes the *sine qua non* of the Christian faith, so Israel in the post-Holocaust Jewish mindset embodies the totality of Jewish hopes for survival and constitutes the quintessence of all Jewish affirmations.

While it is blasphemous to link the two events in such a manner as to regard the State of Israel as some sort of divine recompense or atonement for the Holocaust, the fact that Jews went from the darkest and deepest abyss to the greatest, brightest heights in a matter of a few years cannot be casually ignored. The road to Jerusalem was paved with ashes from the Holocaust. For many Jews, Israel is God's final chance to redeem himself from his breach of the covenant in the Holocaust.

While there is no answer to the Holocaust, Israel enables the Jew at least to bear the burden of its agony. As the Bible states, "For the LORD has comforted his people, he has redeemed Jerusalem" (Isa. 52:9). Heschel poetically noted that after the Holocaust, Jews were mourning widows. However, after Israel, Jews became brides again.

Condemning anti-Semitism, feeling remorse for past incidents of persecution against Jews, and shedding tears over the tragedy to befall the Jews in the Holocaust—such feelings are regarded by Jews as admirable but insufficient Christian responses to the history of anti-Semitism culminating in the Holocaust. A strong commitment backed up by action toward ensuring the present and future survival of Israel and the Jewish people is also essential. Christians must be especially sensitive not to sever the link that Jews themselves make between death and resurrection, granting Jews a condition of suffering and affliction but not of life reborn. Supporting the beleaguered State of Israel after the Holocaust is one of the most profound acts of friendship Christians can extend toward Jews. Franklin Littell, noted Christian historian, expressed this idea best when he stated:

> The threat of a Second Holocaust (the destruction of Israel), the pressure upon Russian Jewry to assimilate and vanish, the ideological attacks of Neo-Nazis and Communists and some self-styled "liberal Christians" upon the Jews' continued survival, make Israel—the people, the land, the state—the focal point of present debate. It is not possible to love a "Spiritual Israel" and hate the earthly Israel. It is not possible to honor and obey the God of Abraham, Isaac and Jacob and wish evil to the Jewish people. To lay it on the line: it is not possible to side with those who seek Jerusalem's destruction and be numbered a faithful Christian. It was not possible in the Germany of the Third Reich, and it is not possible today in America.[12]

Jews believe very deeply that to turn one's back on Israel and the Jewish people is to rebel against God and to fail to heed his harkening cry calling out from the *sheol* of dry bones of Auschwitz to ensure Jewish survival! To abandon Israel—the nation and people—is to desert both God and the Bible. Christians, no less than Jews, must declare, *"am Yisrael chai veyichyeh"*—"the Jewish people lives and shall live." They, no less than Jews, must pray for the peace of Jerusalem and for the welfare of its inhabitants.

The Holocaust was one of the most shattering events ever experienced by the Jewish people, perhaps *the* most shattering—both in terms of its magnitude and its lasting impact on Jewish life and psyche. Whether it be the State of Israel's policies and obsession for security, Jewish anxieties over the eruption of incidents of anti-Semitism, Jewish attitudes toward non-Jews, the Jewish religion today, indeed, Jewish life as a whole—all are equally incomprehensible to the outsider when not viewed through the value-transforming prism of the seminal Holocaust event.

Conclusion

The primary imperative Jews have elicited from the Holocaust is to live, and never to allow a similar Holocaust to occur again. This resolve has prompted them to grapple with the issue of the moral uses and abuses of power as they have not grappled with it for nearly two thousand years. The Holocaust has also forced Jews to struggle with many fundamental doctrines and affirmations that have guided Jewish life for generations. Nothing less than the very existence of the covenant with God has been brought into question. Remarkably, indeed, miraculously, Jews and Judaism have survived the cataclysm and have even undergone a renewal and rejuvenation. Jews remain resolute in bearing the message of God and in serving as his witnesses in this, as yet, unredeemed world. They continue to pray, hope, and work for the coming of the Messiah and salvation of the world.

The primary imperative to be elicited by Christians from the Holocaust is equally as compelling as is that of the Jews—to expunge any and all traces of anti-Semitism and anti-Judaism from their midst. Christians no less than Jews must struggle with their traditions and cardinal affirmations in light of the challenges posed by the Holocaust. They, too, are divinely obligated to ensure Jewish survival and to prevent a future Holocaust.

In truth, any lessons to be derived from the Holocaust actually transcend any parochial perspectives that might separately guide either the Christian or Jewish communities. We live today in a nuclear reality. Now, more than ever before, it is imperative that humankind break the vicious cycle of war and violence, and learn to live together in peace. The Holocaust must shock us into a new sobriety. It must serve as an alarm signaling man to alter fundamentally his ways and outlook. For whatever else the Holocaust may be, it is a warning—perhaps humankind's last—to ensure his very existence.

Chapter 7

ISRAEL:
THE DAWN OF REDEMPTION

I have loved you with an everlasting love;
    therefore I have continued my faithfulness to you.
Again I will build you, and you shall be built,
    O virgin Israel! . . .
For there shall be a day when watchmen will call
    in the hill country of Ephraim:
"Arise, and let us go up to Zion,
    to the LORD our God."

For thus says the LORD:
"Sing aloud with gladness for Jacob,
    and raise shouts for the chief of the nations;
proclaim, give praise, and say,
    'The LORD has saved his people,
    the remnant of Israel.'
Behold, I will bring them from the north country,
    and gather them from the farthest parts of the earth,
among them the blind and the lame,
    the woman with child and her who is in travail, together;
    a great company, they shall return here.
With weeping they shall come,
    and with consolations I will lead them back,
I will make them walk by brooks of water,
    in a straight path in which they shall not stumble;

for I am a father to Israel.
>   and Ephraim is my first-born."
Thus says the LORD:
"Keep your voice from weeping,
>   and your eyes from tears;
for your work shall be rewarded,
>   says the LORD,
>   and they shall come back from the land of the enemy.
There is hope for your future,
>   says the LORD,
>   and your children shall come back to their own country.
(Jeremiah 31:3-4, 6-9, 16-17)

Jewish Bonds with the Land

The Jewish attachment to Israel is a profound one, dating back almost four thousand years to the time when God told Abraham to leave the comfort and security of his homeland, Ur Kasdim, and to go "to the land that I will show you" (Gen. 12:1). Abraham had such great faith and trust in God that he left his home and community, reassured by God's promise that ". . . I will bless you, and make your name great, so that you will be a blessing. I will bless those who bless you, and him who curses you I will curse; and by you all the families of the earth shall bless themselves" (Gen. 12:2-3). Israel is known by a number of different names. The Bible alternately refers to it as Canaan, Eretz Yisrael, Zion, or simply as *ha-aretz,* meaning "the land," as a sign of its belovedness and significance. It is "the Holy Land."

As part of the divine covenant with Abraham, God promised that he and his descendants would inherit the land of Israel as an eternal possession. "On that day the LORD made a covenant with Abram, saying: 'To your descendants I give this land . . .'" (Gen. 15:18). The rabbis point out that the term *natati,* or "I give," is in the past tense, implying that God had already given the land to the Jews at some earlier time. Yet, this is the first record of such a promise. They, therefore, suggest that God had set aside this land for his people, Israel, already at the time that he created the world.[1]

The Torah elaborates on this covenantal agreement between God and Abraham. "And I will establish my covenant between me and you and your descendants after you throughout their generations for an everlasting covenant, to be God to you and to your descendants after you. And I will give to you, and to your descendants after you, the land of your sojournings, all the land of Canaan, for an everlasting possession; and I will be their God" (Gen. 17:7-8). The rabbis note that the Torah's stress on the everlasting nature of the covenant emphasizes the eternal and unconditional nature of the Divine-Abrahamic promise. God made a twofold promise to Abraham—that his descendants would become a great nation and that they would inherit the land of Israel as an *everlasting* possession. He renewed this promise with Abraham's grandson, Jacob, the last of the patriarchs. "The land which I gave to Abraham and Isaac I will give to you, and . . . to your descendants" (Gen. 35:12). And while God established a covenant with Abraham's son Ishmael, too (Ishmael is regarded as the father of the Arab people), this included only the promise of nationhood, not of land.

Israel, however, was not only a divine promise, it was also a fulfilled reality. Abraham, Isaac, Jacob, Sarah, Rebekah, Rachel, and Leah—the foreparents of the Jewish faith and people—all lived, died, and were buried in Israel (except Jacob, who died in Egypt but was buried in Israel, see Gen. 47:30). From that time on there has always been a Jewish presence in the Holy Land. Jewish bonds with the land of Israel are, therefore, rooted in the fact that the very founders of the faith lived and died there. These bonds are also rooted in the fact that this particular land constitutes an essential part of the convenantal promise in the present, as well as in the future messianic era. Eretz Yisrael, in other words, is at the core of Jewish identity and peoplehood; the land shapes the Jews' very character as a community covenanted with God. The Jewish love for Israel, noted Heschel, "was due to an imperative not to an instinct, not to a sentiment. There is a covenant, an engagement of the people to the land. We live by covenants. We could not betray our pledge or discard the promise. . . . Intimate attachment to the land . . . is part of our integrity, an existential fact. Unique, *sui generis* it lives in our hopes, it abides in our hearts. . . . To abandon the land would make a mockery of all our longings, prayers, and commitments. To abandon the land would be to repudiate the Bible."[2]

The history of the Holy Land is a familiar one. After leaving Egypt and wandering in the desert for forty years, the Israelites conquered Canaan and divided the land among the twelve tribes, two and a half of which settled on the East Bank of the Jordan River. Under King David (circa 1000 B.C.E.) the city of Jerusalem became the capital of Israel. The kingdom split after the death of Solomon, with the Northern Kingdom falling in 722 B.C.E. and Judea in the south being conquered by the Babylonians in 586 B.C.E.

That first exile from Eretz Yisrael was undoubtedly a most traumatic Jewish experience, one that left the Jews with feelings of sorrow and depression, loneliness and estrangement. They felt abandoned by God. "By the waters of Babylon, there we sat down and wept, when we remembered Zion. . . . How shall we sing the LORD's song in a foreign land?" (Ps. 137:1, 4). The Jewish exiles, yearning to return to their homeland, vowed always to remember it. "If I forget you, O Jerusalem, let my right hand wither! Let my tongue cleave to the roof of my mouth, if I do not remember you, if I do not set Jerusalem above my highest joy!" (Ps. 137:5–6). That oath, made some twenty-five hundred years ago, is as compelling today as it was then. Indeed, the profound Jewish attachment to the Holy Land and pledge to return was reaffirmed in each generation. The Jewish people never renounced their right and title to that land, nor did Israel ever cease being an intimate part of their consciousness.

Some forty-seven years after the Babylonian exile, King Cyrus of Persia conquered Babylonia and allowed the Jews to return to Israel and build the second temple. Many, in fact, did so under the leadership of Ezra and Nehemiah, although others decided to remain in Babylonia. It was at that point that the first "Diaspora" Jewish community came into existence. (The term "exile" refers to the condition in which a people is forcibly evicted from its land and forbidden to return. "Diaspora," on the other hand, implies a voluntary separation and intentional choice not to return.) From the time of the exile and the destruction of the second temple by the Romans in 70 C.E., until the birth of the State of Israel in 1948, Jews did not enjoy sovereignty over the land of Israel. They made a last ditch effort at gaining such sovereignty with the Bar Kochba rebellion in 132 C.E. Bar Kochba was believed by many, including by some of the leading rabbis at the time, to be the promised Messiah. When the rebellion failed and God's kingdom was not established on earth, however, he was rejected like all others who failed in this regard. For almost two millennia thereafter, Jews wandered rootlessly and defenselessly around the world. They never forgot their dream and their vow to return to their ancient homeland.

Fearful that the elapse of time and separation from their land might lead Jews to forget the Holy Land or to weaken their love for it, the rabbis introduced the theme of a return into virtually every aspect of the Jew's daily life and routine. The three daily prayer services, as well as grace after meals, for example, were injected with references to Zion and to God's promise to bring about a return. When the Jew prayed, he faced in the direction of the Holy Land. Moreover, he concluded the Passover Seder meal and Day of Atonement service with the fervent oath reiterated by Jews over the centuries, *lishanah ha-baah b'Yerushalayim,* meaning "next year in Jerusalem!"

Jewish prayers for redemption and for the coming of the Messiah are also inextricably linked with the notion of a return to the land and an ingathering of the exiles. Pious Jews often slept with their clothes on and with their canes at their side so that in the event that the Messiah came that evening they would be prepared to quickly follow him to Jerusalem. Some Jews today still follow the custom of not playing musical instruments in the city of Jerusalem (even though music was an integral part of ancient temple worship), to demonstrate that their joy remains incomplete so long as Jerusalem and the temple are not rebuilt and all Jews are not ingathered onto their land. For the same reason, it is customary for the groom to break a glass at a Jewish wedding ceremony and for Jews living in the Diaspora to leave a corner (or brick) of their home unfinished as an indication that their residence there is temporary and that only in Eretz Yisrael does a Jewish domicile have real permanence. Annually, a day of fasting and mourning, Tisha b'Av, is held to commemorate the destruction of the temples and the Jewish exile, for in the words of the rabbis, those who mourn over the destruction of Jerusalem will merit living to see it on the day it is rebuilt.

Israel for Jews is far more than a mere abstraction or antiquated theological proposition. It is "the Holy Land," the heart and lifeblood of the Jewish people. It is also God's land and "vineyard," "the beloved of my [God's] soul" (Jer. 12:10, 7). It is the land where divine providence is especially manifest, where "the eyes of the LORD . . . are always upon it, from the beginning of the year to the end of the year" (Deut. 11:12). It is an exceedingly good land" (Num. 14:7); a blessed land (Deut. 33:13); "the most glorious of all lands" (Ezek. 20:6). God's love for Israel, the land, is intertwined with his special love for Israel, his people. "I will rejoice in Jerusalem, and be glad in my people" (Isa. 65:19).

Jews are, in fact, biblically commanded to live in the land of Israel, although those residing in the Diaspora often believe they can fulfill their obligation vicariously by supporting their brethren living there. Over the centuries, countless Jews have gone to considerable lengths, often at great personal risk, to move to the Holy Land or at least to walk on its terrain and to be buried in its soil.

The Jew remains incomplete and his religious observances remain unfulfilled so long as he does not live in Israel. A number of biblical laws pertaining to the land, such as the commandment to tithe produce and to leave the fields fallow on the Sabbatical and Jubilee years, also could not be observed outside the Holy Land. Nachmanides, the great twelfth-century Jewish mystic and biblical scholar who himself moved to Israel despite the risks and hardships involved, made the absolutely astonishing claim that the entire body of Jewish law had genuine, intrinsic validity only when practiced in the land of Israel and that those performing the mitzvot or commandments outside Israel never completely fulfill their Jewish obligation. In other words, the entire function of the law in the Diaspora is to prepare the Jew for the time when he will, in fact, live in Israel. Only then and there can the Jew hope to find religious fulfillment.

The prominence of the theme of the Holy Land in rabbinic law and tradition is echoed in Jewish lore and literature, as well. The mystical tradition, for example, claimed that the very air of Israel makes one wiser and even that a Jew living outside the land is as if he has no God and worships idols! The land of Israel, the mystics also suggested, would stubbornly "refuse" to bear fruit unless the Jews, its natural partners and authentic, compatible inhabitants for whom it was created, dwelled on it and cultivated it. Indeed, Palestine was for centuries a land of desert and swamp until the modern Zionists came and at tremendous sacrifice began tilling its soil. Only then did the land give forth its produce: "For the LORD will comfort Zion; he will comfort all her waste places, and will make her wilderness like Eden . . ." (Isa. 51:3). In truth, the Jewish love for the land of Israel and attachment to it is so profound and compelling that it defies articulation—it is ineffable.

It was the inexorable bond between the people and land of Israel, reinforced in the Jew's daily life and routine through prayer and Torah study, that enabled the miracle of a Jewish return to occur two centuries after their dispersion. Throughout the intervening turbulent centuries, the Jews' passionate yearning to come home never wavered; their love for Israel never waned.

The twentieth-century birth of the State of Israel marked the partial fulfillment of the Jewish dream. It is the outgrowth of a convergence of both ancient Jewish culture and religion with the forces of modernity, pragmatism, and political activism on behalf of a national Jewish homeland.

Modern Zionism

> Thus says the LORD God: Behold, I will take the people of Israel from the nations among which they have gone, and will gather them from all sides, and bring them to their own land. (Ezekiel 37:21)

> The LORD said to Moses: "Why do you cry to me? Tell the people of Israel to go forward." (Exodus 14:15)

Zionism can be described as the modern political movement and national ideology of the Jewish people giving expression to the age-old dream of living in their historic homeland, Eretz Yisrael. The term "Zion" is found in the Bible, antedating its modern usage by centuries. While the Zionist movement sought to actualize many elements of the traditional messianic dream, it also contained new secular nationalistic dimensions not found in those earlier messianic expectations. Its primary goal was to build a national homeland for the Jewish people through human initiative and not to wait for God to send his Messiah.

Modern Zionism originated in the late nineteenth century amidst the tumultuous rise of European nationalism and the deteriorating plight of world Jewry. Western European Jewish hopes that enlightenment and emancipation might bring an end to anti-Semitism and a genuine advancement of the Jewish condition were shattered by incidents such as the Dreyfus Affair in France (see below). Meanwhile, the Jewish predicament in Eastern Europe had become especially acute as incidents of pogroms increased in both number and intensity. Something desperately needed to be done to ameliorate the Jewish situation and to ease their wretched plight. Millions of Jews opted to remain in Russia. For millions of others, the answer was to emigrate to America. For still thousands of others, the only solution was to move to Palestine.

In the mid-1800s, Jewish intellectuals began writing of the need to resettle Palestine and to rejuvenate nationalist feelings. In 1862, Zevi Hirsch Kalischer, an Orthodox rabbi, wrote a book, *Derishat Zion,* in which he insisted that, contrary to the prevalent tradition, redemption would come about through human initiative and natural causes rather than through God's intervention and miracles. He urged Jews to colonize Palestine and to cultivate the land. That very same year Moses Hess, a German-Jewish socialist living in Paris, wrote *Rome and Jerusalem* in which he wrote that "the Jews have lived and labored among the nations for almost two thousand years, but nonetheless they cannot become rooted organically within them. . . . We shall always remain strangers among the nations. What we have to do at present for the regeneration of the Jewish nation is, first, to keep alive the hope of the political rebirth of our people and, next, to reawaken that hope where it slumbers."[3] The only way to solve the Jewish predicament, argued Hess, was to create a national center in Palestine.

A third major nineteenth-century Jewish spokesman for the Zionist cause was Leon Pinsker, an enlightened physician who was deeply provoked and stirred by the vicious pogroms directed against Jews in Russia. Like most others who were involved in the Zionist movement at this stage of its development, Pinsker came from an assimilated background and was alienated from Jewish life. His disillusionment with prospects for the complete integration and equality of Jews in other societies, however, led him and others to reverse their earlier calls for Jewish assimilation. In his book *Auto-Emancipation* (1881) Pinsker diagnosed anti-Semitism as an incurable disease. He urged Jews therefore to seek a national homeland. "No matter how much the nations are at variance with one another, no matter how diverse in their instincts and aims, they join hands in their hatred of the Jews; on this one matter all are agreed."[4] For Pinsker and many others, it was essential that Jews affirm their own nationalism since they would never be totally accepted by Gentile society. They could rely neither on the good will of man nor on the beneficence of God. "Help yourselves," said Pinsker, "and God will help you." The call for Jewish nationalism by people such as Kalischer, Hess, and Pinsker led to the founding of the movements *Hovevei Zion* (or "Lovers of Zion") and *Bilu* (an acronym for the biblical phrase "House of Jacob let us go forth") that colonized Palestine in the late 1800s. The ideological seeds for the founding of political Zionism were sown. It remained for Theodor Herzl to bring the idea to fruition and to turn the dream into a reality.

In 1894, Theodor Herzl, an assimilated Jewish Viennese journalist, was in France covering the trial of Alfred Dreyfus for his newspaper. Dreyfus, a Jew, was a captain in the French army who was accused of trumped-up charges of spying for Germany. The trial stirred the anti-Semitic passions of the French people and fanned the flames of hatred against the Jews. Herzl was traumatized by the fact that such displays of anti-Semitism, particularly the mob's cries of "down with the Jews," could take place in France, one of the most cultured and enlightened nations of its time. The Dreyfus Affair, as it came to be known, was the turning point in Herzl's life and, consequently, in the Zionist movement.

Herzl was totally unfamiliar with the earlier Zionist writings of people like Kalischer, Hess, and Pinsker. In 1896 he wrote *The Jewish State* in which he echoed their views but also developed a practical approach to the Zionist idea:

> We have sincerely tried everywhere to merge with the national communities in which we live, seeking only to preserve the faith of our fathers. It is not permitted us. In vain are we loyal patriots, sometimes superloyal; in vain do we make the same sacrifices of life and property as

our fellow citizens; in vain do we strive to enhance the fame of our native lands in the arts and sciences, or her wealth by trade and commerce. In our native lands where we have lived for centuries we are still decried as aliens, often by men whose ancestors had not yet come at a time when Jewish sighs had long been heard in the country. The majority decide who the "alien" is; this, and all else in the relations between peoples, is a matter of power. . . . In the world as it now is and will probably remain for an indefinite period, might takes precedence over right.[5]

Herzl arrived at the conclusion that, "It is without avail, therefore, for us to be loyal patriots." Instead, he claimed, the Zionist plan must be put into action. "Let sovereignty be granted us over a portion of the globe adequate to meet our rightful national requirements; we will attend to the rest. To create a new State is neither ridiculous nor impossible."[6]

Herzl's call for a world Zionist convention to take place in Basel, Switzerland, in 1897, brought together hundreds of delegates from throughout the world. He later wrote, "In Basel I created the Jewish state. Were I to say this aloud I would be greeted by universal laughter. But five years hence, certainly fifty years hence, everyone will perceive it."[7] Herzl died at the young age of forty-four before his dream of a Jewish state was actualized. His almost prophetic remarks were realized in 1948 when Israel was declared a state, fifty-one years after the first World Zionist Congress, just one year later than he had predicted.

The political Zionism espoused by people such as Hess, Pinsker, and Herzl, which sought to create a national Jewish homeland that would serve as a haven for oppressed Jewry, was complemented by another current of Zionist thought led by philosopher Asher Ginsberg, whose pen name was Achad Haam, meaning "one of the people." This school of Zionist ideology maintained that Palestine should serve, not only as a place of Jewish refuge, but also as a spiritual and cultural center for the

Jewish people. In this way, Israel would bring vitality to Jewish life throughout the Diaspora and be at the heart of Jewish culture, ethics, religion, and peoplehood. For, "from Zion shall come forth Torah and the word of God from Jerusalem."

In 1903 the Zionist movement became deeply divided over whether or not to accept the offer of Uganda, Africa, as a temporary Jewish haven. The idea was particularly attractive since the Jews in Russia were then suffering from terrible persecution, most notably the Kishinev pogroms that had taken place earlier that year. Although many Zionists were willing to accept the offer, the notion of "only Palestine," the Holy Land of the Bible, ultimately prevailed.

In 1917, Britain, which had just received control of Palestine from the Turks, issued the famous Balfour Declaration that stated, "His Majesty's Government view with favor the establishment in Palestine of a national home for the Jewish people." The declaration became the first internationally recognized political document legitimizing the Jewish claim to a state of their own in their ancestral homeland. Thus, many Jews decided to emigrate to Palestine. They came primarily from eastern Europe, although also from the West. There they cultivated the barren, often swamp-infested land and made it bloom. When America imposed a quota in the mid-1920s limiting immigration to the United States, Jewish emigration to Palestine increased even more.

Meanwhile, Arab nationalism was beginning to ferment and to have a serious influence on British foreign policy. Promises were made to the Arabs that often conflicted with ones made to the Jews. Violence and unrest erupted in Palestine. Despite British attempts to hamper Jewish resistance, Jews organized into self-defense forces to protect themselves from Arab riots and attacks. Finally, Britain established a series of commissions to investigate the causes of Arab rioting and to offer solutions to the clash between Arab and Jewish nationalisms. In 1939 they issued a "white paper" calling for the revocation of the Balfour Declaration and its promise of a Jewish homeland. In addition, the document restricted the sale of land to Jews and limited Jewish immigration to 75,000 for the ensuing five years—precisely at the time that Jews fleeing Nazi Europe needed a haven most.

Even after World War II and the extermination of six million Jews in the Holocaust, Britain stubbornly refused to lift her blockade on Jewish immigration. The doors to Palestine and to every other country in the world remained shut. Rather than being sent back to displaced persons' camps in Europe, however, Jews risked breaking the British blockade by illegally smuggling Jewish immigrants into Palestine. The most famous of these attempts was described by Leon Uris in his book *Exodus*.

Yielding to the internal pressures at home calling for their withdrawal from Palestine, the British handed over the problem to the United Nations, which on November 29, 1947, approved a resolution calling for the partition of Palestine into separate Jewish and Arab states. Five months later, the British left Palestine, and on the fifth day of the Hebrew month of Iyar, May 14, 1948, Israel became an independent nation. That date continues to be celebrated today as a national Jewish holiday, Israel's Independence Day.

Ten minutes after Israel declared itself a state, President Truman extended to it de facto United States recognition. Ever since, America has been Israel's greatest and most dedicated friend.

The Hebrew language was revived after some two thousand years and became the official language of the new Jewish nation. The Zionist dream was realized—the State of Israel, a bastion of democracy and Western values in the Middle East, had become a world-endorsed political reality.

The first act of the Knesset, or Israeli parliament, following the recitation of the traditional blessing thanking God for sustaining the Jewish people and for enabling them to live to reach that moment, was to annul the white paper. Later on, the Knesset passed the "law of return," which gave automatic citizenship to all Jews settling in Israel. Over a million Jewish refugees from European and Arab lands were to stream into the fledgling state on the heels of its independence. Israel accepted the United Nations' partition plan despite the fact that she received only one-sixth instead of one-half of the land originally to be divided into separate Arab and Jewish states.

The Arab nations, on the other hand, rejected partition and five of them proceeded to attack Israel from all directions. The Jewish population of six hundred thousand was outnumbered twenty to one. Arab residents living in Israel were urged by their Arab brethren to leave their homes and evacuate the area of conflict, confident of a victorious return soon thereafter when Israel would be routed. Tragically, unlike the hundreds of thousands of Jewish refugees who were forced to flee Arab countries and who were warmly welcomed into Israel, these Arab refugees became pawns of Arab governments, even to this day. Rather than being accepted by any of the twenty-one oil-wealthy Arab nations, the refugees were forced to live in wretched conditions with the promise that one day the Jews would be thrown out of Israel and they would return to their homes.

Despite the tremendous numerical and military odds against her, Israel miraculously was able to drive off her attacking enemies. In 1949 an armistice was signed, bringing an end to what came to be known as the Israeli War of Independence. As an outcome of the war, the Jews lost control over East Jerusalem and the West Bank, which was overtaken by Jordan. Despite the many internationally guaranteed assurances to the contrary, Jordan restricted Jews from visiting their holy sites in that portion of the land. Indeed, the entire West Bank of Judea and Samaria, containing some of the holiest sites cherished and revered by Jews, became *Judenrein*, no Jews allowed, until it was recaptured nineteen years later in the 1967 Six-Day War.

In 1956, Israel joined with French and British forces in breaking the Egyptian blockade that had been imposed on their shipping rights. Under strong pressure from the United

States, however, Israel gave back the Sinai Peninsula that it had conquered, without ever receiving substantial guarantees that a similar blockade would not be imposed in the future or that the Sinai would not be used again as a staging ground for Arab attacks on Jewish settlements. As many had predicted, in a few years Israeli villages bordering Egypt as well as Syria and Jordan were relentlessly attacked by terrorist infiltrators and shelled by Arab artillery.

In 1967, Egypt imposed another blockade on the Straits of Tiran to the tremendous glee of frenzied Arab mobs calling for the destruction of Israel. A *jihad,* or "holy war," was declared with the objective being to throw the Jews into the sea. Egyptian President Nasser moved his troops and armor deep into the Sinai and entered into a military pact with Jordan. War again erupted between Israel and her Egyptian, Jordanian, and Syrian adversaries. In a lightning victory, Israeli forces conquered Gaza and the Sinai from Egypt, Judea and Samaria (the West Bank) from Jordan, and the Golan Heights from Syria. Even then, however, the Arab nations refused to sit down and negotiate peace with Israel, nor would they accept her right to exist in their midst. A "war of attrition" followed in which Egyptian forces persistently bombed Israeli positions on the Israeli side of the Suez Canal.

In 1973 the Arab armies of Egypt and Syria staged a massive surprise attack on the embattled State of Israel. It was Yom Kippur, the Day of Atonement, the holiest day in the Jewish year. The Israeli Defense Forces were initially pushed back, but after mobilizing (Israel has a very small standing army and draws its strength from civilians who can be mobilized within a few days), they succeeded in entrapping the Egyptian Third Army and in pushing the Syrian forces to within ten miles of Damascus. At the insistence of the Soviets, who were reluctant to intrude so long as Israel was losing but eager to bring the fighting to a halt once Israel took the upper hand, the United Nations brought about a cease-fire. Later, an armistice was signed bringing the Yom Kippur War to a halt. The Arab nations, meanwhile, began to pressure many of the world's nations who were dependent on them either for their oil or petrodollars to break relations with Israel and to align themselves with the Arab cause.

In 1977, Egyptian President Anwar Sadat made his historic trip to Israel where he was enthusiastically welcomed by her people, who had been thirsting for peace for almost thirty years. His heroic and valiant cry of "no more war" played no small part in his being tragically gunned down by Moslem extremists a few years later. As of this writing, his successor President Hosni Mubarak and Jordan's King Hussein are the only Arab leaders to publicly and unequivocally recognize the existence of the State of Israel and enter into peace negotiations with her.

A process of normalization between Egypt and Israel was set into motion at Camp David with the assistance of President Jimmy Carter and the United States. As part of its agreement, Israel for the second time gave up the Sinai desert, including the oil fields that she had discovered and drilled, and that were so crucial to her energy independence. In addition, she relinquished the sophisticated airfields she had built. Even Jewish settlements that had served as a bulwark against attack were disbanded, a most controversial decision that met with much internal agony and opposition. Israel gave up the very strategic depth and buffer that had saved her from destruction in 1973, all for the *possibility* of peace.

The Soviet armed and trained Palestine Liberation Organization, which had systematically engaged in hundreds of terrorist attacks against both Jewish and non-Jewish civilians, was thrown out of Jordan in 1970 in a bloody war. The PLO implanted itself in Lebanon, which until then had maintained good relations with Israel, and turned it into a battleground. Civil war brought havoc and destruction to Lebanon, once one of the most beautiful, Westernized, and peaceful countries in the Middle East. In 1982, Israel launched an assault against the PLO, which by then had virtually established itself in Lebanon as a state within a state and which for years had engaged in terrorist incursions into northern Israel.

In 1993 the Oslo Agreements, as they have come to be known for the secret meetings held in Oslo, Norway, were signed by Israel's Prime Minister Yitzhak Rabin and PLO Chairman Yasir Arafat. For the first time, peace and reconciliation seemed to be on the horizon following the famous Rabin-Arafat handshake on the White House lawn in Washington, D.C. Tragically, Yitzhak Rabin was assassinated by a zealous Jew. While Shimon Peres, one of the architects of the Oslo Agreements, picked up the prime minister's mantle and continued implementing the accords, a spate of terrorist bombings against Israeli civilians drove him out of office and brought the entire "peace process" into question. As of this writing, Israel's Prime Minister Benjamin Netanyahu and PLO Chairman Arafat have not completed a peace agreement and remain locked in battle on a host of issues, primarily the question of Jerusalem.

As of this writing, with the exception of Egypt and Jordan, peace still has not come to Israel and her Arab neighbors. Israel remains a pariah among many of the nations of the world, with the United States remaining her staunchest, most steadfast ally. Israel continues to train a civilian army and to give each soldier both a gun and a Bible when they are inducted. She continues to hope that only the Bible will be used.

Chapter 8

THE RISE OF
JEWISH DENOMINATIONS

From Ghetto to Enlightenment

The outbreak of the American and French Revolutions in the latter part of the eighteenth century signaled the dawning of emancipation and the beginning of the modern period for western European and American Jewry. For centuries, Jews had been scorned, ridiculed, scapegoated, and persecuted by their European host nations, sometimes tolerated, sometimes not, but always viewed essentially as aliens. Their wretched condition was, in fact, often contrasted with that of Christians and seen as proof of the superiority of the Christian faith and truth of its message. For centuries the Jews of Europe were forced to live in ghettos and were excluded from most trade associations or guilds, with commerce being one of the few areas open to them. On the other hand, they were usually permitted to control their own religious and social institutions. The little contact that existed then between Jews and Christians usually was limited either to business matters or to appeals by Jewish leadership to the political authorities. In contrast, the Puritan ethic that found expression on American shores tended to be more favorably disposed toward Jews, who were identified as the Israelites of the Bible.

The dawning of the Enlightenment, spearheaded by the Renaissance and the French and American Revolutions, dramatically improved the Jewish condition. A new climate, which was far more tolerant of Jews and hospitable toward them than before, emerged in western Europe. Centuries of political discrimination and social repression were suddenly lifted as nations emancipated their Jews and granted them the rights and privileges of citizenship. For the first time, Jews became viewed by society not so much in terms of their distinctive faith, but on the basis of their common humanity and nationality. In fact, it was the breakdown of religion and the supplanting of religious rule with secular authority that finally rendered an improved Jewish condition. Whereas in the past, religion had served as the central integrating force of individuals (and nations), now it was viewed as a private concern and but one compartment of their character and ideological makeup. Religion, moreover, was not expected to spill over into all areas of life but was to be restricted to the home, the church, and the private domain. The spread of nationalism in the late eighteenth and early nineteenth centuries also favorably impacted upon the Jewish situation, since it, too, urged people to disregard the question of one's religion and to form a cohesive nation on the basis of other factors held in common. It was the forces of progress, reason, universalism, liberalism, secularism, and humanism that made possible the improved situation in which Jews were treated first and foremost as human beings and only secondarily as members of a different faith.

Not surprisingly, with tremendous zeal and fervor, Jews grasped these ideological currents sweeping across western Europe. For it was the breakdown of public religion and the disintegration of its hold on Western man that shattered the debilitating walls of the ghetto, freed the Jews from oppression, and enabled them to participate as full-fledged members in society. This fact has not been forgotten by Jews today, most of whom would subscribe to the notion that Jewish life flourishes best within societies whose public policies are guided by secular, albeit biblically rooted, principles and within those which separate the realm of the church from that of the state.

Jews seek a society rooted in the principles of liberalism, universalism, and humanism, one that posits a sharp division between sectarian religion and public policy. For Jews recognize well that it was these redemptive ideological forces that finally provided them with the opportunity to participate equally in society and to practice their faith freely, rights they did not always enjoy in earlier centuries.

Jews have had to pay a heavy price, however, for affirming these ideals. While the ghetto was, indeed, culturally insular and socially stifling, it did enable them to preserve their religious autonomy and communal cohesiveness. In choosing to leave the constraining ghetto, however, Jews elected to forfeit those very ingredients that had ensured their survival as a distinct faith community for centuries. Their admittance into a free and open society induced them to shed their distinctive Jewish traits in order to blend in and gain acceptance among Gentiles. Unfortunately, what began among Jews as a legitimate concern that (Christian) religion might be dictated or imposed upon them has evolved into an ethic, professed by many Jews and non-Jews alike, that would seek to ban religion as a significant element influencing public policy. The pervasiveness of forces such as secularism, materialism, and assimilation, and the diminution of religious observance, is an indication of the high toll Jews have paid and continue to pay for their decision to leave the ghetto.

As a result of their emancipation, Jews felt the need to reappraise their ancient faith and to reinterpret it both to the outside world and to themselves. By the turn of the nineteenth century, however, their religious options were limited. They could voluntarily remain cloistered and segregated, while preserving pre-emancipation Jewish observances and social mores. They could convert to Christianity and thereby improve their socioeconomic station in life. Or finally, they could simply drop out of religious life entirely. There was a pressing need for new forms of expression that would conform to the ancient Jewish heritage and tradition, but that would be congenial to the modern condition, as well. It was that vacuum that gave rise to Jewish denominationalism.

While the various denominations were formed in response to the spiritual crisis created by modernity, they differed in the manner in which they tried to balance universalism with particularism, tradition with modernity, progress with rootedness in the past, and the biblical and rabbinic traditions with contemporary sensibilities. And while each of the new religious movements brought fundamental changes to Jewish life, none ever completely severed ties with its past. In short, the major question confronting Jews as they stepped out of the walls of the ghettos and into the modern world was whether and how they could live in a secular, open, and pluralistic society while remaining steadfast in their commitment to their ancient Jewish faith, culture, and religious heritage.

Moses Mendelssohn (1729–1786), friend of poet-playwright Gotthold Lessing and associate of Enlightenment philosopher Immanuel Kant, was the first Jew to mediate between Jewish and Western cultures. Mendelssohn sought to bring enlightened German culture to Jews and Jewish culture to German society. For him, the Jewish response to emancipation and modernity was simple: "Comply with the customs and the civil constitutions of the countries in which you are transplanted, but at the same time, be constant to the faith of your forefathers."[1]

Precisely how one balances these two ideals and shapes them into a creative dialectic was, of course, the challenge facing Western Jewry. They met this challenge by developing new Jewish interpretations and by forming new denominational structures for expressing those understandings. The first attempt to develop a new interpretation of Judaism came in the form of the Reform movement. It was followed by the (neo) Orthodox, Conservative, and Reconstructionist movements. While the movements differ, at times radically, there remains an underlying unity and cohesiveness to their worldviews and to their concern for God, Torah, and Jewish peoplehood, which should not be lost sight of. All segments of Judaism today draw their spiritual sustenance from the same biblical and rabbinic traditions and experiences; all express the singularity of the Jewish people and faith.

Reform Judaism

Reform or Liberal Judaism began in early-nineteenth-century Germany and was the first group to reassess the character of Judaism and to adapt it to the changing modern world. It did so by providing a radical response to the question of Jewish integration and adaptation into the Gentile world and by breaking with tradition on a variety of matters. Perhaps Reform's most serious and fundamental break with the past, however, was its rejection of the divinity of the Torah and of the binding authority of the rabbinic tradition. These sources of religious authority, which traditionally were understood as originating in divine revelation, were reinterpreted as human creations, products of Jewish "genius" and "inspiration." In addition, a number of drastic changes were introduced in the synagogue worship service that were contrary to Jewish law and tradition. Men and women, for example, were permitted to sit together rather than separately during prayer service; the organ was used on Shabbat; Hebrew was replaced with the vernacular; decorum was instituted; the number of prayers recited was reduced; the tallit, tefillin, and kippah were eliminated. Some Reform temples even switched the Shabbat day from Saturday to Sunday.

Many other traditional Jewish precepts also were reappraised by the Reformers. The belief in a physical, personal Messiah, for example, was rejected, as was the concept of the resurrection of the dead; the kosher dietary regulations were discarded; and other distinctive rituals and customs setting the Jew apart also were eliminated. Most importantly, *halakhah,* or Jewish "law," was no longer considered binding for these Reformers. Much like the early antinomianism of Christian critics that viewed Judaism as enshackled by excessive legalism, early Reformers feared that halakhah would transform inner piety into outer formalism and divert man's spiritual energies from true inner religiosity. Over against the authority of the oral tradition and Jewish law that had guided Jewish life for centuries, the Reformers sought to reconstruct a modernized Judaism harmonious with the times by stressing the ethical teachings of the prophets. The Jewish mission, in their eyes, was to be a "light unto nations," a duty they would fulfill by teaching the world ethical monotheism.

Isaac Mayer Wise (1819–1900) was the prime force behind the rise of Reform Judaism in America. He founded the Union of American Hebrew Congregations (UAHC), a centralized organization representing Reform congregations, and the Central Conference of American Rabbis (CCAR) for Reform rabbis. Wise also established Hebrew Union College, the Reform rabbinical seminary, and published a prayer book for Reform congregations. In one of his earliest essays, Wise wrote that Judaism had become "a set of unmeaning practices, and the intelligent Jew either mourns for the fallen daughter of Zion or has adopted a course of frivolity or indifference. Therefore," he insisted, "we demand reforms. All unmeaning forms must be laid aside as outworn garments."[2] He offered a number of principles to help guide the Reform refashioning of Judaism:

> All forms to which no meaning is attached any longer, are an impediment to our religion and must be done away with. . . . Another principle of reform is this: Whatever makes us ridiculous before the world as it now is may safely be and should be abolished. . . . A third principle of reform is this. . . . Whatever tends to the elevation of the divine service, to inspire the heart of the worshiper and attract him, should be done without any unnecessary delay. . . . A fourth principle of reform is this, whenever religious observances and the just demands of civilized society exclude each other, the former have lost their power. . . . Last, or rather first, it must be remarked, the leading star of reform must be

the maxim, "religion is intended to make man happy, good, just, active, charitable, and intelligent." Whatever tends to this end is truly religious, and must be retained or introduced if it does not yet exist. Whatever has an effect contrary to the above must be abolished as soon as possible.[3]

The guiding principles of Reform were officially formulated at the 1885 convention in Pittsburgh, Pennsylvania. They became known as the Pittsburgh Platform.

1. We recognize in every religion an attempt to grasp the Infinite, and in every mode, source, or book of revelation held sacred in any religious system the consciousness of the indwelling of God in man. We hold that Judaism presents the highest conception of the God-idea, as taught in our Holy Scriptures and developed and spiritualized by the Jewish teachers, in accordance with the moral and philosophical progress of their respective ages. . . .

2. We recognize in the Bible the record of the consecration of the Jewish people to its mission as the priest of the one God, and value it as the most potent instrument of religious and moral instruction. . . .

3. We recognize in the Mosaic legislation a system of training the Jewish people for its mission during its national life in Palestine, and today we accept as binding only its moral laws, and maintain only such ceremonies as elevate and sanctify our lives, but reject all such as are not adapted to the views and habits of modern civilization.

4. We hold that all such Mosaic and rabbinical laws as regulate diet, priestly purity, and dress, originated in ages, and under the influence of ideas, entirely foreign to our present mental and spiritual state . . . their observance in our days is apt rather to obstruct than to further modern spiritual elevation.

5. We recognize, in the modern era of universal culture of heart and intellect, the approaching of the realization of Israel's great Messianic hope for the establishment of the kingdom of truth, justice, and peace among all men. We consider ourselves no longer a nation, but a religious community, and therefore expect neither a return to Palestine, nor a sacrificial worship under the sons of Aaron, nor the restoration of any of the laws concerning the Jewish state.

6. We recognize in Judaism a progressive religion, ever striving to be in accord with the postulates of reason. . . . Christianity and Islam being daughter religions of Judaism, we appreciate their providential mission to aid in the spreading of monotheistic and moral truth. We acknowledge that the spirit of broad humanity of our age is our ally in the fulfillment of our mission, and therefore we extend the hand of fellowship to all who cooperate with us in the establishment of the reign of truth and righteousness among men.

7. We reassert the doctrine of Judaism that the soul is immortal, grounding this belief on the divine nature of the human spirit, which forever finds bliss in righteousness and misery in wickedness. We reject as ideas not rooted in Judaism the beliefs both in bodily resurrection and in Gehenna and Eden (Hell and Paradise) as abodes for everlasting punishment and reward.

8. In full accordance with the spirit of Mosaic legislation, which strives to regulate the relation between rich and poor, we deem it our duty to participate in the great task of modern times, to solve, on the basis of justice and righteousness, the problem presented by the contrasts and evils of the present organization of society.

Classical Reformers were children of nineteenth-century enlightenment. They tenaciously believed in the ideological currents of liberalism, rationalism, optimism, humanism, universalism, and nationalism. The verities of the twentieth century, most notably the eruption of the Holocaust and birth of the State of Israel, shook Reform to its very foundations and prompted it to radically alter much of its previously sacrosanct ideology.

Fifty years after issuing their Pittsburgh Platform, the Reform rabbis met again in Columbus, Ohio, this time under considerably different circumstances than in 1887. America, not Europe, was now the center of the Diaspora, while Germany, the fountainhead of classical Reform, was being swept away by Hitler and the forces of Nazism. One of early Reform's ideological pillars, anti-Zionism, had by then given way to the wide acceptance of a Jewish state and to Reform's embrace of Jewish nationalism. When the Balfour Declaration was issued in 1917, for example, the Reform rabbinate stated, "We are opposed to the idea that Palestine should be considered the homeland of the Jews. Jews in America are part of the American nation."[4] In 1937, in Columbus, however, they declared, "We affirm the obligation of all Jewry to aid in its [Palestine's] upbuilding as a Jewish homeland." And while in 1917 they rejected Jewish nationalism and proclaimed, "We look with disfavor upon the new doctrine of political Jewish nationalism which finds the criterion of Jewish loyalty in anything other than loyalty to Israel's God and Israel's religious mission,"[5] in 1937 they embraced both Zionism and the Jewish mission which they explained was "to cooperate with all men in the establishment of the Kingdom of God, of universal brotherhood, justice, truth and peace on earth."[6]

The Columbus Platform also proffered a more traditional approach than did early Reform toward the questions of law, ritual, Torah, revelation, and messianism. "Judaism as a way of life," it declared, "requires in addition to its moral and spiritual demands, the preservation of the Sabbath, festivals and holy days, the retention and development of such customs, symbols, and ceremonies as possess inspirational value, the cultivation of distinctive forms of religious art and music, and the use of Hebrew, together with the vernacular, in our worship and instructions."[7] By 1937 the concept of "Jewish peoplehood" had come to assume the same centrality in Reform doctrine as that of "ethical monotheism."

Ironically, while early Reform rejected Jewish nationalism, insisting instead that Jews were a faith community whose mission was to serve God, today Reform Jews are among the staunchest moral, political, and financial supporters of the State of Israel. Indeed, the major challenge facing Reform Judaism today is that it has swung perhaps too far toward Jewish nationalism. Israel, for many Reform Jews today, is the central and sometimes even the only Jewish commitment they have, while worshiping God, studying Torah, and practicing the mitzvot are often reduced to secondary significance. Thus, whereas classical Reform treated Judaism as a faith rather than a nationality, today ethnic nationalism, more than religious faith, worship, or observance, often serves as the sole mode of Reform Jewish expression. The beginnings of change are just now becoming evident, particularly in light of Reform's disillusionment from Israel due to that government's refusal to accept Reform as a legitimate form of Jewish expression.

While Reform Judaism remains the liberal branch of American Judaism, in recent years it has shifted dramatically to the right, not only on the question of Israel and Jewish nationalism, but on matters of traditional Jewish ritual, law, and theology as well. Circumcision is now usually performed, Hebrew as well as English is used in prayers, and even the kippah, tefillin, and tallit are sometimes worn in prayer services, especially by the younger generation of committed Reform Jews. Tradition in Reform circles has come to assume the seat of importance that was once occupied by radical change. According to the National Jewish Population Study conducted by the Council of Jewish Federations (CJF), of the approximately six million Jews currently living in the United States (there are about fourteen million worldwide), roughly 30 percent describe themselves as Reform.

Orthodox Judaism

While there was general Jewish agreement over the need to reappraise traditional Judaism to make it more congenial to modern conditions and palatable to enlightened sensibilities, many Jews felt that the response provided by Reform was far too extreme. In the eyes of these Jews, the Reformers brought about change through the abandonment of tradition rather than through its reinterpretation and reconstitution.

It was to meet the needs of these modern nineteenth-century German traditionalists, who were emotionally and intellectually attracted to both tradition and modernity and who wished to counteract the inroads being made by Reform, that the neo-Orthodox movement, under the leadership of Rabbi Samson Raphael Hirsch (1808–1888), was founded. Hirsch maintained that it was possible to uphold traditional Judaism while at the same time being fully immersed in modern secular German culture. He was the first major Jewish spokesman to advocate an enlightened traditionalism in which tradition and modernity would be brought together without compromising either. Rabbi Hirsch was also the first who felt comfortable both in the European university and in the traditional yeshiva, or seminary.

Hirsch sought not only to make Torah and secular knowledge compatible, as his predecessor Moses Mendelssohn had attempted to do, but to synthesize them as well. Although he advocated that Jewish law be adapted to meet the ever-changing circumstances of life, he resolutely refused to compromise the strict observance of the law. Hirsch was a vehement opponent of Reform Judaism. He advocated "separatist Orthodoxy" and refused to join together with Reform rabbis, not only on religious matters, but on communal affairs as well, lest it appear that he sanctioned their movement or recognized their rabbinic authority. Like the Reformers, however, he and many of his Orthodox coreligionists were also bitterly opposed to political Zionism, believing that such an allegiance conflicted with their German nationalism. But while Reform discarded the doctrine of Jewish nationalism entirely from its religious vocabulary, claiming instead that Judaism was only a faith, even those in the Orthodox camp who rejected political Zionism insisted that Jews remained a nation, but that God had first to send the Messiah to bring the Jews back to Israel. Such a return, they felt, could not be initiated by man himself and certainly not by irreligious Jews who, by and large, constituted the leadership of the Zionist movement. Needless to say, twentieth-century Orthodoxy, along with all other denominations, has warmly and enthusiastically embraced Zionism.

With the massive influx of almost two and one-half million eastern European Jews to the United States between 1880 and 1925, Orthodoxy, or "Torah-true" Judaism, as it sometimes refers to itself, found an excellent opportunity to gain new members. Unlike their enlightened western European coreligionists, these Jewish immigrants were by and large ignorant of Western culture and mores. They came, for the most part, from countries where they had lived in enclosed, self-contained villages and where they had often suffered violent persecution and pogroms.

Unlike their western European counterparts, these Jewish immigrants were often traditionally religious Jews with a strong proficiency in Hebrew, the language of the Torah and prayer book, and with an abiding commitment to Jewish law and ritual. Many of them, however, abandoned their faith upon arriving in America in order to fully integrate into the American melting pot. Some of those who sought to take full advantage of the opportunities America had to offer, but who did not wish to abandon their Jewish heritage, found Reform an attractive option. A third segment, also seeking integration, found Reform Judaism radical and inauthentic. It was they who formed the core of American Orthodoxy.

The Orthodox movement established a network of day schools throughout the country where children received both religious and secular educations. It also founded Yeshiva University as its main seminary and institution of higher learning. As a result of these and other factors, the denomination grew beyond all expectations.

In the aftermath of World War II there was a second influx of European Jews to America consisting primarily of Holocaust survivors, many of whom were Orthodox fundamentalists. They established their own separate seminaries, synagogues, and school systems and tended to look upon secular education and even liberal Orthodoxy (let alone Reform and Conservative Judaism) with suspicion and, often, disdain. There has been a noted resurgence of this segment of Orthodoxy in recent years.

Liberal or modern Orthodox Jews today share much in common with their Conservative and Reform colleagues, at times even more than they do with their own right wing. But despite the differences dividing Orthodoxy, it is united in its shared belief in the divinity of the Bible and in the binding authority of the Talmud and other forms of rabbinic literature. Orthodox Jews constitute the Jewish conservatives theologically, and often socially and politically, as well.

Orthodoxy affirms the centrality of halakhah and the need to organically apply its invariable principles to life's ever-changing conditions. Its function, in the words of the late Rabbi Joseph Soloveitchik from whom I received my Rabbinic ordination and who was then the acknowledged world leader of modern Orthodoxy, is to establish standards and to objectify the amorphous and often fluctuating emotions of man. "The halakhah which was given to us at Sinai is the objectification of religion in the shape of the fixed and lucid molds, in clearly outlined laws and definite principles. It converts subjectivity into objectivity and into a fixed pattern of lawfulness."[8] Orthodox Jews do not regard their dedication to law as either unwarranted or excessively legalistic, but as a commitment rooted in love, joy, and spirituality. They believe deeply in a commanding God, one who seeks a human response to his divine revelatory initiative. The written and oral traditions remain binding and authoritative for the Orthodox Jew today; the study and practice of Torah and Talmud remain his loftiest spiritual ideals.

American Orthodoxy is centered in major cities such as New York, Miami, Los Angeles, Boston, and Chicago.

According to the previously cited CJF study, 11.4 percent of American Jewish households define themselves as Orthodox.

Conservative Judaism

At the turn of the twentieth century, Reform and Orthodox Judaism were the only two religious Jewish options available to Western Jews, and neither satisfied the spiritual and cultural needs of many of them. At that time, there existed no centrist alternative for Jewish expression. Many of those Jews seeking a modern, reformulated Judaism were at odds with the extreme positions of Reform, which they felt advocated the abrogation of Jewish law and tradition rather than its reappraisal. Many also rejected Orthodoxy, which they regarded as too rigid, static, and overly preoccupied with Talmud and law over against God and Jewish peoplehood. It was in response to this vacuum that Conservative Judaism, the centrist school of thought, was born. Conservatives sought to revitalize the Jewish faith by preserving traditional Judaism and adapting it to modern conditions, albeit through moderate change.

While the Conservative movement had its ideological roots in mid- to late-nineteenth-century Germany, it is largely a product of the American scene. When Reform leaders declared their radical proposals at the rabbinical conference in Frankfurt, Germany, in 1845, particularly their desire to eliminate Hebrew from the prayer service and to substitute it with the vernacular, a group of men led by Rabbi Zecharias Frankel who supported moderate rather than radical reforms, stormed out of the meeting and withdrew from the convention. The seeds of what later came to be known as Conservative Judaism and what then was called the "Positive Historical" or "Moderate Reform" school of thought were planted with that act of protest.

In 1887 a group of American moderate reformers of like mind with Frankel's group in Germany established the Jewish Theological Seminary in New York, largely as a protest against the radical Pittsburgh Platform declaration that had been adopted by Reform leaders just two years earlier. That act initiated a third Jewish movement or denomination in America, Conservative Judaism.

In 1902, Rabbi Solomon Schechter joined the Jewish Theological Seminary as its president and in a short time turned it into the center of Conservative Judaism in America. In 1913 he founded the United Synagogue of America, the umbrella association for Conservative synagogues. The fact that Conservative Judaism is today the largest Jewish group in America, comprising 40.5 percent of Jewish households according to the CJF survey, is, in no small measure, due to Schechter's charismatic leadership. It is also due to the fact that it had broad appeal to the many eastern European Jews who sought acculturation in America and who wished to pray in a modern, elegant, and sophisticated setting, but who also sought to retain traditional Jewish principles and practices. Conservative Judaism offered such people a compromise setting.

Conservative leaders were initially very much opposed to sectarianism. For many years they sought to heal the rifts between the two denominational extremes and to mediate between them rather than to start a separate denomination. They were deeply committed to Jewish peoplehood and to the centrality of what Schechter called "Catholic Israel," in the sense of the totality of the community of Israel. In time, however, Conservative Judaism evolved into a separate Jewish movement.

While Reform Judaism focused on the God idea (ethical monotheism) and Orthodoxy emphasized Torah and law, Conservatives stressed the concept of Jewish peoplehood without which, they maintained, the other two legs of the Jewish triad, Torah and God, could not stand or find expression. Precisely what the Conservative group affirmed beyond that, however, remained deliberately unclear for many years. For Judaism, in the Conservative view, is not so much a creedal system as it is a peoplehood whose faith must express the sum total of the Jewish experiences. Conservatives are, therefore, very reluctant to box themselves into a particular doctrinal cast or to reject any part of Jewish tradition, preferring instead to emphasize one aspect of it or another. This type of open-ended, yet circumscribed ideology, which greatly cherished both tradition and moderate change, strongly appealed to Jews living in a modern, pluralistic, nondogmatic world. It provided them with a broad, middle-of-the-road position from which Jews of varying viewpoints could draw.

Conservative Judaism can be described as a critique of both Reform and Orthodoxy. In contrast with both those groups, which had rejected political Zionism in their early years, the Conservative movement endorsed it enthusiastically from its inception because it was so amenable to the movement's overriding commitment to Jewish peoplehood.

Unlike Reform, Conservatives maintained that Jewish law and tradition remained binding and authoritative and constituted the concrete application of prophetic ideals to life's situations. In the words of Alexander Kohut (1842–1894), one of the early leaders of Conservative Judaism in America, "Our religious guide is the Torah, the law of Moses, interpreted and applied in the light of tradition. . . . A Reform which seeks to progress without the Mosaic-rabbinical tradition is a deformity—a skeleton without flesh and sinew, without spirit and a heart. It is suicide; and suicide is not reform. We desire a Judaism full of life."[9]

Conservative Judaism also rejected early Reform's positions that only the moral teachings of the Torah remained authoritative and that ritual and halakhah were no longer valid. Instead, they maintained that ceremonial practices were to be revitalized and given new meaning in light of modern circumstances, and new rituals that did not violate halakhah were to be created.

In contrast with Orthodoxy, Conservatives are more inclined to revitalize Jewish law by adapting it to modern conditions, insisting that such an approach is entirely consistent with historic Judaism, which also introduced change and innovation both to and through the law. That very law, they insist, is to be treated as a fluid rather than a static system in need of constant reexamination in light of the sentiments of the peoplehood of Israel. And while Orthodoxy also views changes in the law as possible, it is far less inclined to tamper with tradition than is Conservative Judaism, which generally seeks out the liberal, more lenient position.

Conservatives regard the Talmud and other parts of the oral tradition as authoritative because they constitute the historical response of the Jewish people to God's revelation. Laws, they assert, are to be understood against the backdrop of the historical conditions present at the time they were introduced. Thus, while both Orthodox and Conservative Judaism accept the divinity of the Torah and authority of the rabbinic tradition, Conservatives are more likely to adapt them to life-oriented changes in light of the principle of Jewish peoplehood than Orthodoxy would allow in light of its commitment to law and tradition. And since Conservatives generally have a less literalist view of revelation than their Orthodox coreligionists, they tend also to be more liberal on issues such as the inerrancy of Scripture, and on man's right to modify talmudic law to suit changing social conditions.

Reconstructionism

Reconstructionism, the youngest of all the denominations, originated just a few decades ago as a left-wing offshoot of the Conservative movement. Like the other movements, Reconstructionism was rooted in the belief that Judaism was in need of regeneration and revitalization. It was founded by Mordecai Kaplan, a former professor at the Jewish Theological Seminary who died in 1983. Most people (including Jews) are not very familiar with this group or its philosophy, and many of those who are, view it essentially as part of the Conservative movement rather than as a separate, fourth denomination, since the philosophies of the two groups share so much in common. Although few in numbers, Reconstructionism today has its own seminary and rabbinical association separate from the Conservative denomination from which it originated.

Reconstructionism's uniqueness stems from the facts that

it is the only Jewish group to define itself on the basis of the philosophy of a single individual, the only one to originate in the twentieth century, and the only one truly born in America. Reconstructionism essentially affirms a religious naturalism rather than supernaturalism. It defines religion as "the need for communing with the Power . . . which makes for salvation," and as something created by man to maintain his ethnic identification. It views Judaism not so much as a faith, but as the all-inclusive, evolving religious civilization of the Jewish people bringing together the various historical expressions of the Jewish community and molding them into an organic unity of faith, culture, and peoplehood. The various Jewish customs, rituals, laws, mores, and institutions are not understood by Reconstructionism as revealed truths, but as religious folkways that evolved from the primordial life of the Jewish people as aids in their quest for self-expression. God, too, is understood not so much as a divine being but more pragmatically, as a "process that makes for salvation . . ." who can be found in the natural order of the universe. He is "what the world means to the man who believes in the possibility of maximum life and strives for it."[10] Those who try to live morally and responsibly exhibit the presence of God in their lives and exemplify the striving toward salvation.

Hasidism

The condition of Jews living in eastern Europe in the late eighteenth and early nineteenth centuries was radically different from that enjoyed by those living in western Europe. The Jews in the east suffered from anti-Semitic legislation and persecution, as well as from day-to-day poverty. Entire Jewish communities were at times annihilated by the Cossacks or by peasant uprisings. These abysmal conditions were especially prevalent in southeast Poland during the time of the Cossack revolt and Chmielnicki massacres of 1648–1649 and Haidamack persecution later on, in which thousands of Jews were slaughtered and thousands of others were forced to accept Christianity.

It was during this period of extreme chaos, suffering, and instability that Shabbetai Zevi (1626–1676) proclaimed himself the Messiah. Shabbetai Zevi had tens of thousands of followers in Turkey, Italy, and Poland who fervently believed that he was the long-awaited Messiah who would bring about God's kingdom on earth and lead the Jews to the Promised Land. Turkish authorities finally ordered Shabbetai Zevi either to convert to Islam or be put to death. His decision to convert rather than to undergo martyrdom disillusioned most (but not all) of his followers and proved that, like the many other pseudo-messiahs before him, he too was a fraud.

A terrible malaise and despair set in following the Shabbetai Zevi affair as the condition of eastern European Jewry grew more and more bleak. Their situation was aggravated even further by the fact that, due to the hardships of their lives, most Jews found it increasingly difficult to fulfill the mitzvah of studying Torah and Talmud, the very foundation of Jewish spirituality. Instead, the rigorous study of the law, which in earlier years was widespread, had become relegated to select groups of elitist scholars. Meanwhile, the masses were left to languish in spiritual and intellectual despair without the means to serve God fully. A schism erupted between the Torah scholars who constituted Jewish leadership, and the poor, often ignorant masses who tended to be looked upon disparagingly by the scholars. Jewish morale sank to the crisis level.

It was within this setting that Hasidism, a grass roots pietist movement, was born. (The term *hasid* means a pious and righteous individual.) Hasidism was founded in the 1730s by Rabbi Israel ben Eliezer, or the *Baal Shem Tov,* meaning "Master of the Good Name," as he came to be known. His charismatic personality and inspiring teachings gave the common folk new hope by providing them with a dignified means of expressing their Jewish spirituality other than through the rigorous, intellectual study of Talmud. Faith, prayer, joy, purity of the heart—these were the characteristics that Hasidism claimed were equal to, and perhaps of even greater importance than, the study of

Talmud; these were the things all Jews could participate in equally; and these were the values that could lift the masses from their lives of drudgery and give them reinvigorated spiritual meaning. The Baal Shem Tov's followers also believed him to possess supernatural powers of healing and to be capable of performing miracles and even expelling demons and evil spirits. He could actually alter God's decrees through his prayers! An entire legendary tradition evolved around the great rabbi's amazing powers and visions.

Although Hasidism drew heavily from Kabbalah, or Jewish mysticism, it tended to downplay the messianic elements of that literature as a result of the persisting disillusionment over the Shabbetai Zevi affair. Hasidism spread like wildfire throughout Poland, the Ukraine, Galicia, and even into Lithuania, the very center of the yeshiva world where intellectual scholarship of Talmud and Jewish law was strongest.

The movement met tremendous resistance, however, from the *mitnagdim,* as those who opposed Hasidism were called. The fear that Hasidism might continue to spread led the Vilna Gaon, one of the most saintly, learned rabbis in modern times, to excommunicate the group and to ban intermarrying or doing business with them. On occasion, mitnagdim brought false charges to government authorities against Hasidim, leading to their incarceration. There were even incidents of book burning!

The mitnagdim opposed a number of aspects of the Hasidic movement. First, they viewed its stress on prayer over and above the study of Torah and Talmud as a deviation from historical Judaism. They also regarded its belief in the miraculous visions and abilities of the Hasidic rabbi as coming dangerously close to idolatry of a human being. The ecstatic singing and often frenzied dancing of Hasidism during prayer was also strongly disapproved of and regarded as undignified. In truth, much of the distrust of Hasidism stemmed from bitter memories of the Shabbetai Zevi affair and grew out of a concern that Hasidism also would become a sectarian group with messianic overtones. Western European Jews, needless to say, also vehemently opposed Hasidism, criticizing it as a reactionary group that was not yet enlightened. Despite the tremendous opposition it faced, the Hasidic pietist movement swept throughout eastern Europe, gaining devotees wherever it went.

Following the death of the Baal Shem Tov, the popular movement was led by Rabbi Dov Baer of Mezhirech (1710–1772) who consolidated Hasidism and oversaw its rapid proliferation. Dov Baer's disciples, in turn, became *rebbes,* or leaders of different Hasidic dynasties in various centers throughout Europe and Israel. The mantle of leadership and succession became hereditary from then on, passing from father to son, or if there was no son, to the son-in-law, in dynastic tradition. In this way Hasidism branched out, diversified, and propagated into a great mass movement. The large emigration of eastern European Jews in the late 1800s and early 1900s brought Hasidism to the United States, as well. In time, the strong opposition of the mitnagdim toward Hasidism waned as they realized that the pietist group remained true to Jewish law and tradition.

At the core of Hasidism's teachings is the notion that the Jew must always strive for *devekut,* or "union with God," especially during moments of prayer when his soul quests to return to its divine origin. Hasidism stresses the notion that joy, self-worth, and spirituality should be attained through the material world, since pleasure can generate profound religious experiences. Both asceticism and melancholia are frowned upon and regarded as hindrances to the service of God. The *zaddik,* or "dynastic leader," is usually regarded as possessing the magical ability to mediate between his followers and God. He offers his Hasidim (followers) advice on all sorts of matters, even those that are not religious per se, such as whether or not to marry a particular person, whether to have surgery, and even whether or not to enter into a major business deal.

There are more than a dozen different Hasidic groups today, generally known by the name of the European city from which the founding rabbi came. Some, such as the Habad or

Lubavitch group, based in Brooklyn, New York, are known for their tolerance toward others, their commitment to Torah and Talmud study, and their overall sophistication and worldliness. Lubavitch Hasidim are located in almost every American city in which there are Jews, especially on college campuses, where the Lubavitch are committed to counteracting Jewish assimilation and to bringing back alienated Jewish youth to their ancient heritage. They are the "Jewish missionaries," the counterparts to Christian Evangelicals in their zeal to spread Judaism, although they focus exclusively on bringing alienated Jews back to the fold. No attempt is ever made to proselytize among non-Jews, since that would constitute a violation of Jewish law and tradition. They are also the groups whose *Rebbe* [leader] was, before his recent death, believed by many of his followers to be the Messiah. Other Hasidic groups tend to be more isolated, sectarian, and intolerant. They constitute the extreme right fringe of the Jewish denominational spectrum. There are even a few Hasidic groups opposed to the political sovereignty of the State of Israel, believing that redemption must come from God and the Messiah, not through human initiative, and certainly not at the hands of secular Jews.

There is friction, and at times hostility, between the more liberal Hasidic groups such as Lubavitch, whose love and tolerance has brought them widespread popularity and support even among non-Orthodox Jews, and the more radical, rigid, and sectarian groups that are estranged from the rest of the Jewish community. While there remain many social as well as theological differences between Hasidism and other segments of Orthodoxy, both are today generally accepted as legitimate forms of Orthodox Jewish expression. The distinctive Hasidic garb, sidelocks and beards, however, sets them apart from all other Jewish groups. The fact that Hasidism never broke with the system of Jewish law, as Conservative and Reform Judaism are viewed to have done, accounts for the Hasidim being considered part of the overall Orthodox denomination rather than as an entirely different group.

The writings of Martin Buber, Abraham Heschel, and other Jewish as well as Christian thinkers who were fascinated by this Jewish pietist movement and its stress on joy, song, dance, and mysticism, have profoundly increased the ubiquitous awareness of Hasidism and broad appreciation for it. Hasidism is today a vibrant Jewish force and a meaningful way of life for hundreds of thousands of Jews throughout the world. Its main centers are in Israel and in New York.

Cultural and Institutional

The five groups described so far provide Jews with a number of different ways in which they can express their religious commitment to Judaism. To be a Jew, however, unlike being a Christian, involves much more than being a member of a faith community. While Christianity involves the adherence to a creed, the belief in a redemptive experience, the participation or affiliation with a church, and most notably, the faith in Jesus as Lord and Savior, Judaism is a variegated way of life that bids the Jew to sanctify life and transform the mundane and the secular into holiness.

Unlike Christians, Jews are a people linked together not only by their common faith, which assumes varying degrees of importance among different people, but by their shared history, culture, nationality, ethnicity, and indeed, intertwined destiny. The fact is that not all Jews who identify themselves as such and who are committed to Jewish life, express themselves Jewishly through any of the religious categories or movements described above. And while most Jews today affiliate with one synagogue or another, many, in fact, do not. Furthermore, of those who do affiliate with a synagogue or temple, many unfortunately do not attend services more than a handful of times during the year, usually on the High Holy Days. However, since Judaism is more a way of life than it is a faith, and since it entails more than prayer and synagogue, it is highly questionable methodologically to use synagogue attendance and affiliation alone as a measurement of a Jew's commitment in the same way that a

Christian's church membership is often viewed as the standard of his commitment.

In truth, even Jews themselves have difficulty agreeing on the question of who is a Jew and how to define Jewishness. The classical Jewish response is that a Jew is one who is born of a Jewish mother or who converts into the faith and peoplehood. The various denominations, however, have different standards of conversion so that many Orthodox Jews do not regard Reform or Conservative conversions as valid. This problem is particularly nettlesome today in Israel where all official questions pertaining to religion are determined exclusively by Orthodox rabbis who reject the authority and legitimacy of non-Orthodox rabbis.

Judaism comprises more than the sum total of its parts. Indeed, the ties that bond Jews throughout the world are intangible, transcending their bonds of faith. Despite their many ethnic, cultural, religious, racial (there are black Jews, too), and socioeconomic differences, Jews are one organic unit, linked together by their mutual faith, heritage, and responsibility to serve as their brothers' keepers. Jewish community and solidarity, even in this post-tribalism age, is a very real commitment for most Jews today. It goes to the very core of what it means to be a Jew, especially for the secular Jew. Just as the domains of the sacred and the profane are inextricably intertwined in Judaism, so the secular Jew who acts on behalf of Jewish causes actually engages in the religious act of sanctifying life. As difficult as it may be for Christians to comprehend (and for many Jews to accept), a Jew can be deeply devoted to his Jewishness while actually being devoid of any religious faith.

For many Jews, being Jewish represents an ethnic identification alone, a civil religion, wherein they give charity to Jewish (and other) causes. Beyond that, they identify only minimally in a religious sense. The concept of *tzedakah*, or "charity," is a very real one for such Jews, deeply ingrained into their Jewish psyche. In most instances, however, even such secular and unaffiliated Jews mark life-cycle events such as birth, death, bar mitzvah, and marriage, through religious observance and with the presence of a rabbi. Insufficient as such commitments to secular and cultural Judaism are, they nevertheless constitute another way in which Jews today affirm their Jewish identity. This is particularly the case regarding the secular Jew's commitment to the State of Israel. As Irving Greenberg has noted, "The most bitterly secular atheist involved in Israel's upbuilding is the front line of the messianic life force struggling to give renewed testimony to the Exodus as ultimate reality."[11] The lines separating secular and religious Jewish institutions are also blurred and intertwined. The same commitments that may be made by Orthodox Jews out of a belief that God requires it of them, can be made by secular Jews for ethnic, cultural, or sociological reasons. Most Jewish organizations today have among their active membership Jews who are motivated by either religious or ethnic factors or both.

There are a number of different Jewish organizations in America, (see page 265 for a list of several such organizations) including those which are service and fraternal oriented, social welfare groups, religious organizations, and those which are devoted to educational and cultural activities. Still others are geared toward community relations activities and toward protecting the rights and security of Jews in America and abroad. And while virtually every Jewish organization and institution today works in some measure on behalf of Israel, there are also groups that are exclusively devoted to Zionist efforts. More than being merely secular organizations, however, these groups exemplify some of the most profound Jewish commitments and compelling Jewish ideals. They may be secular in orientation, but they remain distinctively Jewish, nonetheless.

Part 2

WHERE DO WE GO FROM HERE?

>-+◆>-0-<+-<

WHERE DO WE GO FROM HERE?

After learning of the burdens of history and becoming aware, perhaps even ashamed, of the way their forebears treated the Jewish people in the past, how shall Christians who today seek to extend their hand in friendship to Jews do so? After learning of the Biblical feasts and other scripturally based practices still guiding Jewish life to this day, how can Christians rediscover their own roots in Judaism and reclaim their Jewish soul? After realizing that they are the branches that, by God's grace, were grafted onto the rich olive tree of Judaism, as Paul maintains, how can Christians live out, in practical terms, that expression of unity with the Jewish people and oneness with Judaism, the "mother faith?" And how shall Jews, many of whom still bear in their hearts the scars of past historical encounters with Christians, relate to their Christian neighbors and colleagues? Can suspicions ever be supplanted by trust? Can their feelings toward Christians and perceptions of them ever be changed for the better? In short, how can we, today, reverse the sad and tragic fratricidal history in which Christians and Jews have related to one another? Put differently, where do we go from here?

The burden of history falls on Christians to initiate the rapprochement and to study those pages of their history that brought Jews so much pain and suffering, a history with which Christians, even to this day, are largely unfamiliar. Ara

Tjevidgian, an Armenian Christian whose son is married to Billy Graham's daughter, told me when we first met that the very first thing Christians should do when meeting Jewish people is to "ask forgiveness for all that was done to their community in the name of the Lord, Jesus Christ."

Jews have been historically conditioned—some by direct experience in the Holocaust—*not* to trust others. They are accustomed to being rejected, scorned, and persecuted. Even in an open and free culture such as the United States, Jews can feel marginalized and defensive as the result of accusations of "Jewish conspiracies" in the media and financial worlds or the desecration of Jewish sacred places or the silence of Christians on issues close to the Jewish heart. Many feel paranoid or, at least, awkward and suspicious, even of Christians who effusively profess their "love" for them, often without even knowing them. Of course, that is a much better starting point than the reverse. Most Jews, however, simply want to be treated by others with dignity, warmth, and respect. It will be hard for them to shed their suspicions and come to believe that their neighbor does not, in all likelihood, bear them malice or prejudice. To the contrary, they probably wish them well. Some would even risk their lives on their behalf. It will be difficult for Jews to trust in their neighbor and believe in and, certainly, rely upon, the goodness of man.

Changes in gestures and attitudes toward one another will not come easily to either community. And while we ought not hold ourselves or one another responsible for the evils and misdeeds of past generations, it is incumbent upon us to reverse the bloodstained record of that past. We are divinely commanded to shatter the stereotypes we have of one another and to expunge from our hearts the vestiges of prejudice and residues of antipathy that may remain. Such is not an easy task. Indeed, achieving it may be beyond the scope of our generation. And yet, it is our duty to begin the healing process.

I recall well a tour I once took with a group of Christians to Yad Vashem, the Holocaust Memorial Museum in Israel.

They were visibly moved and felt very uncomfortable as they tried, most for the first time, to come to grips with the reality of anti-Semitism unleashed. They were also overcome with grief and pangs of guilt for what "baptized Christians" in the heart of enlightened "Christian Europe" had done to the Jewish people, both in this century and over the past two millennia. I remember being concerned about their response. Could their trauma and guilt eventually lead to anger and hostility toward Jews for "laying a guilt trip on them"? Their emotions needed to be channeled in a constructive direction and into beneficial action. They needed to be led out of the darkness of guilt onto a path that would empower them to feel like they were reversing the past and doing good for the Jewish people.

Where should they and we be directed? The answer, while simple enough, has eluded us for centuries. The answer is love. It is our duty to extend love toward one another—to ask ourselves at every moment how we can build bridges of understanding, reconciliation, and healing between our communities; love our neighbors as ourselves; and bring *shalom*, peace, to our world.

Christians should be neither surprised nor hurt if Jews, at times, spurn their gestures of friendship and reject their overtures of love. For many Jews, the Talmud expressed best the guarded relationship they ought to have with non-Jews: "respect them and suspect them."

I hope Christians will be patient with Jews as they slowly build trust in others. I hope they will understand Jews' insecurities and need for constant acts of reassurance. And I hope they will recognize that the key ingredient in birthing and nurturing trust in Jews' hearts is their instilling confidence in the relationship by examining the genuineness and purity of their motives for reaching out to the Jewish people.

Jews are suspicious and disdainful of Christians' "conditional love" which is contingent upon their "coming to Christ." Jews have been afflicted by such "love" for centuries, as they have been subjected to pain and persecution, expulsion and affliction, all in the name of Jesus, the one who came in love. Not only has it proven to have horrific consequences, it has not succeeded in the past, nor will it today. However we explain it, whether in New Testament terms that a supernaturally imposed hardening of the heart has come over the Jews, or that they simply do not respond to such disingenuous and insincere outreach, Christians have not succeeded in "bringing the Jews to Christ," though they have attempted to do so for 2,000 years.

While Christians who feel mandated to share their faith with others ought to be able to do so, they should do so in legitimate and responsible ways, sensitively and with unconditional love. I believe deeply in the distinction between witnessing and proselytizing, affirming the former and condemning the latter. Proselytizing involves manipulation, deception, coercion and overly zealous and targeted techniques. While the precise line between the two is sometimes difficult to ascertain, it does exist.

Chrisitians should also be humbled knowing that attempts to convert the Jews in the past were not only harmful but also unsuccessful. Ultimately, they should trust in the sovereignty of God who knows what he is doing and has a divine plan in store for Israel and for his people. Changing hearts, in orthodox Christian theology, is God's doing through the Holy Spirit, not man's. And God can be trusted. Demonstrating love, compassion, and comfort toward the Jewish people and showing them through one's deeds "the love of Christ"—that is the Christians' duty. "Converting" Jews is best left to God to bring about or not, as he deems fit.

Building trusting relationships with Jews is not a simple matter. There remain many pitfalls to be aware of, even for the sincere, well-intentioned Christian. Once, following my speech at a large Evangelical church in a town with few Jews and only one synagogue, I was called by the rabbi of that community. He was irate and wanted me to know that the members of the church were so inspired by my message of the duty to show love to the Jewish people, that hundreds of them converged on the synagogue Sabbath morning and totally overwhelmed and frightened the roughly forty Jews attending services! Sometimes, well-intentioned actions are insufficient. We still have to learn *how* to love one another sensitively—without smothering them with our love.

In addition to unconditional and sensitive love, Christians ought to beware of extending the kind of love that speaks more of the interests and motivation of the love-giver than of the recipient of that love. This is "selfish love," loving others as *we* want to love them instead of loving them as *they* want and need to be loved. A boy scout who "schleps" an old lady across the street when the old lady does not, in fact, want to cross the street, is not *loving* her but harassing her! For many Jews, the best thing Christians can do to show their love is to leave them and their children alone! Sincere, mature Christians must learn to "hold back" their love and demonstrate it patiently, sensitively, and respectfully in a way that Jews want to be loved. Doing so can slowly inspire reassurance and instill trust. We must always remember that two thousand years of history are difficult, if not impossible, to overcome with one or two acts of goodness. It will take repeated pure gestures of respect, concern, caring, dialogue, solidarity, comfort, and cooperation to produce the sweet, beautiful fruit we seek—God's love between us!

Another false "love" well-intentioned Christians often show to Jews is engaging in a "proof text" debate with them, often even before establishing a relationship with them. Jews easily see through such facades. Their historically attuned "survival antennae" immediately recognize the real intent of the person "loving" them—to convert them. This is not to suggest that Christians be proscribed from sharing their faith with Jews or discussing with them such passages as Isaiah 53, or any other part of the Bible, for that matter. It does mean, however, that they do so in the context of a trusting, nonmanipulative, nonpressured, and nondeceptive relationship, with love and respect and with a commitment to dialogue and to listen at least as much as to preach and speak.

The reality is that there is greater interaction between Christians and Jews today than at any other time in history. The rise in the number of intermarriages, the demographic and geographic changes that have brought them closer together professionally and socially, the celebration of holidays such as Christmas, Hanukkah, Easter, and Passover in society, and the greater intermingling of our children in schools—these and other factors are bringing this subject closer to home for all of us.

How can Christians be good neighbors to the Jews with whom they come in contact? How can they be friends to the Jewish community? Should they ask their Jewish acquaintances at work about their faith and practices? Visit their synagogues? Invite them to their homes? Shall they visit and comfort them in their moments of grief and rejoice with them at their moments of joy? Can Christians disagree with Jews on political issues, religious themes, or matters pertaining to the Israeli-Arab conflict without feeling they are betraying them and without being accused of anti-Semitism? In short, how can well-intentioned, loving Christians seeking to reverse the two-thousand-year history of intolerance and enmity characterizing their forebears' relationship with the Jewish people, relate to Jews today?

There is no simple answer. Each situation requires a different response; each person needs to be treated with a special and unique sensitivity. After all, Jews are people like all others. True, they seek, in varying degrees, to preserve Jewish life, faith, and tradition—no easy task in America today where the pressures of assimilation, materialism, secularism, and intermarriage are so strong. Often, Jews wish to be left alone to bond with others who share their faith and culture and who are part of their narrower Jewish community. Christians should try to understand and respect those parameters, much as they would their spouse's privacy, without interpreting that "separateness" as clannishness, elitism, or an act of rejection. Ultimately, it will take repeated and genuine acts of love to break down the walls of enmity and intolerance that have shaped the Jewish consciousness and separated them from others.

One of the greatest tragedies—and enigmas—to befall Western civilization is that for two thousand years, Christians and Jews, both of whom draw their spiritual sustenance from the same primary biblical command to "love thy neighbor as thyself," have related to one another with the utter absence of such love. How can we explain this? Dietrich Bonhoeffer, one of the Christian martyrs in the Holocaust, spoke of the concept of "cheap grace." Perhaps our fault has been in extending "cheap love" toward one another, relating to one another as "its," to use Martin Buber's terminology, rather than as "thous," objects or commodities rather than people created in the divine image, children of God. Perhaps Christians historically "loved" Jews by viewing them as objects to be converted, bombarding them with the gospel but never seeing or treating them as real human beings. This, as I note earlier, was what the Nazis in this century did before carrying out their extermination plans. They reduced the Jews, and other "undesirable" people, to the level of subhumans and treated them as "its"—vermin, objects for destruction.

But God calls us to lead a life of *imitatio dei*, imitating him and loving *real* people. While it is much harder to love real people than it is to love the idea, or even ideal, of them, God calls us to do precisely that.

I had a friend who marched with me in the 1960s at demonstrations in front of the Soviet Embassy calling upon the Soviet government to stop persecuting Jews and to allow them to emigrate. When some, in fact, settled in America and moved in down the block from him, however, he did little, if anything, to help them adjust to their new circumstances, such as assisting them in finding a job, learning the language, getting a driver's license, and so on. Indeed, it is easier to love a cause than to love real people.

We cannot change the relationships of the past. But we can, and must, reverse the history of Christian-Jewish encounters. We can and must bridge the deep chasm existing between our faith communities by living out the doctrine that serves as the cornerstone of our faiths: love. True love is the gift of our faiths to the world; it is both the process through which we achieve the goal of God's love and the goal itself. Living a life of love is how we can achieve proper relationship with God. It is also the mystery and blessing he showers upon us in return for such a walk.

Critical to this journey toward fostering trust and love between us is trying to view life through the eyes of the other. Judaism teaches that we should not judge others until we have been in their place. For Christians and Jews to ever "love" one another they will need to learn how their partners see themselves and how they look at events. Christians should understand, for example, that Jews perceive themselves as bearers and preservers of an ancient tradition that has stood up to those who sought to wean them away from their heritage or persecute them for practicing their faith. As I suggested in the *Introduction*, Christians should make every effort to learn what brings Jews pain and what brings them joy before reaching out to them. They should try to look at life and events through the glasses with which Jews view the world and as refracted through the prism shaping the Jewish ethos.

When a swastika is spray-painted on a synagogue, graves in a Jewish cemetery are defaced, terrorists attack Jews halfway around the world, what do non-Jews see? What do they feel? And how do Jews look at these same events? When Jews read reports of a rise in nationalism in Russia and the growth of right-wing groups here in America—some even bearing "Christian" names and purporting biblical principles; when they learn that dangerous militia groups are flourishing and incidents such as the bombing of the Federal Building in Oklahoma City erupt; when revisionist "scholars" publish material claiming that the Holocaust never happened—what do non-Jews feel? Are they fearful and insecure? Does the thought enter their mind—even fleetingly or sub-consciously— that maybe "they're next"? That they might be made the scapegoat for the ills of society? Sadly, history has shaped

Jews' sensibilities and triggered their fear in reaction to such trends and events. While often such vandalism and acts of anti-Semitism are merely pranks by a few youth, Jews have learned how easy it is for such events to snowball out of control if they are not confronted head on and nipped in the bud.

In 1978, when a small group of fifteen neo-Nazis sought to march through the village of Skokie, Illinois, where many Holocaust survivors lived (and why it was chosen in the first place), I was on the staff of the Anti-Defamation League (ADL). Our approach at the outset was to try to convince the local Jewish community not to block this group from marching, as that would generate even more publicity and give the neo-Nazis the public relations bonanza they so desperately sought. Moreover, the ADL insisted, this was just a group of ten to fifteen publicity-seeking ruffians, a bunch of thugs, who couldn't hurt anyone. We utterly failed, however, to see these events through the eyes of the Jews living in Skokie, the Jews who survived the horrors of the Holocaust and now sought to lead their lives in the peace and security of America. The Jews in Skokie were frightened and rejected our approach. They reminded us that Hitler began his rallies in the 1920s with just a handful of goons, too. People at that time also advised Jews to ignore them and they would go away. Tragically, they did not.

Needless to say, we subsequently altered our plan and fought this neo-Nazi group in the courts. But I learned an important lesson from that experience: to look at life and events not only through the lens of my own experience but also with the added sensitivity that seeing it through others' eyes can bring. Of course, we will never be able to feel everything others do. As a male, I will never fully grasp events as a woman might. I will never fully comprehend the world view of the African American, nor, I hope, the insecurities of the disabled. And yet, to relate to others we must make that effort.

This lesson applies to the subject of witnessing, too. Judaism does not subscribe to the exclusivist theological view that it alone can bring salvation. Nor, of course, does it accept the classic Christian assertion that only that religion is redemptive. Yet, to understand and relate to Christians, Jews should try to grasp their point of view.

Christians, for their part, ought to be aware of how Jews view proselytizing efforts, particularly in light of their two-thousand-year history of encountering such crusades. While most Christians are probably oblivious to this history, Jewish consciousness is such that they view the simple act of a Christian witnessing to them against such a backdrop, innocent and loving as such "acts of friendship" are intended to be.

While both communities ought to make the yeoman attempt to understand each other's positions and worldview and seek out common ground between them, they ought not feel compelled to compromise their integrity in the process of pursuing this lofty goal of "brotherhood." For it is not by denying our faith that such cooperation can come about but by affirming it. Indeed, if Christians were better Christians and Jews better Jews, we would have a better America and a better world.

There are Christians who have built up a track record of sensitively identifying with the Jewish people, supporting their concerns and respecting their faith commitments while not compromising their Christian convictions one iota. Such people have "earned the right" to criticize Jews and their policies and to have such criticism accepted by them. These Christians are "part of the family," friends who can be trusted.

Finally, deeper relationships between Christians and Jews can evolve by working together on issues of shared concern, cooperating in actualizing our common values, and exploring together God's call on our lives. Much like a couple that can come closer together by focusing their attention and love on the same third party, their child, Christians and Jews can enter into greater fellowship by working together in common ventures and on behalf of shared ideals. It was to achieve this vision of dialogue and cooperation that in 1983, I founded the International Fellowship of Christians and Jews.

Areas such as archaeology, tours to Israel, biblical exegesis and homiletics, for example, offer wonderful possibilities for cooperation and mutual enrichment. This was made clear to me when I conducted a Passover Seder in Washington for United States Senators and their spouses. At one point I explained the commonly given Jewish reason for the Israelites placing the blood of the Paschal lamb on the outside of their doorposts— namely, to publicly defy the Egyptians who deified these animals. One Senator's wife, however, pointed out to me that she always understood the story as Israel's response to God's promise to Abraham who was prepared to sacrifice his son but offered a lamb instead. The placing of the blood, she suggested, was a sign of the continuing covenant between God and Abraham's seed. This wonderful interpretation, which is proffered by some Jewish commentators as well, opened up my eyes to another whole dimension of understanding the biblical text.

Practical areas, such as building a secure Israel; helping the needy and the oppressed; reducing the scourges of violence, drugs, teenage pregnancies, and abortions plaguing our society; bringing greater dignity to the elderly, to name just a few, offer wonderful opportunities for cooperation, as well. Both the Jewish community and the Christian community share the goal of creating an environment in which they can raise their children as members of a faith community without fear of outside imposition of negative values. While they may differ on how this can be accomplished, it remains a common goal. That is why, in 1995, I founded the Center for Jewish and Christian Values, a Washington-based project of the International Fellowship of Christians and Jews, bringing together leaders of both communities to dialogue and cooperate in building a more moral society in America for ourselves and our children.

While dialogue in its pristine sense may elude us, and each community comes to the table with its own agendas, we ought to strive for this ideal, nonetheless. Jews, for example, seek more practical goals, such as building support for Israel and helping Jews from the former Soviet Union emigrate to Israel.

Christians generally come to the table with more theological interests, such as seeking greater understanding of the biblical roots of their Christian faith. But both seek to see that their faith and their families survive and thrive. Both can succeed if each is willing to relinquish the notion that the other's success somehow threatens their own. For dialogue to bear fruit, both sides must strive toward listening sensitively to the other and accommodating their own positions as much as possible.

I am often asked what the most common stereotype is that Christians and Jews have of one another. The answer is easy— who we think the other really is. Christians, who see themselves essentially as a faith community, tend to transpose their categories of self-understanding onto Jews. They assume, for example, that an irreligious Jew without a strong faith in God is not *really* a Jew. This is because they are accustomed to identifying their religion by its faith component. Jews, on the other hand, define themselves as such because they were born to a Jewish mother (or, in current Reform practice, even to a Jewish father) or converted into Jewish life. For them, dimensions such as community and peoplehood play a critical role along with faith. Accordingly, Jews generally make the mistake of believing that people are *born* Christians, and continue to be such, whether they have faith or not. That is why Jews assume that tyrants like Hitler, Stalin and Jeffrey Dahmer were all Christians, albeit evil ones, a notion Christians themselves categorically deny.

Over the more than two decades that I have been building bridges of understanding, healing, reconciliation, and cooperation between Christians and Jews, I have grown in my appreciation for the beauty of the Christian faith. I have also developed a profound awe for the mystery of how God works through, and in, Christians' lives. Rather than detracting from my own Jewish attachment, this awareness has enhanced it. I find my Jewish commitments strengthened and personal spirituality enriched by the friendships I have made with Christians. I have been deeply moved and inspired by the sincerity of their belief, by their abiding commitment to helping the Jewish people, and by their standing in solidarity with Israel.

The Fellowship's "On Wings of Eagles" project, in which Christians sponsor airlifts of Jews from the former Soviet Union to Israel, has raised millions of dollars and enabled tens of thousands of Jews to escape anti-Semitism and begin their lives anew in the freedom and security of Israel. Such tangible acts of love endear Christians to Jews and help create that record of trust that is so critical to further reconciliation. Such acts speak louder than words and more meaningfully than all the tracts Christians distribute of the need to come to faith in Jesus. Indeed, they endear Christians, Christianity, and Jesus to Jews in a way "tract giving" cannot do. Such acts are seen by Jews as genuine, sacrificial, and "for real." They reassure Jews that Christians *do* care about them, that God's love is truly working in their lives, and that they, as Jews, are genuinely accepted by their neighbors.

Few of us, thank God, are called upon to risk our lives for our brothers and sisters as saints such as Corrie ten Boom, Raul Wallenberg, Oskar Schindler, and others did. We Jews will forever be grateful to these and other "righteous gentiles" like them for rejuvenating our faith in God in the face of evil, restoring our faith in man in the face of despair, and reminding us of the ideal of love—true love—we are all called upon to extend toward our brothers and sisters.

It is my greatest hope and prayer, one to which I have devoted my life, that through our efforts and God's blessings, we might merit seeing the day we all long for, when enmity and intolerance will be swept from our hearts, when nation shall not lift up sword against other nation and neither shall learn war anymore, and when there will be love—true love—and fellowship among all of God's children. Amen!

Chapter 1

1. E. P. Sanders, *Paul and Palestinian Judaism: A Comparison of Patterns of Religion* (London: Student Christian Movement Press, 1977), 422–23.
2. Pinchas Lapide, "The Aye and the Nay of the Jews: The Lukan View of the Parting of the Ways," *Face to Face* (Winter-Spring 1982): 25–26.
3. Elie Wiesel, "Jewish Values in the Post-Holocaust Future: A Symposium," *Judaism* vol. 16, no. 3 (1967): 281.
4. Martin Buber, *Hasidism and Modern Man* (New York: Horizon Press Pubs., 1958), 28–30.
5. Abraham J. Heschel, *God in Search of Man: A Philosophy of Judaism* (Philadelphia: Jewish Publication Society of America, 1956), 352.
6. Ibid., 185–89.
7. Ibid., 167.

Chapter 2

1. See Eugene Fisher, "Basic Jewish and Christian Beliefs in Dialogue," *PACE* 13 (Feb. 1983): 2.
2. As cited in Samuel Dresner and Byron Sherwin, *Judaism: The Way of Sanctification* (New York: United Synagogue Book Service, 1978), 91.

Chapter 3

1. Achad Haam, *Al Parashat Derachim* (Berlin: Judischer Verlag, 1930), 4-30.
2. Mordecai Kaplan, *Judaism As a Civilization: Toward a Reconstruction of American-Jewish Life* (Philadelphia:

Jewish Publication Society of America and Reconstructionist Pubns., 1981), 444.

3. Abraham J. Heschel, *The Sabbath* (Philadelphia: Jewish Publication Society of America, 1951), 13.

4. Dayan I. Grunfeld, *The Sabbath: A Guide to Its Understanding and Observance* (New York: Philip Feldheim, 1981), 28.

5. As cited in *Evangelical Newsletter* (June 1978).

Chapter 4

1. Abraham J. Karp, *The Jewish Way of Life* (Englewood Cliffs, NJ: Prentice-Hall, 1962), 150.

2. See Saul Friedman, *Incident at Massena: The Blood Libel in America* (Briarcliff Manor, NY: Stein & Day, 1978).

3. Abba Hillel Silver, *Where Judaism Differed* (New York: Macmillan Publishing Co., 1956), 30.

4. Theodor Herzl, *The Jewish State* (New York: American Zionist Emergency Council, 1946), 156–57.

Chapter 5

1. As cited in Isaac Klein, *A Guide to Jewish Religious Practices* (New York: Jewish Theological Seminary, 1979), 420–21.

2. Milton Steinberg, *Basic Judaism* (New York: Harcourt, Brace & Co., 1947), 160.

3. Herman Wouk, *This Is My God* (New York: Doubleday & Co., 1959), 173.

4. The Zohar as cited in the introduction to Joseph Hertz, *Authorized Daily Prayer Book* (New York: Bloch Publishing Co., 1952).

5. Ibid.

6. Moses Maimonides, *A Guide for the Perplexed,* pt. 3, chap. 48, trans. M. Friedlander (London: George Routledge & Sons, 1928).

7. Ibid.
8. Ibid.
9. As cited in Klein, *Religious Practices,* 302.
10. See Maimonides, *Perplexed.*
1 1. Abraham Ibn Ezra, commentary on Exodus 23:19 in *Mikraot Gedolot Bible* (Jerusalem: Levin-Epstein, 1963).
12. Samuel Dresner, *The Jewish Dietary Laws* (New York: Burning Bush Press, 1959), 24, 27.

Chapter 6

1. Elie Wiesel, *Night* (New York: Hill & Wang, 1960), 43–44.
2. Yehuda Bauer, *The Holocaust in Historical Perspective* (Seattle: University of Washington Press, 1978), 32.
3. David Hartman, "Auschwitz or Sinai?" *Jerusalem Post,* 17–23 October 1982, International edition.
4. As cited in Albert H. Friedlander, ed., *Out of the Whirlwind: A Reader of Holocaust Literature* (New York: Union of American Hebrew Congregations, 1968), 399.
5. As cited in Eva Fleischner, ed., *Auschwitz: Beginning of a New Era's Reflections on the Holocaust* (New York: Ktav Publishing House, 1977), 9, 10.
6. Elie Wiesel, et al., *Dimensions of the Holocaust* (Chicago: Northwestern University Press, 1978), 14–15.
7. Alexander Donat, *The Holocaust Kingdom: A Memoir* (New York: Holt, Rinehart & Winston, 1965), 103.
8. Stanley Milgram, "Some Conditions of Obedience and Disobedience to Authority," *Human Relations* 18 (1965): 57–75.
9. Arthur Morse, *While Six Million Died* (New York: Random House, 1968), 8.
10. Irving Greenberg, "On the Third Era in Jewish History: Power and Politics," *Perspectives* (New York: National Jewish Resource Center, 1980), 3.

11. Wiesel, *Night,* 44.
12. Franklin Littell, Christians Concerned for Israel
    Notebook (April 1971): 1.

Chapter 7

1. See Rashi commentary on Genesis 1:1 in *Mikraot
   Gedolot Bible* (Jerusalem: Levin-Epstein, 1963).
2. Abraham J. Heschel, *Israel: An Echo of Eternity* (New
   York: Farrar, Straus & Giroux, 1969), 44.
3. As cited in Eliezer Ehrmann, *Readings in Jewish History:
   From the American Revolution to the Present* (New
   York: Ktav Publishing House, 1977), 265.
4. As cited in Ehrmann, *Readings,* 268.
5. As cited in Ehrmann, *Readings,* 274.
6. Ibid.
7. As cited in Joseph Blau, *Modern Varieties of Judaism*
   (New York: Columbia University Press, 1966), 66.

Chapter 8

1. As cited in Blau, *Modern Varieties,* 27.
2. As cited in Ehrmann, *Readings,* 36.
3. As cited in Ehrmann, *Readings,* 36–37.
4. As cited in Jacob Agus, "The Reform Movement," in
   *Understanding American Judaism: Toward the
   Description of a Modern Religion,* vol. 2, ed. Jacob
   Neusner (New York: Ktav Publishing House, 1975), 17.
5. Ibid.
6. As cited in Ehrmann, *Readings,* 40.
7. Ibid.
8. As cited in Neusner, *Understanding,* 121.
9. As cited in Ehrmann, *Readings,* 47.
10. Mordecai Kaplan, *The Meaning of God in Modern
    Jewish Religion* (New York: Behrman House, 1937), 328.
11. Irving Greenberg, "Cloud of Smoke, Pillar of Fire:
    Judaism, Christianity, and Modernity after the
    Holocaust," in Fleischner, *Auschwitz,* 43.

Defense - Civil Liberties Groups
American Jewish Congress (AJC) 212-879-4500
American Jewish Committee (AJC) 212-360-1520
Anti-Defamation League (ADL) 212-490-2525

Israel Oriented Groups
American Israel Public Affairs 202-639-5200
   Committee (AIPAC)
United Jewish Appeal 212-980-1000

Religious Denominational Groups
Orthodox Union of America (Orthodox) 212-563-4000 or
   212-613-8100
United Synagogue of America
   (Conservative) 212-533-7800
Union of American Hebrew
Congregations (Reform) 212-249-0100 or
   212-650-4000

Ben-Sasson, Haim H. *A History of the Jewish People.* Harvard University Press.

Dawidowicz, Lucy. *The War Against the Jews 1933-1945.* Bantam Books.

Heschel, Abraham J.
   Man's Quest for God. New York: Charles Scribner's Sons, 1954.
   The Sabbath. NewYork: Harper & Row Pubs, Inc., 1950.
   God in Search of Man: A Philosophy of Judaism. New York: Farrar, Straus & Giroux, Inc., 1955.

Kertzer, Morris. *What is a Jew?* Simon & Schuster Trade.

Kolatch, Alfred. *The Jewish Book of Why.* HIGB.

Lamm, Maurice. *The Jewish Way of Death and Mourning.* New York: Jonathan David Pubs., Inc., 1969.

Prager, Dennis. *The Nine Questions People Ask About Judaism.* Simon & Schuster Trade.

Wiesel, Elie. *Night.* Bantam Books.

Rabbi Yechiel Eckstein has also written extensively on
a variety of subjects including:

Jewish Views of Jesus, Christians and Christianity
Christians and Anti Semitism
Christian Missions and the Jews
Jewish/Christian Relations

►┼◄►─O─◄►┼◄

For information on additional writings by Rabbi Eckstein, or for
questions, comments or further resources on this subject, please feel
free to contact:

International Fellowship of Christians and Jews
28 E. Jackson Blvd. Suite 1900
Chicago IL 60604
telephone: 312-554-0450
fax: 312-554-0490
e-mail: IFCJ@prodigy.net

RABBI YECHIEL ECKSTEIN

Rabbi, author, lecturer, radio and television host, Yechiel Z. Eckstein is Founder and President of the International Fellowship of Christians and Jews, an international organization based in Chicago, and its Center for Jewish and Christian Values based in Washington, D.C. Rabbi Eckstein and his organization are dedicated to building bridges of understanding between Christians and Jews, and to creating a broad network of cooperation and support in areas of shared concern, such as Israel and moral values.

Widely considered the leading Jewish expert on Evangelical Christians and liaison with the Christian community, Rabbi Eckstein lectures frequently in both Christian and Jewish circles, both in America and around the world. As a trusted emissary between communities, he has organized numerous conferences throughout the United States with Catholic, Protestant and, especially, Evangelical groups. Eckstein is the coordinator and driving force behind the annual Evangelical-Jewish Leadership Conference in Washington, DC, and has been the Jewish representative at the National Day of Prayer activities. Rabbi Eckstein has opened sessions of the United States Senate with prayer and, in a historic program, conducted a Passover Seder for the United States Congress. In another historical first, he delivered the benediction at the dedication of the Franklin Delano Roosevelt memorial in Washington, D.C.

Rabbi Eckstein is the author of four highly-acclaimed books: *What You Should Know About Jews and Judaism* (Word, Inc.), *Understanding Evangelicals: A Guide for the Jewish Community*, *Ask The Rabbi*, and *Five Questions Most Frequently Asked About Jews and Judaism*. He has been the subject of numerous articles in newspapers and magazines throughout the world, including a feature article in *People* magazine. He also serves on the National Board of Directors of the American Refugee Committee.

Eckstein has hosted the nationally-syndicated radio program, "Ask the Rabbi," and the nationally-broadcast television special, "Shalom from Israel." Another television special, entitled "While the Door is Still Open," describing the condition of Jews in the former Soviet Union and how concerned Americans can help Jews emigrate to Israel, was produced by Eckstein. Hosted by Pat Boone and featuring several Christian leaders, the program urges viewers to contribute funds toward the emigration of Jews from the former Soviet Union to Israel. He was also co-host with actress Nancy Stafford of the new television special on the same theme. He also served as co-host of the nationally broadcast "On Wings of Eagles" radio program with Debby Boone and Rich Buhler, and in its later version with Steve Brown and Nancy Stafford, aimed at achieving the same purpose. Since 1993, the Fellowship has contributed millions of dollars, raised almost entirely from Christians, to the UJA's Operation Exodus program, as a result of these television and radio specials.

With a wide range of accomplishments to his credit, the Rabbi has also included academic achievements, with master's degrees earned at two prestigious institutions, Columbia University and Yeshiva University in New York City. He was ordained as rabbi at Yeshiva and completed his studies for his doctorate at Columbia. Eckstein has served on the faculty of Columbia University, Chicago Theological Seminary, and Northern Baptist Seminary. He also served on the Chicago Board of Jewish Education, and was instrumental in developing a Holocaust curriculum for the Chicago Public School System.

A gifted singer and musician, Eckstein is a cantor and renowned performer of Israeli-Hasidic music, accompanying his song with guitar. He has performed throughout the United States and in Israel, and has recorded five record albums.

Eckstein and his wife, Bonnie, reside in the Chicagoland area, and are blessed with three daughters: Tamar, Talia and Yael.